Law & Equity

Legal History Library

VOLUME 10

Studies in the History of Private Law

VOLUME 5

The titles published in this series are listed at brill.com/lhl

Law & Equity

Approaches in Roman Law and Common Law

Edited by

E. Koops & W.J. Zwalve

MARTINUS NIJHOFF PUBLISHERS

LEIDEN • BOSTON
2014

Cover illustration: Fresco of citizens in front of the album of the praetor, Museo della Civiltà Romana, Rome. Photographer: W.J. Zwalve.

Library of Congress Cataloging-in-Publication Data

Law & equity : approaches in Roman law and Common law / Edited by E. Koops & W.J. Zwalve.
p. cm. — (Legal history library ; volume 10) (Studies in the history of private law)
Includes index.
ISBN 978-90-04-26219-5 (hardback : alk. paper) — ISBN 978-90-04-26220-1 (e-book)
1. Equity—Great Britain—History. 2. Equity (Roman law) 3. Common law—History. I. Koops, E. (Egbert) editor of compilation. II. Zwalve, Willem Jans, editor of compilation. III. Title: Law and equity.

KD674.L39 2013
346.42'004—dc23

2013035751

This publication has been typeset in the multilingual "Brill" typeface. With over 5,100 characters covering Latin, IPA, Greek, and Cyrillic, this typeface is especially suitable for use in the humanities. For more information, please see www.brill.com/brill-typeface.

ISSN 1874-1793
ISBN 978-90-04-26219-5 (hardback)
ISBN 978-90-04-26220-1 (e-book)

This book is printed on acid-free paper.

CONTENTS

PREFACE

The external structure of English law has much in common with classical Roman law, not because Roman law was integrated into the law of England as it was on the European continent and in Scotland, but because by sheer coincidence English law still has a dual structure closely resembling the dual structure of classical Roman law. In Roman law, two distinct legal sources applied to practically all private law issues: the *ius civile* and the *ius honorarium*, statutory and customary law (*ius civile*) on the one hand and the law as created by Roman magistrates (*ius honorarium*), particularly the praetor (*ius praetorium*), on the other. In English law there is a similar distinction between Law and Equity; between the Law as administered by the Courts of Law on the one hand and Equity as developed in Chancery on the other. There is in fact no better definition of the relation between Law and Equity in English law than that given by the famous Roman lawyer Papinian of the relation between *ius civile* and *ius praetorium* in Roman law:

> D. 1,1,7,1: *Ius praetorium est, quod praetores introduxerunt adiuvandi vel supplendi vel corrigendi iuris civilis.*
>
> Equity is the law developed in Chancery to support, amend and correct the common law.

The peculiar interaction between *ius civile* and *ius honorarium* shaped the law of Rome, as the interaction between Law and Equity did (and does) with English law. This striking similarity between the external structure of classical Roman law and that of English law is illustrated by the differences and similarities which this interaction has produced in the law of property and the law of obligations. This volume contains four contributions on the external historical aspects of the dichotomy between *ius civile* and *ius honorarium* and Law and Equity respectively, and four contributions on issues of substantive law, such as security interests; the evasion of formalities in property law (bonitary ownership compared with equitable ownership); rescission of contracts; and the construction of contracts.

This volume presents the proceedings of the Leiden conference celebrating the semi-centennial anniversary of *Philips van Leyden b.p.*, the Leiden student society for Roman law and European Legal History on Friday, December 16, 2011. The purpose of the conference was to bring together lawyers and legal historians from two different legal traditions, civilians and common lawyers, in order to present their views on a peculiar characteristic common to both English law and Roman law.

The conference was funded by the Dutch Ministry of Justice ('Ministerie voor Veiligheid en Justitie'); the law offices of DLA Piper, Bird & Bird and NautaDutilh; the Leiden E.M. Meijers Institute for Legal Research and the Faculty of Law of Leiden University. The editors wish to express their gratitude to all sponsors.

We are particularly grateful to E.S. Daalder and T.B.D. van der Wal, both for their assistance in organizing the conference and their efforts in preparing the final manuscript.

The editors
Leiden, December 2012

LIST OF CONTRIBUTORS

P. (Paul) Brand is Professor of English Legal History in the University of Oxford and is a Senior Research Fellow and Senior Dean of All Souls College, Oxford. His books include *The Making of the Common Law* (London, 1992) and *The Origins of the English Legal Profession* (Oxford, 1992). He is the editor and translator of four volumes of The Earliest English Law Reports published by the Selden Society (1996–2007) and is working on further volumes with reports from the second half of the reign of Edward I. He is also working on a volume of the Oxford History of the Laws of England covering the period 1216–1307.

F. (Frits) Brandsma is Professor of Roman Law at the University of Groningen. His research concentrates on the comparative history of Property Law and the Law of Contract, with a particular focus on the European *ius commune* and English law, as well as the Byzantine legal tradition. He has authored books on Byzantine law (*Dorotheus and his Digest translation*, 1996) and Roman-Frisian law (*Roman-Frisian Law of the 17th and 18th Century*, 2003, with J.H.A. Lokin and C.J.H. Jansen).

J. (John) Cartwright is Professor of the Law of Contract at the University of Oxford, and Tutor in Law at Christ Church, Oxford; and Professor of Anglo-American Private Law at the University of Leiden. He specializes in English and comparative private law, teaching Contract, Comparative Law, Land Law, Roman Law and Tort. His research interests lie in the Law of Contract, Comparative Law (especially French Law) and Property Law. He has written extensively in these areas, including books on *Misrepresentation, Mistake and Non-Disclosure* (3rd ed., Sweet & Maxwell 2012) and *Contract Law: An Introduction to the English Law of Contract for the Civil Lawyer* (2nd ed., Hart Publishing 2013), and as co-editor of *Anson's Law of Contract* (29th ed., Oxford University Press 2010) and of *Cheshire and Burn's Modern Law of Real Property* (18th ed., Oxford University Press 2011).

D. (David) Ibbetson is Regius Professor of Civil Law in the University of Cambridge, having formerly taught at Magdalen College, Oxford. He has written widely on the history of English law between the 13th and the 20th century, and has a particular interest in the relationship between English law and the European *ius commune*.

E. (EGBERT) KOOPS is assistant professor of Property Law at the University of Groningen. He has written on the various 'Modes of Subsidiarity' with regard to security interests (2010, in Dutch, which won the Premio Speciale dell'Università di Camerino in 2013) and has co-edited books on *The past and future of money* (2008) and 'The massification of private law' (2010, in Dutch).

M. (MIKE) MACNAIR is Ann Smart Fellow and Tutor in Law at St Hugh's College, Oxford University. He is author of *The Law of Proof in Early Modern Equity* (Comparative Studies in Continental and Anglo-American Legal History, vol. 20, Berlin 1999) and of a number of articles and essays on topics in the history of equity and of evidence and procedure.

H.L.E. (HENDRIK) VERHAGEN is Professor of Private International Law and Comparative Law at the Radboud University Nijmegen; and Professor of Roman Law (Conrat chair) at the University of Amsterdam. He is also a member of the Amsterdam bar, practising with the law firm of Clifford Chance (Amsterdam, Finance and Capital markets). His publications include books on agency and assignment in private international law and contemporary Dutch law, as well as articles on contracts, security interests, insolvency and unjust enrichment in private international law, comparative law and Roman law.

W.J. (WILLEM) ZWALVE is Professor of Legal History in the Faculty of Law of Leiden University, where he reads on Roman law and the Roman law tradition in contemporary continental European private law. He previously held the chair of Jurisprudence and Comparative Private Law in the Faculty of Law of the University of Groningen, where he still holds a chair in Anglo-American Private Law. He writes about the history of Roman law and comparative legal history.

LIST OF ABBREVIATIONS

AC	Appeal Cases
All ER	All England Law Reports
Amb.	Ambler's Chancery Reports
Art.	Article
BGB	Bürgerliches Gesetzbuch
BL	British Library
Bro. Parl. Cas.	J. Browne's Cases in Parliament
Burr.	Burrow's King's Bench Reports tempore Mansfield
BW	Burgerlijk Wetboek (Dutch civil code of 1992)
c.	*circa*
C.	*Codex Iustinianus*, ed. stereotypa P. Krüger, 11th ed. (Berlin: Weidmann, 1954)
C.Th.	*Codex Theodosianus*, ed. Th. Mommsen and P. Meyer (Berlin: Deutsche Akademie der Wissenschaften, 1905)
Cc	Code civil (French civil code)
Ch. (D.)	Chancery (Division)
Chan. Rep.	Reports in Chancery
CLJ	*Cambridge Law Journal*
CP	Common Pleas
CRAI	*Comptes-rendus des séances de l'Académie des Inscriptions et Belles Lettres*
D.	*Recueil Dalloz*
D.	*Iustiniani Digesta*, ed. stereotypa Th. Mommsen, 16th ed. (Berlin: Weidmann, 1954)
Decr.	Decretum Gratiani
ed.	edition; editor(s)
e.g.	*exempli gratia*
EELR	*The Earliest English Law Reports*, ed. P. Brand (London: Selden Society, 1996–)
Eng. Rep.	English Reports (London/Edinburgh: Stevens & Sons/ W. Green & Son, 1900–1927)
Eq. Ca. Ab.	Equity Cases Abridged
et al.	*et alii*
etc.	*et cetera*
EWCA	England and Wales, Court of Appeal

EWHC	England and Wales, High Court
f.	folion
FIRA	*Fontes Iuris Romani Antejustiniani I–III*, ed. S. Riccobono *et al.* (Florence: Barbèra, 1940–1943)
FLR	Family Law Reports
Gaius	*Gai Institutiones*, ed. M. David (Leiden: Brill, 1964)
Gl.	Glossa
H	Hilary term
HEL	W.S. Holdsworth, *A History of English Law* (London: Methuen, 1903–1945)
HL	House of Lords
HLB	*Harvard Library Bulletin*
HLR	*Harvard Law Review*
Hob.	Hobart's King's Bench Reports
HR	Hoge Raad (Dutch Supreme Court)
ibid.	*ibidem*
i.e.	*id est*
i.f.	*in fine*
ILR	*Illinois Law Review*
Inst.	*Iustiniani Institutiones*, ed. stereotypa P. Krüger, 16th ed. (Berlin: Weidmann, 1954)
JLH	*Journal of Legal History*
KB	King's Bench
L&HR	*Law & History Review*
LQR	*Law Quarterly Review*
LR	Law Reports
[1] LT	Law Times Reports
M	Michaelmas term
[1] Mod.	Leach's Modern Reports
MS.	Manuscript
NJ	*Nederlandse Jurisprudentie* (Dutch law reports)
Nov.	*Iustiniani Novellae*, ed. R. Schöll and W. Kroll, 6th ed. (Berlin: Weidmann, 1954)
OBW	Oud Burgerlijk Wetboek (old Dutch civil code, 1838–1992)
ODNB	*Oxford Dictionary of National Biography*
OHLE	*Oxford History of the Laws of England* (Oxford: Oxford University Press, 2003–)
OJLS	*Oxford Journal of Legal Studies*
P	Paschal term
P & CR	Planning and Compensation Reports

P. Wms.	Peere-Williams' Chancery & King's Bench Cases
Plow.	Plowden's Reports
QB	Queen's Bench
r.	*recto*
S.	section
subs.	subsection
s.n.	*sub nomine*
s.v.	*sub verbo*
Swanst.	Swanston's Chancery Reports
T	Trinity term
TvR	*Tijdschrift voor Rechtsgeschiedenis / The Legal History Review*
UKHL	United Kingdom, House of Lords
UKPC	United Kingdom, Privy Council
v.	*verso*
Vern.	Vernon's Chancery Reports
Ves. Sen. / Jr.	Vesey Senior's / Junior's Chancery Reports
WLR	Weekly Law Reports
X.	Liber Extra, Decretals of Gregorius IX
YB	Year Books
ZSS	*Zeitschrift der Savigny-Stiftung für Rechtsgeschichte* (*Romanistische Abteilung*)

PART ONE

INTRODUCTION

INTRODUCTION: THE EQUITY PHENOMENON

W.J. Zwalve and E. Koops

The 'equity phenomenon' is approached in this book from two different angles. The first concerns two systems of substantive positive law, classical Roman law and English law, both consisting of two different branches: *ius civile* and *ius honorarium* in Roman law, and Common law and Equity in English law. In both systems Equity and *ius honorarium* served the same end. They were developed in order to support, amend and correct the other branch of the law, *ius civile* in Roman law and the Common law in English law. In this approach, Equity and *ius honorarium* ('Roman Equity')[1] are treated as the settled outcome of an historical process inducing Roman law and English law to develop the law along two separate lines: custom and statutory law (*ius civile* and the Common law) as construed by judges (English law) and *iuris periti* (Roman law) on the one hand and the amendments and corrections made by the Lord Chancellor (English law) and Roman magistrates, in particular by the praetor (Roman law), on the other.

The traditional dichotomy of English law has not been unavoidable. Equity only grew into a separate branch of English law after the Common law courts ceased to apply 'equitable' considerations in the decision-making process. Here the word 'equity' is used in a different, Aristotelian sense. It does not indicate a separate branch of positive law, but designates *aequitas*, reasonableness and fairness, as applied by a judge in construing the law and interpreting the facts of a case at hand. As Paul Brand shows in his contribution, early English justices did not hesitate to apply equity to reach a just result. Continental justices in the highest sovereign courts applied equity, which was more often than not found in Roman law and canon law, as a matter of course when deciding a case on the basis of customary law, which was also the primary source of law in medieval continental Europe. They continued to do so, as Willem Zwalve shows, until the end of the legal 'ancien régime' on the continent. Consequently, there

---

[1] H.F. Jolowicz, *Roman Foundations of Modern Law* (Oxford: Clarendon, 1957), 56, fnt. 5.

has never been an incentive on the continent for the introduction of a separate branch of the judiciary responsible for the subjection of the law to equitable standards. The highest courts on the continent applied Aristotelian equity as a matter of course. However, dissatisfaction with the 'equity' of continental European sovereign courts was widespread on the continent since the 16th century. It was perceived as an arbitrary and therefore unpredictable standard of law, as expressed in the legal proverb 'de l'équité des Parlements, Dieu nous garde'. Similar objections to the equitable jurisdiction of the English Lord Chancellor in his Court of Chancery were made in England at the same time, most prominently by John Selden. Mike Macnair deals with the problem of predictability and the arbitrariness of early English Equity in his contribution to this volume.

Unlike their continental counterparts, the justices of the Common law courts in Westminster, when in or about 1530 encouraged to do so by none other than the Lord Chancellor, Sir Thomas More, explicitly refused to apply henceforth what has been called 'geometric equity', meaning 'an amendment or correction of the law'.[2] This gave rise to the Court of Chancery as a Court of Equity. In the early years of Chancery's involvement in the development of the law, considerable energy was spent by English theorists to define Equity and thus provide a basis for the Chancellor's involvement in the law and a theoretical framework for his decisions. As David Ibbetson shows, these efforts failed to reach a satisfactory result, primarily because the Aristotelian concept of *epieikeia* falls short, leading Mike Macnair to contend that 'Chancery bar equity is perhaps the *least* 'equitable', in the Aristotelian *epieikeia* sense of 'flexible', branch of English law'. Most of the contributors to this volume (Ibbetson, Macnair, and Zwalve) agree that 'Conscience' would have been a better approach, since English Equity always operates on the conscience of a defendant. It has at its root the subjective civilian concept of *bona fides* ('goede trouw', 'guter Glaube', 'bonne foi'), rather than the objective civilian concept of *aequitas* or *epieikeia* ('redelijkheid en billijkheid', 'Treu und Glauben', 'reasonableness and fairness', 'équité'). It consists of the sum of the legal consequences (most notably the imposition of a constructive trust) that the courts of Equity have drawn over time from this conscience-test, which is, as Mike Macnair stresses, traditionally at the heart of their activity. In the end—all efforts to define English Equity on a substantive basis having

---

[2] On the More-incident and 'geometric equity' see J.H. Baker, *The Oxford History of the Laws of England* VI: 1483–1558 (Oxford: Oxford University Press, 2003), 46–47.

failed—there is but one, circular, definition to which everyone may and does agree. It is Maitland's famous definition: 'Equity is that body of rules which is administered only by those Courts which are known as Courts of Equity'.[3] As with democracy, it may be quite unsatisfactory, but there is no better option. Or is there?

It seems that Papinian's definition of *ius praetorium* in D. 1,1,7,1 may still claim to describe, *mutatis mutandis*, English Equity. It is the law developed in the Courts of Equity to support, amend and correct the Common law, since 'equity follows the [Common] law', but 'it will likewise go beyond'.[4] The reason so many English lawyers and legal historians avoid using this definition rests primarily on the fact that there is, or rather was, prior to 1876, an important difference between the activities of a Roman praetor, and the English Lord Chancellor and other Equity judges, as stressed by Mike Macnair in his contribution. A Roman praetor amended Roman Common law (*ius civile*) primarily, though not exclusively, by announcing new rules of law in his annual *edictum*, that is to say by acts of legislation. True as this may be, it does not account for all praetorian interferences with Roman Common law. As noted by Mike Macnair, the praetor could also interfere by adapting the *formula* issued by him and used by the *iudex privatus* at the trial, in order to protect an interest which was not enforceable at *ius civile*, thus acting in accordance with the famous maxim of English Equity that 'Equity will not suffer a wrong to be without a remedy'.[5] There is another difference, though, of even greater importance. Unlike the Lord Chancellor in his Court of Chancery, a Roman praetor did not under normal, Republican, circumstances have a court of his own administering *ius praetorium* exclusively.[6] He never *decided* cases solely on the basis of his *ius praetorium*. Instead, he instructed a judge (*iudex privatus*) to decide the case on the basis of *ius praetorium* as laid down in his annual edict; on the instruction as contained in the *formula* issued by him; *and*

[3] F.W. Maitland, *Equity, a Course of Lectures*, ed. J. Brunyate (Cambridge: Cambridge University Press, 1936), 1. Maitland was well aware that this definition only applied to English law before 1876. After the fusion of the courts of Common law and Equity by the Judicature Acts 'we are driven to say that Equity now is that body of rules administered by our English courts of justice which, were it not for the operation of the Judicature Acts, would be administered only by those courts which would be known as Courts of Equity' (Maitland, ibid.).

[4] *Paget v Gee* (1753) Amb. 807, at 810; 27 Eng. Rep. 511, at 512 *per* Lord Hardwicke.

[5] On this maxim see R. Megarry and P.V. Baker, *Snell's Equity*, 27th ed. (London: Sweet & Maxwell, 1973), 27–29.

[6] On this point see W.W. Buckland, *Equity in Roman Law* (London: University of London Press, Hodder & Stoughton, 1911), 1 *seq.*

on the Common law (*ius civile*). Roman judges therefore applied Roman Common law *as well as* Roman Equity, much like English judges do after the Judicature Acts. It is primarily due to this circumstance that Roman Equity has always been closer to Roman Common law than was the case in English law prior to the Judicature Acts. Consequently, the Roman praetors were not able to develop substantive legal institutions independent of the Common law (*ius civile*) in the way English Chancellors were, as is illustrated by the latter's development of the trust, allowing for a more or less permanent separation of the equitable title of a beneficiary and the legal title of a trustee.[7] It is certainly no coincidence that practically the only instance where a Roman praetor had his own court and decided cases on his own, inevitably led to the introduction of precisely such a substantive new legal institution, developed independently of Roman *ius civile*. It was that of the *praetor fideicommissarius*, who developed the law of *fideicommissa*, the only construct of Roman law (remotely) resembling the Anglo-American trust.

> Romanists may object that the concept of dual ownership was not alien to Roman law since ownership 'at law' (*dominium ex iure Quiritium*) could coincide with a kind of ownership recognized by Roman Equity (*ius praetorium*), in some cases even overriding the title of the owner at law, i.e. according to the *ius civile*. The creative use of Roman bonitary (praetorian) ownership is even demonstrated in this volume by John Cartwright and felicitously compared with the ways in which English Equity made use of similar constructs in order to evade comparable legal formalities. It should be stressed however that under Roman law the coexistence of two different kinds of title to one and the same object was *always* a temporary, as a matter of principle transitory, incident. It was an anomaly, sooner (classical Roman law) or later (post-classical Roman law) to be eliminated, since praetorian ownership always resulted in ownership at law by the process of acquisitive prescription, reuniting the legal title with the equitable title. Roman law has always strived to prevent a permanent separation within the right of ownership itself;[8] the institution of acquisitive prescription, not coincidentally an alien construct to Anglo-American law, was primarily aimed at preventing such a separation. Consequently, Roman law was unfavourable

7 On this see *Wortley v Birkhead* (1754) 2 Ves. Sen. 571, at 574; 28 Eng. Rep. 364, at 366 *per* Lord Hardwicke: 'It could not happen in any other country but this: because the jurisdiction of law and equity is administered here in different courts, and creates different kinds of rights in estates.'

8 Whenever a permanent or temporary separation of rights of ownership and rights of enjoyment (or security) was called for, Roman law employed special proprietary interests (*iura in re aliena*), such as usufruct, quitrents (*emphyteusis*) and hypothecation.

to constructs resembling the Anglo-American trust in any way.[9] The only exception was the law of *fideicommissa*.

In dealing with the problem of predictability and the arbitrariness of English Equity, Mike Macnair implicitly reveals another striking similarity between Roman Equity and English Equity. In the pre-1876 era, the Lord Chancellor was the most important official administering Equity. Like his counterpart, the Roman praetor, he was primarily a political figure. Consequently, Chancellors came and went with every changing political wind and, more importantly, were not by necessity specialists in the branch of the law, Equity, that they were supposed to administer. The same held true for a Roman *praetor urbanus*. He was never appointed on account of his special abilities as a lawyer. Many praetors were elected each year,[10] but their respective 'provinces' were only assigned to them by lot. Accordingly, most, if not all, praetors administering justice in Rome were advised and guided by the learned members of their *consilium* or even by professional assistants (*assessores*).[11] It is interesting to learn that, in the process of stabilizing Equity in England, similar methods were at one time employed.

Stabilizing English Equity into a system of reliable substantive law was a necessity, if only because immense wealth was placed into trusts, which were ruled by Equity rather than the Common law. Predictability was therefore of the greatest importance. This is one of the main reasons, if not *the* reason, why 'Chancery bar Equity' eventually turned out to be 'the least 'equitable' branch of English law' (Macnair, *infra*, 79). In describing that stabilizing process from an external perspective, Mike Macnair summarizes the history of English Equity by pointing to the importance of the relatively slow emergence of reports of Equity cases, the development of a specialized Chancery bar and the introduction of appeal in Chancery cases. The crucial factor was that precedents became as decisive in Chancery as they were in the Courts of Common law. In the second half of the 17th century, the importance of precedent in Chancery was emphasized by Sir Orlando Bridgeman (1606–1674), Lord Keeper of the Great Seal between 1667 and 1672, in the following words:

---

9 See Buckland, *Equity*, 15 *seq*.

10 The praetors were elected by the people in republican times and by the Senate under the empire.

11 There is an instructive story in Seneca's *De tranquilitate animi* (3,4) that a praetor merely repeated the words dictated to him by his *assessores*, who were learned in the law. As the standing of the office of praetor declined, the importance of his assistants increased, causing the Roman lawyer Paul to write a book *De officio assessorum* and a related treatise *De conceptione formularum*.

> Precedents are very necessary and useful to us; for in them we may find the reasons of the equity to guide us; and besides, the authority of those who made them is much to be regarded. We shall suppose they did it upon great consideration, and weighing of the matter; and it would be very strange and very ill if we should disturb and set aside what has been the course for a long series of time and ages.[12]

The emergence of a series of reliable Equity reports and a specialized Bar and Bench have ensured the reliability which English Equity attained in the 19th century. A 'codification' of English Equity was therefore unnecessary. It is doubtful whether the stability of Roman Equity was ever achieved by means of codification, or something resembling it. The stability of Roman Equity was ensured by the *communis opinio* of the lawyers as expressed in their *libri ad Edictum.*[13] This particular development is illustrated by Verhagen's contribution on security interests, which shows that the innovative role of the *ius praetorium* was taken over by the imperial rescript practice (*ius novum*) after the consolidation of the praetorian edict under Hadrian.

After 533, Roman Equity ceased to exist, since it was incorporated in Justinian's *Digests* and was consequently raised to the level of statutory law. From this point on the equitable review of the law became the exclusive preserve of the legislator, the emperor. Judges in any court within the empire were explicitly forbidden to assess the equity of the law (C. 1,14,1). After the reception of Roman law on the continent the imperial privilege was extended to the highest Courts of Appeal of the various principalities. As Willem Zwalve shows, the exercise of equitable discretion by these courts had a destabilizing effect on the law, especially in France. This primarily occurred because judicial decisions were as a rule unmotivated, thus preventing the emergence of reliable reports of equity cases, which had been the instrument by which English Equity was stabilized into a body of coherent *law*. The French monarch Louis XIV put a (partial) stop to this practice by prohibiting his courts, especially the sovereign courts ('Parlements'), to deviate from royal legislation 'sous prétexte d'équité', in a repetition of Constantine's ban from C. 1,14,1.

After the French revolution, the iniquity or deficiency of a statute could only be amended by legislation. This was considered to be a consequence

---

12 *Fry v Porter* 1 Mod. 300, at 307; 86 Eng. Rep. 898, at 902.

13 Macnair writes that it is 'trite' that Hadrian promulgated 'a codified form of the Edict drafted by the jurist Julian', but see W.J. Zwalve, "Einige Bemerkungen zur Constitutio Tanta/Dedooken § 18", *TvR* 51 (1983), 139–145.

of the doctrine of separation of powers, preventing a return to the arbitrariness of the ancient 'Parlements' abolished in 1790. As the memory of arbitrary decisions on the basis of equity dwindled in France, the highest judicial authority, the 'Cour de Cassation', slowly and cautiously though on occasion surprisingly blatantly[14] encroached upon the preserve of the legislator, by introducing new remedies not provided in the Code civil. For the most part, however, the exercise of equity in modern French case law occurs within a context that Anglo-American lawyers would identify as construction of the law according to the 'equity of the statute', to which David Ibbetson pays attention in his contribution. It is only in the Netherlands that a really remarkable development has occurred. Although Constantine's ban on the equitable review of statutory law is still in force there,[15] the new Dutch civil code of 1992 explicitly provides that 'a rule binding upon [obligor and obligee] by virtue of *law* [...] does *not* apply to the extent that, in the given circumstances, this would be unacceptable according to the standards of reasonableness and fairness.'[16] Willem Zwalve contends that this rule is the result of the muddling of two different kinds of equity: the conscience-based subjective concept of *bona fides* ('English Equity') and the objective concept of *aequitas* or *epieikeia*. By replacing the former concept with the latter in the law of obligations, the Dutch legislator, though stressing that this equitable discretion is a power to be used most sparingly, has in fact opened the way for a new phenomenon, Dutch Equity. Whether this new form of equity will eventually be harnessed into a system of reliable substantive law, remains to be seen.

Four contributions are present to substantiate the interaction between *ius civile* and *ius honorarium* (and *ius praetorium* in particular), and Common law and Equity, in Roman law and English law respectively. Two relate to the law of property and the other two to the law of obligations.

As far as the law of property is concerned, Roman Equity has been instrumental in overcoming formalities imposed by Roman Common law. John Cartwright deals with what certainly is one of the most important incidents in classical Roman law, i.e. the correction of a transfer of title to

14 The introduction of the *actio de in rem verso* in the 'Boudier'-case (*Patureau-Miran c. Boudier*, Req. 15 June 1892, *D.* 1892,1,596) is the most obvious example. It is less well known that this decision is now practically overruled in France by subsequent case law on the basis of the principle of 'enrichissement *sans cause*'.

15 Art. 11 of the Statute, containing General Principles of Legislation (1830).

16 Art. 6:2 subs. 2 of the Dutch civil code (BW).

res mancipi (cattle, slaves and Italian land) which had failed because the formality required by the *ius civile, mancipatio*, had been disregarded in favour of an informal *traditio*. In this instance, on condition that all the requirements of a valid transfer by way of *traditio* were met, the praetor protected the interest of the transferee against all claims by the transferor (and his successors) and against third parties encroaching upon his possession by an ingenious mix of praetorian remedies (*actio Publiciana* and the *exceptio* (*replicatio*) *rei venditae et traditae*), thus turning the possession of the transferee into *de facto* ownership ('bonitary ownership'). In English law, Equity has operated similarly by correcting some formalities required by Law on the basis of the maxim 'Equity considers as done what ought to be done', exemplified in *Walsh v Lonsdale*.[17] Although the concept of bonitary ownership has been expunged from the civil law ever since Justinian abolished *mancipatio* in favour of the informal *traditio*, modern civil law still stands in need of it.

> A good example is the following problem of modern Dutch law. For the valid transfer of title to land, Dutch law requires a valid consideration (*causa*) and a transaction in front of a notary which has to be registered in the Land Register to complete the transfer. What happens, when transferor and transferee have done everything in their power to perfect the title of the transferee, but the notary fails to register? English law (Equity) will apply the rule in *Walsh v Lonsdale* (see for example *Re Rose*),[18] but Dutch law fails to provide a satisfactory solution. The transferee will acquire title by acquisitive prescription after ten years (Art. 3:99, subs. 1 of the Dutch civil code), but what happens if the transferor fails within that period and his trustee in bankruptcy wishes to lay claim to the land as belonging to the assets of the bankrupt at law, to be sold on behalf of his creditors? Only by recognizing remedies like the ancient praetorian *exceptio rei venditae et traditae* (and, consequently, the possibility of bonitary ownership) can modern Dutch law escape from this predicament.

The Roman law of security interests as we know it, contained in Justinian's Corpus Iuris, is practically entirely the product of praetorian intervention and later imperial legislation, while the English law of security interests has largely been molded by Equity. Hendrik Verhagen draws attention to parallel lines of development in Roman law and English law. He sets out by comparing charge-based security in Roman law and English law, with an emphasis on the floating charge. This is interesting because

[17] (1882) 21 Ch.D. 9.
[18] [1952] Ch. 499.

continental civil law has turned its back on the old Roman floating charge since the promulgation of the modern codes in the 19th century. These are all based on the so-called 'specialty'-principle, implying that security interests can only vest in specifically identifiable separate assets of a debtor, thus excluding not only the floating charge, but also the general hypothec ('Generalhypothek') on *all* the assets of a debtor. 19th-century continental legislators concurred with the opinion of Lord Mansfield that the assignment of an entire estate for security purposes 'tends to defeat the whole system of bankrupt laws'.[19] However, since the second half of the 19th century Lord Mansfield's sound principle has been overruled by the rise of floating charges, 'and a great scandal it is'.[20] It is not unusual in Anglo-American legal literature and court decisions to characterize (fixed and floating) charges as forms of 'hypothecation'[21] since they leave the legal title to secured property with the chargor while vesting a special proprietary interest in the chargee, just like a Roman hypothec did and a modern civilian hypothec does. Roman hypothecs were the product of Roman Equity and English charges are a typical product of English Equity, since they are mainly though not exclusively inspired by the construct of the declaration of trust. In modern business transactions, where corporations are prominently present, fixed and floating charges have now practically superseded the old security interests of the Common law, chattel mortgages and pledges, just like the ancient *fiducia* of Roman Common law was supplanted by a non-possessory security interest of praetorian origin, the hypothec.

From a continental perspective, the problem with English 'contract law' is that there are really two kinds of contract law, rather than one. One is quite familiar, even to civilians. It is the law of simple contracts, informal agreements. The other is less familiar to continental civilians, but nevertheless of equal importance. It is the law of covenants, agreements embodied in a formal written deed, a document traditionally 'signed, sealed and delivered'. Once an agreement is reduced into a deed many doctrines peculiar to the law of simple contract, including the doctrine of consideration, cease to apply, since the agreement is merged into the document.

---

19 *Wilson v Day* (1759) 2 Burr. 827, at 830; 97 Eng. Rep. 583, at 585.

20 *Salomon v A. Salomon & Co. Ltd.* [1897] AC 22, at 53 *per* Lord Macnaghten. We should stress that modern continental banking practice has practically eliminated the 'specialty-principle' through the construct of a comprehensive transfer of all after acquired property (as in Germany) or similar stratagems.

21 See, for example, *In re Slee (ex parte North Western Bank)* (1872) LR 15 Eq. 69.

From that moment on it is the deed rather than the underlying agreement that conveys interests in property or creates obligations. It is a construct closely resembling the *contractus litteris* of classical Roman law.[22] Frits Brandsma refers to it in the introduction to his contribution on rescission of contracts in classical Roman law and English law. He reveals another striking similarity between classical Roman law and English law. Neither was developed on the basis of general principles of substantive law, but on the basis of forms of action in the broadest sense, meaning active and defensive procedural remedies rather than rights, available either at Law (*ius civile*) or in Equity (*ius praetorium*). Like the English Lord Chancellor in his Court of Conscience, the Roman praetor was instrumental in providing remedies not available at Law, such as the *exceptio doli* in cases like that of the Roman *eques* Gaius Canius who was subjected to fraud by the crafty Sicilian Pythius.

The praetorian origins of many remedies of modern continental civil law are still clearly recognizable. Modern civil law still deals with a contract concluded by fraud as valid at law, though voidable at the instance of the defrauded party. Whether or not in Roman law avoidance had an effect *in rem*, affecting third parties, did not depend on any general principles of conceptual jurisprudence typical of modern continental civil law (retroactivity and the ensuing reversion of title), but on the nature of the remedy involved. Sometimes it had an effect *in rem*, as with duress, sometimes it had not, as with fraud. In English Equity, conversely, the guiding principle in granting equitable relief against third parties was and is not the nature of the remedy involved, the question whether it was *in rem* or merely *in personam*, but the conscience of the party against whom equitable relief was sought, amounting to the question whether or not his conduct implied a constructive trust on behalf of the party seeking relief. In this respect at least, the Lord Chancellor was much more consistent than the Roman praetor.

In the final contribution, Willem Zwalve returns to the theme of Aristotelian *epieikeia* and substantive law by addressing the history of the provision of D. 17,1,26,6 since the reception of Roman law on the continent. That history contains a rare example of the inconsistency of Aristotelian equity on the one hand and the creative function of misinterpretation in the law on the other. A casual remark in the Accursian gloss seduced some medieval civilians to contend that the provision of D. 17,1,26,6, by

[22] Gaius 3,128–133.

denying a commissioner a claim against his principal for the reimbursement of accidental losses incurred while executing his commission, was so inequitable that it should not be applied by the courts. This contention was rejected by most of the medieval Italian commentators, but approved by the French Parlements ('nous suivons la glosse') resulting in a provision in the French civil code of 1804 making the principal liable for *all* losses incurred by a commissioner in the execution of his commission (Art. 2000 Cc). This provision was copied in the Dutch civil code of 1838, replacing the French Code civil in the Netherlands. A hundred years later it was regarded by many Dutch authors as so obviously inequitable that it was replaced by the original rule of D. 17,1,26,6 in the new Dutch civil code of 1992, albeit with an added distinction originating with the early glossator Aldericus (Art. 7:406 BW). The history of this provision confirms Celsus's famous dictum that in deciding cases on purely equitable considerations 'pernicious errors are frequently committed by relying too much on the authority of jurisprudence'.[23]

[23] D. 45,1,91,3 (Paulus, *libro decimo septimo ad Plautium*): *esse enim hanc quaestionem de bono et aequo: in quo genere plerumque sub auctoritate iuris scientiae perniciose inquit erratur.*

PART TWO

EXTERNAL HISTORICAL ASPECTS

CHAPTER ONE

THE EQUITY OF THE LAW: LAW AND EQUITY SINCE JUSTINIAN

W.J. Zwalve

Introduction

The medieval clerks of the oldest still functioning European court of law, the *Audientia Sacri Palatii Apostolici*, the *Rota Romana*, were notoriously corrupt. It was common knowledge throughout medieval Europe[1] and it raised an interesting question, discussed by the eminent civilian Jacques de Revigny († 1296), professor of civil law at the University of Orléans. 'Suppose', he writes in his influential *Lectura Codicis*, 'that I am representing your interests and you send me to the *curia romana*, where the clerks rob me. I come home to my employer ruined and I say: "I am your representative and it is in your service that I have been robbed. I demand that you compensate me for my losses." Equity and good manners suggest a positive answer, the law, however, says the contrary.'[2] For this latter statement, Revigny refers to D. 17,1,26,6, where the Roman lawyer Paul states that an agent has a right to be compensated by his principal for the losses he has incurred in executing his assignment, but not for all losses, explicitly excluding losses caused by robbery and shipwreck.[3] The contrast between law and equity, as stressed by Revigny in this case, was

[1] See the interesting anonymous *Dialogus inter euntem ad curiam et venientem a Roma de malis moribus curie*, published as an appendix in: P. Herde, *Beiträge zum päpstlichen Kanzlei- und Urkundenwesen im dreizehnten Jahrhundert*, 2nd ed. (Kallmünz: Lassleben, 1967), 247–251: *res est notoria* (at 251, *f.* 96*v*.).

[2] Jacques de Revigny, *Lectura super Codice* (ed. Paris, 1519, incorrectly attributed to Pierre de Belleperche by the Parisian publisher = *Opera iuridica rariora* I, ed. D. Maffei, E. Cortese and G. Rossi (Bologna: Forni, 1967)) on C. 1,14,1 (*f.* 32*v*.): *Sum procurator tuus. Mittis me ad curiam romanam. Spoliant me breviarii. Redeo ad dominum nudus. Dico: ego fui procurator tuus et in tuo servitio fui spoliatus. Peto ut resarcias mihi damna mea. Equitas dictaret quod sic et curialitas. Ius dicit contra: ff. Man. l. Inter causas, § non omnia.*

[3] Paulus, *libro trigesimo secundo ad edictum. Non omnia, quae impensurus non fuit mandator<i> imputabit, veluti quod spoliatus sit a latronibus aut naufragio res amiserit vel languore suo suorumque adpraehensus quaedam erogaverit: nam haec magis casibus quam mandato imputari oportet.* See on the emendation *infra*, 177, fnt. 2.

not emphasized by him alone.[4] It already occurred in the Accursian Gloss (*c.* 1250)[5] and was continually referred to throughout the later Middle Ages[6] as the classic case where equity and law are at odds, usually, as Revigny does, in commentaries on a provision of the emperor Constantine, reproduced by Justinian in his Codex as C. 1,14,1. The provision reads as follows:

> It is our duty alone, as it is permitted to us alone, to look into matters involving equity and law.[7]

Constantine's decree on the privilege of the emperor to rule on the equity of the law marks an important event in Roman legal history. It pins down the exact date (3 December 316) on which the powers of a Republican Roman magistrate of ancient standing, the *praetor urbanus*, to correct Roman common law (*ius civile*) on equitable grounds (*aequitatis gratia*) had finally come to an end, to be replaced by the powers of an absolute monarch to dispense justice in his own right. On this date the traditional dual structure of Roman law (*ius civile* as opposed to *ius praetorium*) definitively ceased to be a dynamic and formative factor in the development of substantive Roman law. In this contribution, I intend to show first how the civil law lost the dual structure of classical Roman law and

---

4 Nor is the example he gives new. An elaborate version is also found in the commentary on C. 1,14,1 by Odofredus († 1265), the rival of Accursius: *Lectura super Codice* I (ed. Lyon, 1552 = *Opera iuridica rariora* V.1, ed. D. Maffei, E. Cortese and G. Rossi (Bologna: Forni, 1968)), on C. 1,14,1 (under no. 5, *f.* 35*v.*). Odofredus ascribes this example to the 'Ultramontani'. This must be one of the first references to academic legal education in France by one of the Italian *doctores*.

5 See Gl. 'Iusque' on C. 1,14,1.

6 See, for example, Cinus Pistoiensis (*c.* 1270–1336), *Lectura codicis* (ed. Venice, 1493), on C. 1,14,1 (but for Cinus' opinion on D. 17,1,26,6 see also *infra*, 185, fnt. 35); Jacobus Butrigarius (*c.* 1274–1348), *Lectura super Codice* (ed. Paris, 1516 = *Opera iuridica rariora* XIII, ed. D. Maffei, E. Cortese and G. Rossi (Bologna: Forni, 1973), on C. 1,14,1; Albericus de Rosate (*c.* 1290–1354), *Commentarii in secundam Digesti Veteris partem* (ed. Venice, 1585 = *Opera iuridica rariora* XXII, ed. D. Maffei, E. Cortese and G. Rossi (Bologna: Forni, 1977)) on D. 17,1,26,6: *Rigorosus est iste § et contra aequitatem*; Bartolus (1314–1357), *Commentarii super prima parte Codicis* (ed. Venice, 1526), on C. 1,14,1; Paulus de Castro (*c.* 1362–1441), *In primam Codicis partem Commentaria* (ed. Venice, 1582), on C. 1,14,1.

7 Constantinus, 316: *Inter aequitatem iusque interpositam interpretationem nobis solis et oportet et licet inspicere*. Constantine's provision is also reproduced, in a somewhat extended version, in the *Codex Theodosianus*, from which Justinian took it: see C.Th. 1,2,3. On the antithesis between *aequitas* and *ius scriptum* in the writings of the medieval glossators of Roman law, see: E.M. Meijers, "Le conflit entre l'équité et la loi chez les premiers glossateurs", *TvR* 17 (1941), 117–135 (= *Etudes d'Histoire du Droit* IV, ed. R. Feenstra and H.F.W.D. Fischer (Leiden: Universitaire Pers Leiden, 1966), 143–156); H. Lange, "Ius aequum und ius strictum bei den Glossatoren", *ZSS* 71 (1954), 319–347.

secondly how it came to introduce a ban on an equitable review of the law, only to end up, at least in my own country of the Netherlands, with an equitable discretion of judges that would have dumbfounded classical Roman lawyers and will most certainly flabbergast common lawyers.

From Classical Roman Law to the Middle Ages

Modern civilians can scarcely imagine the fundamental change in legal paradigm caused by the promulgation of Justinian's Digests in 533. The richly varied and stratified system of sources of law in force until then[8] was instantly changed into a monolithic system, concentrating on but one source of law, statutory law, since Justinian had, as he emphasizes, 'reduced the total to one'.[9] The most obvious consequence of this reduction was the elimination of the old distinction between *ius civile*, Roman statutory and customary law as well as the learned literature[10] on the one hand and *ius honorarium*, the law developed by the Roman praetor and other magistrates, on the other. The primary source of *ius praetorium* was not so much the *naturalis ratio*, which was embodied in the *ius gentium*, but, more directly, the *naturalis aequitas*.

> Ulpian explicitly refers to *aequitas naturalis* when he comments on the praetorian edict awarding *restitutio in integrum* to someone under the age of 25 in spite of the fact that, according to the *ius civile*, a man came of age at 14.[11] In fact he does so frequently, for example when commenting on the famous praetorian edict *pacta conventa servabo*, whereby the praetor awarded certain legal consequences to informal agreements not enforceable 'at law'.[12] In all these instances praetorian equity operates on the basis of an act of 'legislation', since the praetor introduced remedies to correct the rigor of the *ius civile* in his *edictum perpetuum*, the jurisdictional edict published by him as the first act of his term of office and containing the principles by which he would be guided in the exercise of his office. Famous examples are the remedies for fraud (*actio de dolo* and *exceptio doli*) introduced by Cicero's friend Aquilius Gallus during his term as praetor. There were however other, more subtle ways to let praetorian equity prevail over the *ius civile*, most notably in cases where the *ius civile* did not provide an action, but where the praetor granted a plaintiff an 'action on the facts of a case' (*actio in factum*),

[8] See Gaius 1,1–7.

[9] *Const. Tanta/Dedoken*, 1.

[10] D. 1,1,7 pr. (Papinianus): *Ius autem civile est, quod ex legibus, plebis scitis, senatus consultis, decretis principum, auctoritate prudentium venit.*

[11] D. 4,4,1 pr. (Ulpianus): *Hoc edictum praetor naturalem aequitatem secutus proposuit.*

[12] D. 2,14,1 pr.: *Huius edicti aequitas naturalis est.*

> or a special extension of an already existing action (*actio utilis*). I will give but one example in order to illustrate this important mechanism. According to the *ius civile*, a contract of mandate (*mandatum*) was terminated by the death of one of the contracting parties.[13] This rule could lead to inequitable results whenever a mandatory incurred expenses in executing his assignment without knowing that his principal had already died. According to the rigor of the law, he could not bring an action against the heir of his principal, since, at law, the contract was terminated by the demise of the principal. We know that, in the time of Cicero, some praetors allowed the mandatory to bring an action against the heir of the principal, whereas others, clinging to the rigor of the law, did not.[14] By the time of Gaius, however, it was generally held that the praetor should award an action in such cases.[15] This development is important, since it shows that *bona fides*, 'good faith', motivated the praetor to intervene long before it was settled that a mandatory had a claim against the heir of his principal on account of it.[16]

By the continuous interaction between 'law' and 'equity', Roman law attained an impressive flexibility, supervised and controlled by the praetor, who developed a complex system of rules meant to, as Papinian has it, 'support, amend and correct' the *ius civile*.[17] However, by the time Justinian ascended to the throne, the *viva vox iuris civilis*,[18] the instrument of equity in Roman law, had been reduced to complete silence. There were still praetors in Rome, but their office was, as a German scholar phrased it, 'zur absoluten Bedeutungslosigkeit herabgesunken'.[19] The judicial functions of the praetor had long since been taken over by an imperial official, the *praefectus urbi*, and his most important function, the development of equitable remedies necessary to support, complement and correct the *ius civile*, had equally long since been taken over by the emperor himself. Ever since the end of the 2nd century AD, the development of Roman law was in the hands of nameless civil servants in the imperial chancery, preparing the countless imperial *rescripta* surviving in Justinian's *Codex*. Though Roman law at least theoretically still had a dual structure (*ius civile* and *ius praetorium*), the *naturalis aequitas* had ceased to be expressed by

---

[13] Gaius 3,160; D. 17,1,26 pr.

[14] Auctor ad Herennium II,13,19: *M. Drusus pr. urbanus, quod cum herede mandati ageretur, iudicium reddidit, Sex. Iulius non reddidit.*

[15] Gaius 3,160; see also D. 17,1,26 pr.

[16] See on *bona fides* also *infra*, 178.

[17] D. 1,1,7,1: *Ius praetorium est, quod praetores introduxerunt adiuvandi vel supplendi vel corrigendi iuris civilis gratia propter utilitatem publicam.*

[18] D. 1,1,8 (Marcianus): *Nam et ipsum ius honorarium viva vox est iuris civilis.*

[19] G. Wissowa *et al.*, ed., *Pauly's Realencyclopedie der classischen Altertumswissenschaft* XXII.2 (Stuttgart: Metzler, 1952), s.v. 'Praetor' (G. Wesenberg), col. 1603.

praetorian remedies, but was articulated by imperial legislation instead. Constantine's decision of 316 confirms that the development of Roman equity was to be the preserve of the emperor, the legislator, rather than the ordinary judiciary. When seen from this perspective, it was only one last step to advance all the law to the august level of imperial legislation. Be this as it may, from the contemporary perspective the final step, taken by Justinian in 533, to raise *all* law to the level of imperial legislation, implied a rethinking of the making of law, a consequence none was so keenly aware of as Justinian himself.

Justinian instructed the judiciary on the use of his new legislation in his famous bilingual *Constitutio Tanta/Dedoken* one of the introductory statutes to the Digests. In this statute he deals with the problem of *lacunae* in the law. Since Justinian, or rather his brilliant minister Tribonian, was certainly not as naive as some continental legislators of a later age, he understood that the assessment that the law has a *lacuna* is based on a specific interpretation of a statutory provision within a specific factual context. And so he recommends a judge, who thinks he has stumbled upon a *lacuna*, to rethink his interpretation of that provision or even to look elsewhere, thus forcing him to proceed *de similibus ad similia*[20] in finding a solution to his problem.[21] However, in the unlikely case that this *modus operandi* does not provide a satisfactory answer to the problem at hand, a referral to the emperor himself is called for, meaning that the judge must leave the interpretation of the provision to the emperor so that the case may be decided on the basis of the imperial instruction (*relatio ante sententiam*):[22]

> If any such case arises let a remedy be sought from the Emperor, because God has set the imperial function over human affairs so that it should be able, whenever a new contingency arises, to correct and settle it and to subject it to suitable procedures and regulations.[23]

---

[20] See the rule in D. 1,3,12 (Julianus): *Non possunt omnes singillatim aut legibus aut senatus consultis comprehendi: sed cum in aliqua causa sententia eorum manifesta est, is qui iurisdictioni praeest ad similia procedere atque ita ius dicere debet.*

[21] There is an interesting discussion in the Gl. 'Non possumus' on D. 1,3,12 on the question whether reasoning by analogy was still allowed when the emperor was near at hand and could easily be consulted.

[22] The procedure was not introduced by Justinian. It is to Constantine, again, that it is to be credited: see C. 7,61,1 (319).

[23] Const. Tanta/Dedoken, 18: *Si quid igitur tale contigerit, augustum imploretur remedium, quia ideo imperialem fortunam rebus humanis deus praeposuit, ut possit omnia quae noviter contingunt et emendare et componere et modis et regulis competentibus tradere.*

It is within this context that Constantine's provision in C. 1,14,1 is to be read. The assessment that a statutory provision leads to inequitable results rests on an interpretation of that provision which seems incorrect *prima facie*, since the law always aims at *aequum et bonum.*[24] That is why a referral to the emperor is called for in this case as well, allowing the emperor to decide on the equity of the law and if necessary provide an equitable solution to the problem at hand.[25] In this way, the *aequitas naturalis* of classical Roman law hardened into an *aequitas scripta*, to which a judge was only allowed to refer if a statutory provision (i.e. the imperial decision) explicitly allowed him to do so.

> The emperor took cognizance of such cases in his capacity of the only legislative authority *and* in his capacity of the highest judicial authority.[26] This may have given Justinian the idea to outright abolish the incident of *relatio ad principem.* As it seems, the instruction of the emperor enabled the judiciary to relieve itself of the burden of deciding hard cases by shifting that responsibility to the emperor. This may have been the reason why, some years after the promulgation of the new Codex Justinianus (534), Justinian issued a statute (Nov. 125, 543) prohibiting the judiciary from further disturbing, as he says, his *serenitas* with such questions and ordering them to dispense justice as they thought best.[27] He explains this decision on the grounds that the true construction of the law or even a decision on the equity of the law in a particular case will finally come to his attention anyway, by way of the ordinary means of appeal. However, Nov. 125 has made less of an impression on the western legal tradition than the original statutory provisions of Constantine, Valentinian and Justinian ordering a *relatio ad principem* in cases of doubt about the equity of the law or the true construction of the law, which were still to be found in the Codex Justinianus, especially in C. 7,61 *rubr.* (*De relationibus*). A medieval excerpt (*authentica*) from the 6th century Latin translation (the so-called *Authenticum*) of this originally Greek Novel was indeed added to the provision of C. 7,61,1 in the medieval manuscripts of the Codex Justinianus,[28] but it was generally construed as

---

Translation taken from A. Watson ed., *The Digest of Justinian* I (Philadelphia: University of Pennsylvania Press, 1998).

24 D. 1,1,1 pr.

25 See also C. 1,14,9 (Valentinianus and Marcianus, 454): (*post alia*) *Si quid vero in isdem legibus latum fortassis obscurius fuerit, oportet id imperatoria interpretatione patefieri duritiamque legum nostrae humanitati incongruam emendari.*

26 On the equation of legislative and judicial powers of the emperor, see Justinian's constitution in C. 1,14,12.

27 On the relation between the provision of C. 1,14,1 and Nov. 125 see N. van der Wal, *Manuale Novellarum Justiniani, aperçu historique du contenu des Novelles de Justinien*, 2nd ed. (Groningen: Chimaira, 1998), no. 1188 (184 and fnt. 112 there).

28 Authentica 'Novo iure' on C. 7,61,1: *Novo iure causa perfecte examinata sententia terminetur; quae exsecutioni legitimae demandatur, nisi ab ea fuerit appellatum.*

merely meaning that judges were not entitled to shift the burden of deciding hard cases onto the highest judicial authority by ordering a *relatio ante sententiam* without due consideration of the matter.[29] Accordingly, *relatio ante sententiam* was never abolished in the West. In fact, it occurred frequently in procedures at canon law, where the pope was always available as the highest authority. Many, if not most of the papal decretals collected in the *Liber Extra*, the codification of pope Gregory IX (1234), contain legal advice (*sacrae iussiones*) given at the request of lower authorities. One can only speculate about the possible development of continental civil law if medieval German emperors had been in a position to play a similar role.

From the Middle Ages to the French Revolution

Fortunately, we can pass over the five centuries during which Western Europe descended into the abyss of the Dark Ages. Having reached the beginning of the 12th century, we can return to our question as it was raised in Italy at that time. The five miserable centuries in between did, however, have their effect on the nature of that question. It was not, as it had been in the days of Justinian, whether a judge could rule on the equity of a statutory provision, but whether a judge could rule on the equity of the law as it was understood by then. After five centuries of decline, the system of sources of law had fundamentally changed once again. Instead of Roman law, which had been exclusively statutory law ever since Justinian, customary law had become the primary source of law in the Middle Ages and the question therefore was whether a judge was free to rule on the equity of customary law. As it happens, the Roman Catholic Church—involved in a grand struggle to promote civilized standards in a world lapsed into barbarism—felt that a negative answer to this question would have upheld the uncivilized customs which the predominantly German nations of (Western) Europe called their 'law'. Consequently, a succession of medieval popes entered into a highly successful campaign to eliminate customary law as an autonomous source of law by subjecting it to

29 See, on this construction of the authentica 'Novo iure', the Gl. 'Quoniam' on Coll. IX, Tit. VIII (Nov. 125); Azo, *Summa codicis* (ed. Venice, 1596), on C. 7,61 no. 1. Both authorities refer to D. 5,1,79,1. See also the Gl. 'De inquisitione processu' (*c.* 1265) on X. 2,28,68 and especially the comments of the medieval authority on the law of civil procedure, Guillaume Durant (*c.* 1230–1296), in his *Speculum iuris*, Lib. II, Part. II, Tit. *De relationibus*. It emerges from all of these authorities that whenever a judge was in doubt about the true construction of the law, he was entitled but not necessarily required to refer the matter to a higher authority.

the *aequitas canonica*, starting with the following rebuke directed at the unfortunate bishop Wimund of Aversa by pope Gregory VII (1021–1085):

> If you want to set a conflicting rule of customary law against this, you ought to realize that the Lord says: 'I am the Truth and Life'. He did not say: 'I am the custom', but the Truth. To quote a phrase from Saint Cyprian, any usage, no matter how old and no matter how widely held, must certainly be overruled by the truth and a custom that is contrary to the truth must be abolished.[30]

The papal doctrine culminated in a provision in one of the first real codes of law to appear in Western Europe, the *Decretals of Gregory IX*, or the *Liber Extra* (X.), as it is usually called:

> No one who is in his right mind thinks that natural law can be set aside by a mere custom, since although the authority of an ancient custom is no small thing, it is nevertheless not strong enough to set aside positive law unless it is reasonable and has been legitimately confirmed by an enduring usage.[31]

The tenor of this provision is clarified in the Gl. 'Legitime' in the following way: customary law can indeed set aside statutory law (read: Roman law), provided it is reasonable *and* provided it has been tolerated by a legislator aware of the existence of the custom.[32] The canon law doctrine was of course supported by many medieval civilians,[33] since the provision just cited from the Decretals of Gregory IX was almost literally taken from Justinian's Codex (C. 8,52(53),2):

---

30 Decr. dist. 8, c. 5: *Si consuetudinem fortassis opponas, advertendum quod Dominus dicit 'Ego sum veritas et vita'. Non dixit 'Ego sum consuetudo', sed veritas. Et certe (ut beati Cypriani utamur sententia) quaelibet consuetudo, quantumvis vetusta, quantumvis vulgata veritati omnimodo est postponenda et usus qui veritati est contrarius, est abolendus.*

31 X. 1,4,11: *nemo sanae mentis intelligit naturali iure […] quacunque consuetudine […] posse aliquatenus derogari. Licet etiam longaevae consuetudinis non sit vilis auctoritas: non tamen est usqueadeo valitura, ut vel iuri positivo debeat praeiudicium generare, nisi fuerit rationabilis et legitime sit praescripta.*

32 Gl. 'Legitime' on X. 1,4,11: (*post alia*) *et sciente illo qui potest ius condere*, referring to D. 1,3,32,1.

33 The medieval civilians had a problem here because the Digests clearly stated (D. 1,3,32,1) that customary law equalled statutory law (*inveterata consuetudo pro lege custoditur*), since it rested on the consent of the subjects much like a formal statute (*lex*). Consequently, any formal statute was capable of being repealed by a later contrary custom. The best solution to this obvious contradiction was suggested by the early glossator Placentinus († 1182 or 1192), according to whom (Gl. 'Aut rationem' on C. 8,52(53),2) the text in the Digests referred to ancient times, when the power to legislate still lay with the Roman people, whereas in later times that power was vested in the emperor exclusively. Accordingly, imperial legislation could not be set aside by a later contrary custom.

> The authority of custom and long usage is no mean thing, but it should not prevail to the extent that it overrules reason or the law.[34]

These were also the convictions of the canonists and civilians packing one of the most prestigious courts of law on the continent, second only to the *Rota romana*, the 'Parlement de Paris'. From the second half of the 13th century onward it subjected French customary law to the test of reasonability,[35] more often than not meaning its compliance with Roman and canon law. One of the first victims was the doctrine that a deed, the 'lettre scellée' of French customary law, can only be defeated by another deed, thus allowing a defendant to prove by parole evidence that he had already paid to the plaintiff what was due under the deed.[36]

The authority of the court, the 'Parlement', to interfere with customary law in this way rested on the conviction expressed in the Gl. 'Legitime' just mentioned, that customary law was not binding on the legislator, the King, and consequently not binding on the Court either since the Court was doing justice *vice regis*. Accordingly, it was at liberty to set aside customary law whenever equity seemed to demand it. Since the King was *legibus solutus*,[37] so was his Court.[38] This seems to have been one of

[34] Constantinus, 319: *Consuetudinis ususque longaevi non vilis auctoritas est, verum non usque adeo sui valitura momento, ut aut rationem vincat aut legem.*

[35] J.P. Dawson, *The Oracles of the Law* (Ann Arbor: The University of Michigan Law School, 1968), 296, fnt. 17, mentions six instances from the 'Reports' (*Quaestiones Variae*) of Jean le Coq (Johannes Gallus, †1400), the first French reporter ('arrêtiste'), in which the 'Parlement de Paris' rejected a local custom because it considered that custom unreasonable. See *Quaestiones Johannis Galli*, ed. M. Boulet (Paris: E. de Boccard, 1944), no. 68 (= *Stilus supremae curiae parlamenti*, ed. C. Dumoulin (Paris, 1558), no. 64); 121 (115); 182 (177); 198 (191); 277 (269); 278 (270). In all these instances Le Coq is quite positive about the rejection of a particular custom by the Parlement. The usual expression is *per arrestum non fuit recepta consuetudo*. One wonders how Le Coq could have known this, since the 'Parlement' gave no reasons for its decisions. The answer seems to be that in the oral pre-trial proceedings before the 'Grand Chambre' the advocates of the parties had to indicate their contentions to be proved later point by point (*articulatim*). It could happen that one of the parties contended a custom in its favour. If this assertion was struck by the court from the list of contentions to be proved later on, one can be reasonably sure it did so because it disapproved of the custom.

[36] For this development in France see my article "Sola scriptura, an Essay in Comparative Legal History", *TvR* 80 (2012), 95–128.

[37] D. 1,3,31: *princeps legibus solutus est.*

[38] Jacques d'Ableiges (†1402), *Grand Coutumier de France*: 'la cour n'est liée, ni obligée a aucune loy ne a aucun stille tellement qu'elle ne puisse faire le contraire quant il lui plaist, car c'est la cour capitale du royaume et le roy est empereur en son royaume et y peut faire loys et establissements et deffaire se il lui plaist.' This passage is not in *Le Grand Coutumier de France*, ed. E. Laboulaye and R. Dareste (Paris: Durand and Pedone-Lauriel, 1868), but it is cited from a medieval manuscript (Bibl. Nat. u.a. Fr. 3555, *f.* 169) by P. Guilhiermoz,

the reasons why the 'Parlement de Paris' abstained from giving grounds for its decisions.[39] This peculiar phenomenon is explained *c.* 1337 by an anonymous justice in that court who wrote the following lines in a confidential memorandum intended only for the eyes of other justices in the Parlement:

> The secrets of the Supreme Court are not to be divulged, since the Court sometimes decides contrary to the rigor of the law and sometimes even contrary to the law itself, which does not bind the King, being sovereign and not bound by the law, and this happens frequently.[40]

Be this as it may, the right of sovereign courts, like the 'Parlement de Paris', to overrule customary law (and Roman law for that matter) and dispense justice on equitable grounds was undisputed in France during the 'ancien régime'. It was invariably based on the fact that sovereign courts participated in the Royal Sovereignty and were accordingly entitled to let equity prevail over the law, sometimes even with explicit reference to Constantine's provision in C. 1,14,1.[41] Consequently, there has never been a 'court of equity' as opposed to a 'court of law' in France, nor anywhere else on the continent. There was no need for that since the highest courts of law exercised equitable discretion as a matter of course.

Three consequences of the doctrine at the basis of the equitable jurisdiction of continental courts during the 'ancien régime' need to be emphasized. It implied first of all that only sovereign courts were entitled to let equity

---

Enquêtes et Procès: Étude sur la procédure et le fonctionnement du Parlement au XIVe siècle (Paris: Picard, 1892), 152, fnt. 1.

39 Dawson, *Oracles*, 287.

40 *Style de la Chambre des Enquêtes*, in P. Guilhiermoz, *Enquêtes et Procès*, 221: *Nec debent cuilibet apparere secreta curie supreme [...] quae curia quandoque contra iuris rigorem, vel etiam contra jus aliquociens, ordinat [...] quod ius non ligat Regem, tamquam superiorem et solutum legibus et juribus [...] et hoc frequenter fit.*

41 See Claude-Joseph de Ferrière (*c.* 1680–*c.*1748), *Dictionnaire de Droit et de Pratique* I (ed. Paris, 1771), 543 s.v. 'Droit étroit': 'Il n'y a parmi nous que les Juges souverains qui puissent quelquefois s'écarter dans leurs Jugements de la rigueur de la Loi. [...] La raison est que les Juges des Compagnies Souveraines sont les dépositaires de l'autorité du Prince, auquel il appartient d'être l'arbitre entre la Loi et l'équité' (referring to C. 1,14,1). Ferrière also refers to Louis Charondas le Caron (1534–1613), *Pandectes ou Digestes du Droit François*, Livre I, chap. V (*De l'équité*) (= *Oeuvres de Me Louis Charondas le Caron* II (ed. Paris, 1637), 20), where it is said that 'Je sçay bien toutefois que les Cours souveraines, qui jugent sous l'auctorité du Roy, ont puissance d'interpreter, moderer et suppleer les Loix et Ordonnances: et sont leurs Arrests, principalement ceux qui décident les causes en general, suivis et tirez en exemple et consequence: tellement qu'ils ont effect de Loy et constituent un droit universel et c'est á cause de la souveraineté, que la Roy a departie à ses Parlements et Conseils souverains.'

> prevail over the law. Since this privilege was based on sovereign authority, lower courts were *not* entitled to it.[42] Secondly, not even the sovereign courts, the French 'Parlements', were entitled to rule on the equity of royal legislation ('ordonnances'),[43] and thirdly, whenever a sovereign court had decided against customary law on equitable grounds in an 'arrêt de règlement', this decision, having the force of a royal decree, was binding on lower courts.[44]

There is a remarkable example of the practice of the French 'Parlements' to let equity prevail over the law in their treatment of D. 17,1,26,6,[45] the very text that was traditionally cited as the classic instance where equity and law are at odds.[46] I will deal with it in another contribution to this book.[47]

Dissatisfaction with the Equitable Discretion of Sovereign Courts

The doctrine of the equitable discretion of sovereign courts was not peculiar to France. It was adhered to elsewhere on the continent as well. It is for example well documented for the sovereign principality of Savoy in the very influential *Codex Fabrianus*.[48] I refer to Savoy in particular, since we know that when the transalpine part of that principality had been conquered by the French king Francis I in 1536, the first supplication his subjects made to their new sovereign was to deny the privilege of an equitable jurisdiction to the new 'Parlement de Chambéry' established by

---

[42] See also *infra*, 29.

[43] The 'Parlements' themselves seem to have contested this, which may have caused Louis XIV to explicitly prohibit his 'Parlements' to subject royal legislation to their equitable discretion in his famous 'Ordonnance civil' (1667, Art. 6): see *infra*, 28, fnt. 53.

[44] Charondas, *Pandectes*, quoted *supra*, 26, fnt. 41.

[45] For a recent discussion of this text according to classical Roman law see P. Gröschler, "Schadens- und Aufwendungsersatz bei Julian, Afrikan und Paulus", in *Africani quaestiones, Studien zur Geschichte und Dogmatik des Privatrechts*, ed. J.D. Harke (Berlin/Heidelberg: Springer 2011), 17–36. Since classical Roman law is not at issue here, I will refrain from a discussion of this article, although I do not share some of its conclusions.

[46] See *supra*, 18, fnt. 6.

[47] See *infra*, 177 *seq*.

[48] A massive collection of decisions from the *Senatus Supremus* of that principality, collected by its learned Chief Justice, Antoine Favre (1557–1624), and utilized all over the continent. See *Codex Fabrianus* (I used the edition Geneva, 1649), Lib. 4, tit. 15, *Def.* 33, fnt. 16 (*cognoscit enim senatus vice Principis*, a footnote to the line in *Def.* 33, where it reads that *senatus aequitatis maiorem quam stricti iuris rationem habere soleat*). See also Lib. 7, tit. 14, *Def.* 1, fnt. 8 and Lib. 9, tit. 29, *Def.* 5, fnt. 4 ((*senatus*) *personam repraesentat ac maiestatem Principis*).

Francis in Savoy.[49] Obviously, the Savoyards were afraid to be subjected to the same equitable discretion as the subjects of the Parlement de Paris. Instead they preferred the certainty of their ancient 'coutumes' and Roman law.[50] Dissatisfaction with the equitable discretion of the sovereign courts was widespread in France itself as well, as is testified by a famous legal proverb: 'dieu nous préserve de l'équité des Parlements'.[51] Sometimes this aversion was even shared by the sovereign himself. In his bull *In throno iustitiae* (1561) pope Pius IV (1560–1565) reformed the *Rota* and instructed the justices (*auditores*) of that court to follow their precedents and not to overrule them 'on the pretext of an equity not based on enacted law' (*praetextu aequitatis in iure non scriptae*).[52] In 1667 Louis XIV followed suit by ordering his courts to strictly adhere to royal legislation and not to deviate from it 'sous prétexte d'équité'.[53] In doing so he followed the example of Justinian, as he also did by ordering a *relatio ad principem* whenever there was doubt about the construction of a royal statute.[54] In this way, the equitable jurisdiction of the French 'Parlements' was limited to customary law and Roman law. It was not yet entirely abolished though. Not until the French revolution did the idea, that the equitable jurisdiction of the highest courts was really an expression of the legislative powers of the sovereign in the name of whom they exercised it, lead to decisive steps by a new legislator unwilling to share his authority with the judiciary and, accordingly, in effect restating Constantine's ancient doctrine.

---

[49] On this incident see E. Burnier, *Le Parlement de Chambéry sous François Ier et Henry II (1536–1559)* (Chambéry: A. Bottero, 1862), 13.

[50] Burnier, *Parlement*: 'les Etats, représentés par leur procureur, stipulèrent que les provinces conquises seraient jugées "suivant *la loi et le droit*, et non suivant l'équité".' (emphasis added).

[51] On this proverb, and for a comparison of English and French 'equity', see V.V. Palmer, " 'May God protect us from the Equity of Parlements': Comparative Reflections on English and French Equity Powers", *TLR* 73 (1998–1999), 1287–1308.

[52] *Magnum Bullarium Romanum* II (ed. Lyon, 1673), 58, Pius IV, const. 44 par. 12.

[53] Ordonnance civile, touchant la réformation de la justice, Tit. 1, Art. 6, in *Recueil général des anciennes lois françaises* XVIII, ed. F.A. Isambert *et al.* (Paris: Belin-Leprieur, 1829), 106: 'Voulons que toutes nos ordonnances, édits, déclarations et lettres-patentes soient observées, tant aux jugemens des procès qu'autrement, sans y contrevenir; *ni que sous prétexte d'équité*, bien public, accélération de la justice, ou de ce que nos cours auroient à nous représenter, elles ni les autres juges s'en puissent dispenser ou en modérer les dispositions, en quelque cas et pour quelque cause que ce soit.' (emphasis added).

[54] Ordonnance civile, touchant la réformation de la justice, Tit. 1, Art. 7 (Isambert, *Recueil general* XVIII, 106): 'Si dans les jugemens des procès qui seront pendans en nos cours de parlement et autres nos cours, il survient aucun doute ou difficulté sur l'exécution de quelques articles de nos ordonnances, édits, déclarations et lettres-patentes, *nous leur défendons de les interpréter, mais voulons qu'en ce cas elles aient à se retirer par-devers nous, pour apprendre ce qui sera de notre intention*' (emphasis added).

In concluding this section, I should add that medieval and early modern civilians did *not* believe that equity should play no part in the adjudication process in the lower courts at all. To the contrary: it was generally accepted that any judge, in applying the law, should do so in accordance with natural justice (*aequitas non scripta*).[55] Canon law[56] saw to it that this maxim was widely accepted, because the precepts of the canon law of civil procedure, as expounded in the *Speculum Iuris* by Guillaume Durant (*c.* 1230–1296), contained the guiding principles of medieval continental civil procedure.[57] There was however a restriction in place: a lower judge could not let natural justice prevail over the law, since that was a prerogative of the sovereign (and his sovereign court). Accordingly, in the lower courts there was no ban on an equitable *construction* of the law, but merely on the usurpation of the legislative function under the disguise of interpretation.[58] As far as customary law was concerned, it was generally held by medieval doctrine that inferior courts were not at liberty to overrule it as the sovereign courts could. According to medieval doctrine, Constantine's rule in C. 1,14,1 should not only be applied in the conflict between *aequitas* and *ius scriptum*, but also in the conflict between *aequitas non scripta* and *ius non scriptum*.[59]

From the French Revolution Onwards

During the preparation of the French Code civil a short but bitter conflict arose between the members of the 'Tribunat'[60] on the one hand and the drafters of the Code, Napoleons puppets, on the other, Portalis most prominently among them. It concerned the 'Titre préliminaire' of the Code. One of the bones of contention was Art. 4 of that 'titre', introducing a new criminal offence, 'déni de justice'. It stated that a judge who refused to pass judgement on account of the silence, the obscurity, or the deficiency of the law was guilty of a criminal offence. According to

---

[55] The key text was D. 13,4,4,1 (Ulpianus): *In summa aequitatem quoque ante oculos habere debet iudex*. See also C. 3,1,8 (Constantinus): *Placuit in omnibus rebus praecipuam esse iustitiae aequitatisque quam stricti iuris rationem.*

[56] Decr. causa 4, q. 4, c. 1; Gl. 'De vultu dei iudicium' on X. 3,12,1.

[57] See on this issue Durant, *Speculum*, Lib. I, Part. I, Tit. *De dispensatione* par. 1 ('Aequitas vero') (ed. Basle, 1574, repr. Frankfurt: Vico, 2009), no. 4, p. 59, l. col.

[58] On this issue see Antonio Perez (Perezius, 1583–1673), *Praelectiones in XII libros Codicis* (ed. Amsterdam 1671), on C. 1,14, no. 18.

[59] See the Gl. 'Iusque' on C. 1,14,1: *item potest poni eodem modo in iure stricto et non scripto et aequitate non scripta.* See for some striking examples (all concerning the equity of feudal law) Odofredus in his Commentary on C. 1,14,1 (*supra*, 18, fnt. 4), no. 2–4.

[60] A consultative assembly supposed to advise the French 'législative' and established by the French constitution of 1799, which legitimized Napoleon's 'coup d'état' of the same year. It was suppressed by Napoleon in 1807.

the 'Tribun' Maillia-Garat[61] this was a fallacy, since it forced the judge to commit a far more serious crime, i.e. the offence of interpreting the law,[62] which turned him into a legislator rather than an adjudicator. Garat's opinion is important, since in the course of his 'discours' he refers not only to the equitable jurisdiction of the Roman praetor as unconstitutional, but also to the equitable jurisdiction of the English Lord Chancellor in his Court of Equity. He was well informed on the nature of its jurisdiction by the *Constitution de l'Angleterre*, by the Swiss scholar Jean Louis Delolme,[63] whom he quotes as an authority to inform his audience that such a court, useful though it may be (or may have been) in England, was objectionable in France at the present time 'vu la précision des idées qu'on se forme aujourd'hui'.[64]

> Garat was aware of the fundamental difference between the continental and the English approach to the equity phenomenon. He stresses in his speech that English 'equity' acts *in personam*.[65] It does so because it always operates on the conscience of a defendant,[66] and it is for this reason too that a Court of Equity used to be qualified as a Court of Conscience.[67] Accordingly, it has at its root the subjective civilian concept of *bona fides* ('goede trouw', 'guter Glaube', 'bonne foi'), rather than the objective civilian concept of *aequitas* ('redelijkheid en billijkheid', 'Treu und Glauben', 'équité'). English Equity consists of the sum of all the legal consequences (such as the imposition of a constructive trust) that the Court of Chancery and succeeding courts have drawn over time from this conscience-test that is traditionally at the heart of their activity.[68] Continental civilian 'equity' conversely equals

---

[61] Jacques Joseph Garat, called Maillia-Garat or Garat-Maillia (1767–1837 or 1839).

[62] See his opinion in P.A. Fenet, *Recueil complet des travaux préparatoires du Code civil* VI, (Paris, 1836), 143–170.

[63] Delolme (or De Lolme, 1740–1806) was born and educated as a lawyer in Geneva, but was forced into exile to England, where he studied the constitution.

[64] Garat, in Fenet, *Recueil complet*, 159, quoting Delolme. I found the quote in the first tome of the London 1785 edition of Delolme's *Constitution de l'Angleterre* on 128. There are several editions of this interesting book, which has even been translated into English. The older editions, for example the Amsterdam 1778 edition I consulted, do not have the digression on English Equity which was added by the author in later editions.

[65] Garat, in Fenet, *Recueil complet*, 159–160: 'les publicistes anglais tiennent pour maxime que la cour de chancellerie, qui est la première des cours d'équité, ne saurait porter atteinte aux biens, mais à la personne.'

[66] *Westdeutsche Landesbank Girozentrale v Islington London Borough Council* [1996] AC 669, at 705 *per* Lord Browne-Wilkinson: 'equity operates on the conscience of the owner of the legal interest.'

[67] See M. Macnair, "Equity and Conscience", *OJLS* 27 (2007), 659–681, especially 672 *seq.*

[68] Macnair, "Equity and Conscience", 676: 'From the beginning until 1873–75, this examination of the *conscientia* of the defendant was the absolute centre of the fact-finding procedure of Chancery and other equity-courts.'

> natural justice, or 'reasonableness and fairness', and represents a distinct set of rules directed at the judiciary rather than at subjects. English Equity does *not* equal natural justice.[69] Much harm is done by the fact that continental civilians by and large take for granted that it does.

Delolme was of course referring to the doctrine of separation of powers as attributed to Montesquieu, which was to be enshrined in the 'Déclaration des Droits de l'Homme et du Citoyen' (1789).[70] There was however another element alien to the ideas of Montesquieu contained in that much overrated document, ruling out a fair and equal balance of powers, i.e. the principle of the Sovereignty of the Nation[71] which vested supremacy in the legislature as the voice of the 'volonté générale'. The judiciary, for example, was already brought in line with populist convictions in 1790. The old 'noblesse de robe' and its 'Parlements' were suppressed and replaced by judges chosen by the people for a six-year period.[72] There was no judiciary independent from the legislature in France after that, the less so since judges were instructed to leave all questions relating to the construction of statutes to the legislature, thereby in fact confirming Louis XIV's decree of 1667:

> Décret sur l'organisation judiciaire (1790), Titre II, Art. 12: 'Ils ne pourront point faire de règlemens, mais ils s'adresseront au Corps Législatif toutes les fois qu'ils croiront nécessaire, soit d'interpréter une loi, soit d'en faire une nouvelle.'[73]

A provision such as this is closely connected to yet another consequence of the doctrine of the sovereignty of the people, i.e. the dogma that there can only be one source of law in a society based on that doctrine, statutory law, since in a 'free' society the citizens can only be ruled by a law agreed to by (a majority of) the people or by its representatives in the legislature. In complying with these principles, the new order brought

---

69 See the *caveat* of Lord Greene in *Re Diplock's estate* [1948] 2 All ER 318, at 326: '[...] if the claim in equity exists, it must be shown to have an ancestry founded in history and in the practice and precedents of the courts administering equity jurisdiction. It is not sufficient that because we may think that the 'justice' of the present case requires it, we should invent such a jurisdiction for the first time.'

70 Art. 16: 'Toute Société dans laquelle la garantie des Droits n'est pas assurée, ni la séparation des Pouvoirs déterminée, n'a point de Constitution.'

71 Art. 3: 'Le principe de toute Souveraineté réside essentiellement dans la Nation. Nul corps, nul individu ne peut exercer d'autorité qui n'en émane expressément.'

72 J.B. Duvergier, *Collection complète des Lois, Décrets, Ordonnances, Réglements, Avis du Conseil d'État* I (Paris: Bonnet, 1824), 361 *seq.*

73 Duvergier, *Collection complète*, 363.

about a revolution in the doctrine of sources of law, much like the revolution caused by Justinian in 533. The legal pluriformity of the 'ancien régime' was done away with once and for all and was replaced by a legal uniformity of which an 'absolute' monarch like Louis XIV could only have dreamt.[74] Contemporaries were well aware of this, as is for example clarified by Robespierre himself:

> la législation romaine posait en principe que l'interprétation des lois appartenait à celui qui a fait la loi: *eius est interpretari legem, qui condit legem.* [...] Notre ancien régime avait reconnu lui-même la nécessité de ce principe.[75]

This is a fragment from a speech by Robespierre occasioned by the proposal to establish a Cour de Cassation. It was to be, in the words of Robespierre, 'une dépendance de la puissance législative'.[76] Would it share the equitable powers of the legislature that were once vested in those 'dépositaires de l'autorité du Prince',[77] the ancient 'Parlements'? This was unthinkable under the new constitution. No court of law in France, not even the Cour de Cassation, was to share the equitable jurisdiction of the ancient French 'Parlements' suppressed by the 'Constituante' in 1790. The interpretation of the law as well as the appraisal of the equity of the law was to be the exclusive preserve of the new absolute monarch, the people, as represented by the (majority of the) legislature. Hence the resuscitation of instruments typical of an absolute monarchy such as the *relatio ad principem*, the 'référé législatif',[78] on the basis of the ancient Roman maxim *eius est leges interpretari, cuius est condere.*[79] Consequently, Garat stressed the obvious contradiction between the provision of Art. 4 of the 'titre préliminaire' and the implied ban on interpretation, let alone equitable construction, of the law inherent in the 'référé législatif'. He was right of course, but he was unable to prevent the passing of the 'titre

---

74 On this issue: Albert Rigaudière, "Un rêve royal français: unification du droit", *CRAI* 148 (2004), 1553–1567 and the literature referred to there in fnt. 1.

75 *Archives parlementaires de 1787 à 1860*, première série (1789 à 1860), XV (Assemblée nationale constituante, du 21 avril 1790 au 30 mai 1790) (Paris, 1883), 670.

76 *Archives parlementaires*, ibid.

77 Ferrière, *Dictionnaire*, 543.

78 On the history of the introduction of the 'référé législatif' in 1790 see: P. Alvazi del Frate, *Giurisprudenza e référé législatif in Francia nel periodo revoluzionario e napoleonico* (Turin: Giappichelli, 2005); M. Miersch, *Der sogenannte référé législatif: eine Untersuchung zum Verhältnis Gesetzgeber, Gesetz und Richteramt seit dem 18. Jahrhundert* (Baden-Baden: Nomos, 2000) and Y.L. Hufteau, *La référé législatif et les pouvoirs du juge dans le silence de la loi* (Paris: Presses Universitaires de France, 1965).

79 C. 1,14,12,3 and 5; Const. Tanta/Dedoken, 21 *i.f.*

préliminaire', including the provision of Art. 4, as Napoleon removed him from the 'Tribunat' in 1802. As it stands the 'titre préliminaire' does not contain an explicit ban on equitable construction of the law and neither does it contain a provision that a judge may not assess the equity of the law. It is generally understood that he may not, but for an *explicit* bar on the discretion of a judge to set aside the law whenever equity seems to demand it, we must turn to the Netherlands.

Dutch Equity

The Netherlands fell under the shadow of the French revolution from 1795 onwards and were even part of the Empire since 1810. Consequently, the Code civil obtained force of law in the Netherlands. It remained in force until 1838, when, 25 years after the Netherlands regained independence (1813), it was finally replaced by a 'genuine Dutch product', the 'old' Dutch civil code, repealed in 1992. The 1838 code was based on a draft composed by the Leyden law professor Joan Melchior Kemper (1776–1824). As a matter of course the code had to contain a 'titre préliminaire' on the French model, but whereas Napoleon's code had but six provisions in that 'titre', Kemper's draft provided for no less than 73 sections intended to carefully regulate and restrain a judge's terrible powers of interpretation and construction of the law. It had in S. 49 the precursor of the present Art. 11 of the Statute, containing General Principles of Legislation (1830). It reads as follows:

> Whenever the terms of a statute have a significance clear enough to exclude a different opinion completely, it shall not be at the discretion of the judge to pass judgment on the basis of that opinion against the clear letter of the law, much less so on the basis of a fictitious equity.[80]

Kemper's entire draft was hacked to pieces in Parliament and so was this rather long-winded provision. The new 'titre préliminaire', the 'Statute, containing General Principles of Legislation', was cut down to 14 sections and S. 49 was replaced by the present Art. 11 of that Statute, reading as follows:

[80] Art. 49, Ontwerp 1820: 'Wanneer echter de woorden eener wet eenen zoo duidelijken zin hebben, dat de ondergestelde meening zich op geenerlei wijze met die woorden kan laten overeen brengen, staat het de regter niet vrij, op grond dezer meening, en nog veel minder op grond eener denkbeeldige billijkheid, tegen de duidelijke letter der wet, uitspraak te doen.'

> A judge has to pass judgment on the basis of the law; under no circumstance is he allowed to rule on the intrinsic value or the equity of the law.[81]

A hundred and twenty years later another draft of a new Dutch civil code was presented to the Dutch Parliament. It contained a 'titre préliminaire' as well that was supposed to replace the current Statute, containing General Principles of Legislation. The drafter, the Leiden law professor E.M. Meijers (1880–1954), felt it was necessary to provide some rules on the relation between statutory law on the one hand and other sources of law, such as customary law *and* equity, on the other. In this context he made a distinction between mandatory statutory law (*ius cogens*) and optional statutory provisions (*ius dispositivum*). The latter could be overruled by equity if the circumstances of a case called for it (S. 3 of the draft); the former were incapable of being overruled (S. 1 of the draft). Meijers' 'titre préliminaire' was heavily criticized in the law reviews[82] even before it was brought before Parliament, and it was quietly laid to rest after the untimely demise of the drafter in 1954. However, one provision from his 'titre préliminaire' still survives in the present code, which replaced the old one in 1992. It concerns S. 7 of Meijers' 'titre préliminaire', resurfacing as Art. 3:12 of the present code. It reads as follows:

> In determining what reasonableness and fairness require, generally accepted principles of law, current juridical views in the Netherlands,[83] and the societal and private interests involved in the case must be taken into account.[84]

Originally intended by Meijers as a guide to judges who had to decide a case without the assistance of any provision of statutory law or customary law, the provision has gained quite a different significance in the new Dutch code; a significance that would probably have baffled the drafter,

---

[81] Art. 11 der Wet, houdende Algemene Bepalingen der Wetgeving van het Koninkrijk ('Wet AB'): 'De regter moet volgens de wet regt spreken: hij mag in geen geval de innerlijke waarde of billijkheid der wet beoordeelen.'

[82] See especially the highly critical article by I. Kisch, "Het eerste zevental", *RM Themis* (1955), 137–170.

[83] There is a slight difference in redaction here between Meijers' draft and the final text of the provision in the new Dutch code. Whereas Meijers' draft had the phrase 'current juridical views *of the Dutch people*', the italicized words were replaced by the phrase 'in the Netherlands'. At the time, the legislator felt it was necessary to emphasize that the 'juridical views' of noncitizens residing in the Netherlands were not to be excluded from judicial cognizance: *Parlementaire Geschiedenis van het nieuwe Burgerlijk Wetboek, Boek 3 (Invoering Boeken 3, 5 en 6)*, ed. W.H.M. Reehuis (Deventer: Kluwer, 1990), 1036–1037.

[84] Translations of provisions of the new Dutch civil code are taken from H.C.S. Warendorf *et al.*, *The Civil Code of the Netherlands* (Deventer: Kluwer, 2009).

Meijers, himself.[85] Be this as it may, Meijers' description of the constituent elements of equity, 'reasonableness and fairness', in his 'titre préliminaire' offended one of the direct descendants of the old revolutionary tradition in the Dutch parliament of the time. As a member of the 'steeled cadres' of the former Dutch Communist Party (CPN), Jan Haken (1912–1956) was instinctively aware of his duties under that tradition as well as its Rousseauvian origins.[86] He objected to judges turning themselves into the interpreters of 'the legal convictions held in the Netherlands', since in doing so they acted as legislators by usurping the voice of the people. It is as if the spirit of Robespierre had taken possession of the MP from East-Groningen and was guiding him along the correct revolutionary paths, because he insisted that there was only one proper authority to decide what exactly were 'the legal convictions held in the Netherlands', to wit the representatives of the people as assembled in Parliament.[87] Consequently, he proposed nothing less than a 'référé législatif' any time a judge felt compelled to decide a case on purely equitable principles. He was right of course, but he was not able to prevent the rise of Dutch equity, 'redelijkheid en billijkheid'. Haken, who had survived four years in Buchenwald, died too young in 1956 and was therefore unable to frustrate the introduction of 'Dutch equity' into the law of obligations, most prominently into the following sections of Book 6 (containing general provisions on the law of obligations):

> Art. 6:2 BW
> (subs. 1) An obligee and obligor must, as between themselves, act in accordance with the requirements of reasonableness and fairness.
>
> (subs. 2) A rule binding upon them by virtue of law (*sic*), usage or a juridical act does not apply to the extent that, in the given circumstances, this would be unacceptable according to the standards of reasonableness and fairness.

---

85 As a legislator, Meijers was a representative of the old school by emphasizing the pre-eminence of statutory law over other sources of law such as custom and equity. For this assessment see: J.H.A. Lokin, "De plaats van Meijers in de legistische traditie", in *Rechtsvinding onder het NBW (een Groningse kijk op het nieuwe vermogensrecht)*, ed. C.J.H. Brunner *et al.* (Deventer: Kluwer, 1992), 5–39.

86 For the speech of J. Haken, MP, see: *Parlementaire Geschiedenis van het nieuwe Burgerlijk Wetboek, Invoering Boeken 3, 5 en 6, Voortgang*, ed. W.H.M. Reehuis (Deventer: Kluwer, 1993), 163–165.

87 Haken, in ibid. (my translation): 'What are these 'current juridical views of the Dutch people'? How is a judge to be informed about them? The idea that justice will be done according to the current juridical views of the Dutch people is a fiction. The only place where these juridical views can be properly discussed is Parliament, but that is being sidestepped in these instances.'

> Art. 6:248 BW
> (subs. 1) A contract not only has the juridical effects agreed to by the parties, but also those which, according to the nature of the contract, apply by virtue of law, usage or the requirements of reasonableness and fairness.
>
> (subs. 2) A rule binding upon the parties as a result of the contract does not apply to the extent that, in the given circumstances, this would be unacceptable according to the standards of reasonableness and fairness.

Jan Haken would certainly have objected to these sections. Did they not offer the perfect instrument—ambiguous, imprecise and malleable external standards ('reasonableness and fairness')—to enable the ruling classes and their sinister cronies in the judiciary to further oppress the working classes, much as had been done by German courts only a few years earlier?[88] I cannot speak for Jan Haken, but I do deplore the introduction of external standards in a contractual context, and certainly of imprecise ones such as reasonableness and fairness. Take for example the case advanced by Revigny of the commissioner robbed by the clerks of the *curia Romana*. It purports to be an illustration of the iniquity of the law as expressed in D. 17,1,26,6. But is that provision really as inequitable as many medieval lawyers (Revigny was certainly not the only one) were inclined to believe? And more importantly does the rule expressed in D. 17,1,26,6 even apply to the case advanced by Revigny?

The contract of mandate was, according to Roman law, a *contractus bonae fidei*. Now *bona fides* ('good faith'), unlike Dutch equity, does not refer to objective external standards addressed at the judge directly, to be applied by him as a matter of law, but points to the subjective expectations the contracting parties may mutually have, given the specific circumstances of a specific contract. Consequently, the assessment whether or not a person is *bona fide* or acts *bona fide*, is always a matter of fact rather than law. So it is in the case advanced by Revigny. The rule in D. 17,1,26,6 does not apply to it at all. Not because it is inequitable (it is not), but simply because it does not apply as a matter of *fact*. *Ius est in causa positum*, says the maxim.[89] Now, whenever someone *at that time* accepted a commission to represent someone in a court as infamous as the *Rota romana*, he might expect to be compensated for certain specific losses incurred in

[88] For the abuse of 'Generalklauseln' during that period see the seminal book by B. Rüthers, *Die unbegrenzte Auslegung: zum Wandel der Privatrechtsordnung im Nationalsozialismus* (Frankfurt: Athenäum Fischer Taschenbuch, 1973), generally and especially 210 *seq.*

[89] D. 9,2,52,2 (Alfenus).

the execution of that contract, such as the bribes paid to the clerks, since they were notoriously corrupt. This outcome is borne out by the specific circumstances of the case and good faith (*bona fides*) alone. The Dutch legislator of 1992 has suppressed the concept of 'good faith' in the law of obligations and supplanted it by a different concept, originally not even intended for that purpose at all; a concept—'reasonableness and fairness', to be defined by the objective standards of Art. 3:12 of the Dutch civil code—that is not only equivocal and misleading, but even potentially dangerous; a concept, moreover, that makes a mockery of the provision of Art. 11 of the still obtaining Statute, containing General Principles of Legislation. It seems that modern Dutch law is witnessing a return to the equitable discretion of the courts of the 'ancien régime'. There is one important difference though. Whereas in the old days only the highest courts were allowed to wield their equitable discretion, nowadays any judge in the Netherlands may apply Dutch equity. That is, or ought to be, a disturbing prospect. The often repeated reassuring statement that it concerns a power to be used most sparingly,[90] does not provide comfort at all. We are witnessing all over Western Europe a process wherein the executive power and its henchmen in Parliament are putting the judiciary under constant pressure. We are also witnessing all over Western Europe (and yet again) a related process where populism is on the rise and political discourse, even among the traditional political parties, is reduced to the level of slick one-liners. In an uneasy political atmosphere such as this, it is an uncomfortable feeling that the judiciary has the power to enforce compliance with 'the legal convictions prevailing in the Netherlands' at any time and turn itself into the mouthpiece of public sentiment and resentment. Compliance, *not* legal positivism, was the main weakness of the German judiciary in the dark years between 1933 and 1945.[91] It is not a typically German character trait and so there is no guarantee that the process will not repeat itself elsewhere, certainly not when all the instruments to make it possible are readily available. As with natural law,[92] there is a dark side to equity.

90 See the caveats in: *Parlementaire Geschiedenis van het nieuwe Burgerlijk Wetboek, Boek 6 (Algemeen gedeelte van het Verbintenissenrecht)*, ed. C.J. van Zeben *et al.* (Deventer: Kluwer, 1981), 66 *seq.*: 'only in exceptional cases', 'with great restraint'.

91 On this issue see the important article by W. Ott and F. Buob, "Did Legal Positivism Render German Jurists Defenceless During the Third Reich?", in *Praktische Vernunft, Gesetzgebung und Rechtswissenschaft*, ed. W. Schreckenberger and C. Starck (Stuttgart: Steiner, 1993), 92–105.

92 On this see F. Wittreck, *Nationalsozialistische Rechtslehre und Naturrecht* (Tübingen: Mohr Siebeck, 2008).

CHAPTER TWO

THE EQUITY OF THE COMMON LAW COURTS

P. Brand

Good Faith and Fraud

In Hilary term 1290 Agnes, the daughter of Richard de Brok, brought a suit against Edmund of Navestock in the court of Common Bench at Westminster, the main English court for the hearing of civil litigation. She was claiming chattels (movables) to the value of £66 which he was unjustly withholding from her. We know about this litigation both from the formal official record of the case and from two independent, unofficial law reports of it. I will be editing all of these for a forthcoming Selden Society volume, in continuation of my series of *The Earliest English Law Reports*.[1] Her claim was an unusual, perhaps even an unprecedented one, certainly in the Common Bench. It was for the return of the movable goods (animals, grain, clothes, household linen and money) which her father Richard had handed over to Edmund in December 1277 at Richard's house in Barking in Essex as a marriage-portion, apparently shortly prior to their marriage, and which Edmund had then taken with the agreement of his and her kinsmen to his own house ten miles away at Navestock, and had subsequently treated as his own property. The basis of her claim was that immediately (*statim*) after Edmund had married her he had begun suing for a dissolution of their marriage (*divorcium*) in an ecclesiastical court on the grounds that he had previously contracted marriage with another woman (Elizabeth de Ludehale)[2] and had obtained a dissolution of his marriage to Agnes from the Court of Arches in London on these grounds,[3]

---

[1] P. Brand, ed., *The Earliest English Law Reports* (London: Selden Society, 1996–; hereafter cited as *EELR*). It will be 1290H.1 in vol. 5 of that series. The count is also used as specimen in the pleading manual *Novae Narrationes*, ed. E. Shanks (London: Selden Society, 1963) where it is the basis of B220 (at 115–116) and C261 (at 288–289).

[2] The reports however suggest, more plausibly, that he arranged for Elizabeth to initiate the suit and in the end this is what a jury found to be the case.

[3] The Court of Arches was the main appeal court for the province of Canterbury and it seems likely that there had been prior proceedings in the consistory court of the bishop of London, probably at St Paul's, but this goes unmentioned in the case.

but he had then refused to return the chattels given by her father on the basis of the marriage. Agnes claimed damages of one hundred pounds.

Only the reports, but not the official record, tell us of the various unsuccessful pleas made by Edmund's serjeant (Hugh of Lowther): that, since the chattels had been given in marriage, jurisdiction over the suit belonged to the ecclesiastical court; that, since the original grantor had been her father Richard, action to claim the chattels he had given lay properly only for him or for his executors, and not for Agnes; that, if the chattels had been given in marriage to them both, her claim could only be to half the chattels. All the official record shows is that Edmund denied that Richard had given him any goods and chattels by reason of the marriage and offered to support his denial by wager of law, that is to say denial on his own oath supported by the oaths of eleven compurgators. Since the original grant had not been attested by any written deed this was something that English legal custom of this period would normally have found an acceptable offer of proof. The record, however, shows that it was rejected on the grounds that the initial contract had been *adeo manifestus* ('so public'), the delivery of the chattels also so 'manifest' and their taking to his home so 'manifest' that this was more properly a matter for trial by jury than compurgation by Edmund and (the record adds) by an Edmund who had already rendered himself 'suspect' by the annulment.

The two reports add materially to this. They show that the form of his initial denial was challenged, so that Edmund was forced to amend it so as to deny not just receiving the chattels on a particular day but on any day; and that he was also forced to deny receiving any chattels, not just chattels to the value of what Agnes had alleged he had received. One of the reports also shows that it was her counsel (Roger of Higham)[4] who initially made the *ad hominem* argument against allowing Edmund to make his denial through compurgation, namely that the court should presume he would perjure himself in order to retain the goods and animals since he had previously perjured himself when he had married the lady, presumably by failing to declare that he was already married. It was then chief justice Mettingham who made the point about the publicity surrounding the contract and the delivery of the movables, that the contract could not have been made solely between Edmund and Richard in Edmund's chamber but that the relatives of both parties must have been

[4] Though one report ascribes the speech to William of Gisleham, a justice of the court.

present and that it was likely that many outsiders had seen the movables being carried off and driven away. The second report (perhaps reporting the words of the teacher who used this case in his teaching) noted that by the common law he would have got to his 'law' (compurgation) but that it had been adjudged that the facts be ascertained through a jury verdict out of favour for the woman because she had been deceived and had lost her virginity (*desceu et despocelle*). The jury came the very next term, which was very fast for the appearance of a jury, and found that the chattels had indeed been handed over as Agnes had claimed and, on being questioned, that the annulment had been at the suit of Elizabeth but at the instigation of Edmund. The court then gave a judgment which as enrolled does not make perfect sense, but whose general tenor can be plausibly reconstructed. It held that the chattels would not have been delivered to Edmund in the first place if his fraud and malice had been known, since the contract of marriage was rendered invalid by the prior, but unrevealed, contract and that the chattels ought not to remain with him now since *fraus et dolus nemini debent patrocinari*, here meaning that no one should benefit from their own fraud and deception. Agnes was therefore awarded the value of the chattels (£66) and additional damages assessed by the jurors at £16.

This case illustrates quite nicely one of the ways in which the English common law courts of the later 13th century can be seen acting in an 'equitable' way, doing equity, well before the invention of a separate Court of Equity in England in the second half of the 14th century. The justices of the Common Bench evidently made their judgment in this case in order to undo the consequences of what subsequent events revealed to have been a transfer of valuable chattels obtained by Edmund on the basis of fraud and deceit. In so doing, they were evidently willing to overlook, and perhaps even override, the argument that title to the movables more properly lay in the original grantor or his executors, though they may have had in mind the not wholly convincing analogy with the granting of land as a marriage portion (where land was really granted to both husband and wife) and the consequences of an annulment of the marriage for a marriage portion of land, where the wife might indeed keep all the marriage portion if she was the innocent party. The court was also willing to overrule the general customary rules and practice about proof by insisting that proving or disproving Edmund's denial of the receipt of the movables was a matter for a jury and not for compurgation. Its hesitation about doing this is, I think, shown by its adoption of two quite incompatible justifications for doing so: the one depending on the public or manifest nature of the transactions concerned, the other depending on the presumption that Edmund's previous conduct indicated a high risk of perjury if he was allowed to use compurgation. The court's knowledge that it was doing something outside the normal rules of English custom may also be revealed by its use of the learned law tag (*fraus et dolus nemini debent patrocinari*) which is found in a limited number of other cases but is not part of the normal language of English common law judgments in this, or any other, period.

Something not dissimilar, but a little less complicated, happened in an earlier case heard before royal justices itinerant in Yorkshire in 1279. Again we have both the official record and an early law report, though the latter is much less helpful. I have edited them both in vol. III of my *Earliest English Law Reports*.[5] In this case Denise, the widow of William of Wath, was claiming her dower third share of a sizable holding in the village of Thornhill against one William of Longfield. William made a defence of a kind that is common in such cases. He said that she was not entitled to dower since her husband had not been seised of the holding at the time of their marriage or afterwards. She denied this and the case went to a jury. It did not give a direct answer. It stated the facts and left it up to the justices to apply the law to them. Denise had married William during his father's lifetime by words of present consent and she had then borne William children, but they had never gone through a formal marriage at the church door. When William's father had died and he had succeeded him in his inheritance he had decided that he could do better for himself and had contracted marriage with a second woman also named Denise, this time in a full public ceremony. The first Denise had then brought proceedings in the ecclesiastical court to assert the validity of her own prior marriage and had succeeded in this. William of Wath had then been required by the authorities to resume cohabitation with her and to go through a proper formal marriage ceremony and had been excommunicated three times before finally submitting. He had previously leased these lands now claimed by the first Denise to William of Longfield (the defendant) and before going through with the formal ceremony had

[5] *EELR* III, 82–83 (79–81 Yorks. 5). I have previously discussed this case in P. Brand, "Reasoned Judgments in the English Medieval Common Law 1270–1307", in *Ratio Decidendi: Guiding Principles of Judicial Decisions*, vol. 1, *Case Law*, ed. W. Hamilton Bryson and Serge Dauchy (Berlin: Duncker & Humblot, 2006), 55–56.

enfeoffed William of the land to spite her and to prevent her from getting her dower. On the face of it, this finding of fact should have spelled disaster for the first Denise. To be entitled to dower a widow would normally have to show that her husband had been in possession of the land at the time of the marriage ceremony or had acquired it since. Her late husband had not been in possession. The court nonetheless decided she was entitled. The relevant date, the court held, was to be reckoned not as the date of the marriage but as that of the sentence upholding the validity of the prior, informal marriage when William of Wath had become obliged to marry Denise formally. There was no reference by the court to any prior precedent for this, nor any statutory authority for the rule, merely a general and vague invocation of the fact that *jus dotale* inhered in her from that time according to 'God and all right' (*secundum Deum et omnia jura*). Again the use of the language of the learned law shows that the common law justices were struggling. The judgment was partially based on its perception that the grant to William of Longfield had been made 'maliciously' (*maliciose*) and 'to evade the law' (*in fraudem legis*) in order to deprive Denise of her dower; that William's acceptance of the grant could be similarly characterised; and that the law was there to help those defrauded and also to deter fraudulent behaviour in the future.

Common Law courts might also have 'good faith' and fraud in mind in making other kinds of decision. The obligation of warranty freely undertaken by most grantors when granting land imposed a duty to defend the grantee's possession if it was impugned in legal proceedings and to provide land of equal value in exchange if it was lost in those proceedings. The obligation was normally undertaken on behalf of the grantor and his or her heirs and it passed by inheritance to the heirs of the grantor. The duty to provide an exchange was, however, limited by the rule that it only applied if the warrantor's heir had inherited lands of an equal or greater value from the warrantor. In a Common Bench case of 1286, which is known again both from the enrolment and from a report which I have printed, Luciana of Middleton claimed her dower share of lands at Rothley in Northumberland from the abbot of Newminster.[6] The abbot vouched Walter Scot to warranty for these lands on the basis of a charter granting the lands and promising warranty from Walter's father John of Middleton, whose heir he was. Walter admitted that he was his father's heir but denied that he held

---

6 *EELR* II, 242–244 (1286.4).

any lands by inheritance from his father because he had surrendered all title to the lands he had inherited before the litigation started. The abbot claimed he had deliberately conveyed them to his eldest son to evade the obligation but had effectively remained in possession. The court held that he remained under the obligation. The chief justice (Thomas Weyland) took an even firmer line. Even if the land had been sold to a stranger, if the purchase money had been used to purchase other land, it too would have been under the obligation to provide warranty. What mattered was the substance, not the form; warrantors should not be allowed to escape their obligations through fraudulent conveyances.

In another Common Bench case of the same year Philippa of Dutton was suing Robert of Dutton for the manors of Great and Little Rownall in Staffordshire as her right of the gift of Sir Vivian of Standon (perhaps her father). She claimed that Robert had only gained title to them by the grant of Philippa's former husband John of Cockfield, whose wishes she had been unable to oppose before the annulment of their marriage. The case is again one for which we have both the official enrolment and a law report.[7] Robert vouched John, who was evidently not his father but his stepfather, to warranty. When John appeared he asked to be shown the basis for his voucher. Robert produced a charter in the name of both John and his former wife, the claimant, settling the manors on Robert and the heirs of his body but with only Philippa binding herself and her heirs to warranty. Robert then claimed John was bound to warranty by the fact that he had been a party to the grant. It looks as though mother and son were cooperating to ensure that the mother recovered what had been her marriage-portion and to ensure that the former husband provided lands of an equal value to his stepson. The likelihood that this was indeed the case is increased by the allegation that it was Philippa, rather than her son, who was already in possession of the manors when Robert vouched John to warranty. The justices were divided about the propriety of the voucher and whether Robert should have vouched Philippa as well as John. Ralph de Hengham, chief justice of King's Bench, sitting in on the case, thought that the voucher of John alone should be allowed since, if Robert was made to vouch her as well, she could escape warranty by simply claiming that her participation in the grant had been forced while she was under her former husband's control, and that she could not be

7 *EELR* II, 253–255 (1286.9).

made to warrant something to which she herself had a good claim. Brunton, a justice of the Common Bench, thought that both John and Philippa should have been vouched since they had a joint but several liability or obligation to warranty. Weyland, the court's chief justice, had a more interesting line. He thought the relevant criterion was the purpose of the grant with which the warranty had been promised. If the land had been granted to a stranger there could be no presumption that Philippa had wished or intended to be obliged to warranty, whatever the deed might say. Since the land had been given to her own son it could be presumed that this was what she wanted, and so she should be bound. And Weyland evidently thought that making this kind of judgment was in accordance with something he could see as being 'equity' for he said that 'I see in this case an equity' (*Je regarde en ce cas un equite*).

Equitable Features of the Action of Account

Let me now turn to a different area of later 13th and early 14th-century common law where we can, I think, see equitable features being incorporated into the common law and in which contemporaries seem to show some awareness that this was indeed the case. This is in relation to the common law action of account. The action of account initiated by a writ of account seems to have existed since the later 12th century but prior to the second half of the 13th century seems to have been mainly something heard and determined in local county courts. From then onwards, however, it became an increasingly common action in the Common Bench at Westminster. The ostensible purpose of the action was to require an agent who had controlled the lands, movable goods and cash of another for a certain period of time to make an accounting of the movables and money he had had under his control during this period, and of any payments or transfers he had been authorised to make, before auditors, who would record all of this in a full written account. The auditors would then strike a balance and thereby determine how much the agent owed the principal for whom he had been acting. The agent was then liable to imprisonment until he had paid in full anything that he owed. The principal's main interest was, of course, in ensuring payment of the balance owed to him.

Initially, the action of account was available only against those agents who could be described as being the 'bailiffs' of their principals. The word is not specific in its meaning but the paradigm case seems to have been that of an agent who was in charge of a manor or group of manors, with the 'bailiff' overseeing the direct exploitation of a seignorial demesne (the growing of cereals and legumes on the manorial demesne and their harvesting and the subsequent sale of the crop or its transfer to the lord's household for domestic use; the husbandry of animals on the seignorial demesne and the common pasture of the village to provide meat, dairy products, wool and animals for working the arable lands and for sale) and with receiving rents and other seignorial income from the manorial lord's free and unfree tenants. During the second half of the 13th century the courts and the king's chancery, which drafted and issued the original writs which commenced litigation and warranted the courts hearing that litigation, seem to have cooperated in a deliberate and sustained attempt to extend the availability of the action. As early as 1262 an action of account was successfully brought against an agent as his lord's 'bailiff' when the agent had managed shops in York and Pontefract and had been given 200 marks to buy merchandise and had goods to the value of 1000 marks to sell.[8] From 1289 onwards account was also being regularly used by men who can be identified as vintners or spicers to seek an accounting from the managers of their wine shops or taverns in London,[9] and in various other major towns of provincial England such as Northampton,[10] Coventry,[11] Reading,[12] Gloucester,[13] Oxford,[14] and Huntingdon.[15] In 1291 and 1305 the

[8] *Martin of Ottringham v Stephen of Woodgate*: KB 26/166, m. 26d.

[9] *John Hurel v Roger son of John Silvote of Chelmsford*: for service as his taverner, receiving 19 barrels of wine worth 53s each to sell and answer for value; defendant claims returned six without sale or administration and had accounted for rest: CP 40/96, m. 198d (Michaelmas 1292).

[10] *Robert of Catworth v William son of Hugh le Veise*; handed over 40 barrels of wine worth 100 marks at SJB 1284 and had administration till same day in 1286; denies bailiff in town or administered wine: CP 40/76, m. 35d (Hilary 1289).

[11] *John of Lidgate merchant v John Hikebrid of London*: administration of £20 wine from Easter to Christmas 1288; denies bailiff; but found that was: CP 40/81, m. 15 (Hilary 1290).

[12] *Ralph Tailor of Reading v John de Maunt*: bailiff and taverner in period in 1289 when handed over 19 barrels and one pipe of wine; initially denies his bailiff but jury at xv Trinity 1293 finds was and received all: CP 40/96, m. 64 (Michaelmas 1292).

[13] *Robert Spicer of Gloucester v Robert de Wysham*: on receipt of six barrels of wine received for sale at Martinmas 1292 and alleges received money from sale as bailiff and receiver up to following Advinculation; denied and to jury: CP 40/105, m. 80 (Trinity 1294).

[14] *Richard Spicer of Oxford v John of Boxore junior*: one years' service from Martinmas 1292 when received 70s in money and 3 barrels worth £7 6s to sell for plaintiff's profit: CP 40/105, m. 121d (Trinity 1294).

[15] *William of Bicknor of Huntingdon v John Bagard*: on sale of five barrels of wine and keeping of two silver cups: CP 40/106, m. 82 (Michaelmas 1294).

owners of boats brought actions of account against the masters of those boats (again as 'bailiffs') for the profits of their voyages in the boats.[16] From 1271 onwards the availability of account against bailiffs was also stretched in a different way. When land was granted to a child under age English social practice was for the grantor to appoint a 'guardian' (*custos*) to take possession of it and to manage it until the child came of age. That agent had not been appointed by the grantee whose property it now was, but the courts seem to have found no difficulty in allowing actions brought by the child once he or she was of age against the guardian for an accounting of their period of managing the land.[17] From the later 1280s onwards actions of account also began to specify not that the agent had been the plaintiff's 'bailiff', but the 'receiver of his money'. This was used to cover not just income from ecclesiastical sources[18] but also money entrusted to an agent for trading,[19] for making purchases of movables[20] or of land,[21] or

16 *Nigel of Deepdale merchant v Reginald son of Agnes of Burnham*: sued as bailiff in Burnham for 2 years from Thursday before Martinmas 16 Edward I but is for one boat with all tackle worth £20 and fish and herrings in it to value of £100; he denies bailiff in that time; jury in Hilary 1293 finds was bailiff; handed over boat with tackle *gubernandum tanquam rector navis predicte*; so to render account: CP 40/90, m. 79 (Trinity 1291); *Gilbert Silke of Holkham v John Charles junior* sued as bailiff in Holkham: had care of boat for two years and administration of fish and other things carried in it and sold by land and sea to value of £60 (also parallel action against him as receiver of moneys): CP 40/156, m. 2 (and m. 24 for parallel) (Trinity 1305).

17 The earliest case I have so far found is one in the 1271 Kent eyre (*John son of Bernard v Thomas of Higham*): JUST 1/365, m. 60d. For later cases see *Robert and Richard of Thursford v Ralph Avenel*: CP 40/59, m. 45d (Trinity 1285); renewed at CP 40/92, m. 20 (Hilary 1292); *John Cosyn and wife Alice v Thomas Mountsorel*: CP 40/83, m. 100 (Trinity 1290); *Thomas de Ferrers v Thomas Meverel of Gayton*: CP 40/106, m. 27d (Michaelmas 1294).

18 The earliest pleaded case I have noted is *master Jordan of Wimborne archdeacon of Chester v master William of Wymondham*: CP 40/72, m. 50d (Easter 1288) for income from the archdeaconry; and see also *master Arnald Lupi de Tillio v John de Hakebeche*: CP 40/90. m. 125d (Trinity 1291) for money, corn and other goods received from church.

19 The earliest example I have noted is 89 Wilts. 18 (*EELR* IV, 430–432) (though also movables).

20 The earliest example I have noted is *master Richard of Northampton v Robert of Woore*: CP 40/104, m. 126 (Easter 1294): money handed over to purchase cloth at Exeter fair.

21 See *Michael le Bret v John of Wicken of Burnham Thorpe*: CP 40/145, m. 14 (Michaelmas 1303): money handed over on three separate occasions to purchase land for the benefit of the plaintiff.

for money received from the sale of goods such as mill stones,[22] shoes,[23] rabbit skins,[24] or money entrusted to an agent for legal purposes.[25]

Things did not end there. In 1292 Stephen de Rabaz sued William of Mowsley as bailiff of his manor of North Kilworth. William was able to show that he was the lessee, not the bailiff, of this manor under a sixteen year lease for which they had agreed a fixed annual rent, though he had only held the manor for eleven of the sixteen years. The lord conceded that William was the lessee but said that his lease had excluded the casual income from wardships, reliefs and escheats derived from tenants who held of the manor. The court held him liable to account for the income he had derived.[26] Constructively he was regarded and treated as being Stephen's bailiff, or in later language his trustee, for this income. In a 1306 case John Bacun sued the chaplain Thomas of Lambourne seeking an account for a period as his bailiff at Aythorpe Roding in Essex. What Thomas had evidently been was the parochial chaplain of the church there, of which John was the rector, for a year from Michaelmas 1304. Thomas had not received any of John's parochial revenue. What John wanted was an accounting for the liturgical fittings of the church: three vestments each worth £5, a chalice worth £2, a missal worth £5 and other books worth £2. The court duly adjudged that he should account to John for them. It may not, however, have been irrelevant that John was one of the senior clerks of the Common Bench, the keeper of the rolls and writs of the court.[27] There are also at least three examples of the action of account being used in respect of what look like single transactions, rather than the kind of series of transactions or actions associated with almost all other actions of account. In Easter term 1294 Master Richard of Northampton sued Robert of Woore for an account as the 'receiver of his moneys' on the basis of a single payment made to him on a single day at Northampton to purchase cloth at a fair at Exeter. Robert denied being accountable for any such payment.[28] In Trinity term 1294 Stephen Rabaz

---

22 See *Adam of Manningtree v William Taverner of Ipswich*: CP 40/159, m. 210d (Easter 1306).

23 See *John of Colney v Thomas of Norwich*: CP 40/160, m. 16d (Trinity 1306); *Gilbert of Winchcombe v Vincent of Erdington*: CP 40/164, m. 101 (Trinity 1307).

24 See *John of Bristol v Peter of Denham*: CP 40/161, m. 75 (Michaelmas 1306).

25 See *Agnes widow of Abraham son of Rannulph of Grantham v John Morice of Easton*: CP 40/138, m. 28d (Easter 1301).

26 CP 40/96, m. 164.

27 CP 40/160, m. 91.

28 CP 40/104, m. 126.

sued William le Somter as his 'receiver of moneys' on the basis of entrusting him with a horse worth 25 marks to sell at the next fair in Boston and half a mark he had given to cover for his expenses. The horse had been sold for twenty marks but William had not paid over the purchase price to him. Stephen now demanded an account. William claimed to have purchased merchandise there to the value of twenty marks and to have delivered it to Stephen in his house at Warwick. A jury found that he had only delivered merchandise to the value of five marks and the court adjudged that he should now 'account' for the difference.[29] In 1305 Ralph, son of Simon Parker of Lopham, sued Walter of Upgate of Wilby by Hargham in Norfolk for an account as 'receiver of his moneys' for a single payment of 45 shillings made in 1276 at Wilby to purchase sheep on behalf of Ralph. Again Walter denied receiving any money and the issue went to a jury.[30] These cases suggest that by the final years of the reign of Edward I the courts were allowing litigants to use account to fill in a gap in the range of remedies available where money or a movable had been entrusted to an agent for a single transaction, and that trust had been betrayed. This might well be called an 'equitable' development. It saw the stretching of the common law by disregarding the limited types of relationship covered by the action of account and extending the action to cover a much wider range of relationships and also stretching it to cover not just relationships that lasted over time, but also one-off transactions, and thus providing a more general remedy for certain types of breach of trust.

A second characteristic of the action of account is also relevant here. This is the procedure followed for selecting auditors when the court held that an account was owed by the person against whom the action of account was brought. It would perhaps have been expected that the plaintiff (the principal) would simply appoint the auditors, as he would have done if the agent had accounted out of court, as he should have done. This did not happen. A second possibility was for the court itself to go ahead and appoint auditors to hear the account being rendered, a procedure rendered appropriate by the court having jurisdiction in the matter through the prior litigation on the 'accountability' of the defendant. This is indeed found in a significant number of cases.[31] In others, however,

---

29 CP 40/105, m. 53.

30 CP 40/153, m. 60.

31 For examples see CP 40/51, m. 70: *Milicent de Montalt v Peter de la Rokele* (Michaelmas 1283): *et dati sunt auditores* Nicholas of Stapeleton and Ellis of Beckingham; at octaves of Hilary given different auditors, John of London and Henry of Guildford; CP 40/69, m. 129:

it was not. In at least two cases the assignment of auditors by the court was specifically said to have been made 'with the consent of the parties',[32] while in five the auditors are said to have been chosen by both parties,[33] and in a further three each of the parties is specifically stated to have chosen one (out of two) or two (out of four) of the auditors.[34] An assumption that normally the parties would have at least some say in the choice of auditors is also implied by a 1294 case where the plaintiff was under age and it was for this reason, it was said, that the court 'assigned' auditors.[35] Indeed, an anonymous commentator (perhaps a teacher) noted in a comment on a case of 1302 that in the action of account the auditors were 'quasi arbitrators, that is to do equity to both parties' (*quasi arbitratores sestasaver de fere equite utrique parti*).[36] This not quite 'equity' in the later English sense of that term, but it does recognise that the procedure being

Agnes de Valence v John le Fraunceys (Michaelmas 1287): before Thomas Haliday and William Reygni *auditoribus ad hoc assignatis* at the inn of chief justice Thomas Weyland in London; CP 40/100, m. 91d: *Philip d'Aubigny v William de Cressy* (Easter 1293): *dantur ei auditores per justiciarios*, namely John of Stafford and Richard of Brinkley of Lincs but subsequently at Easter 1294 *de consensu parcium* new auditors appointed, namely said John of Stafford and John of Bradford; CP 40/101, m. 57: *William son of Ralph of Oxwick v John Gunnild of Gatley* (Trinity 1293): *et assignantur eis auditores*, namely Roger of Holm and Thomas of Framingham; CP 40/110, m. 29d: *Elizabeth widow of Oliver of Ingham v Ellis of Norfolk* (Michaelmas 1295): *et assignantur ei auditores*, namely Geoffrey of Norwich and Simon East; CP 40/116, m. 12: *William Haute v Walter Scrapyun* (Hilary 1297): *assignantur eis auditores* namely Robert of Shuldham and Robert atte Bataylle; CP 40/160, m. 91: *John Bacun v Thomas of Lambourne chaplain* (Trinity 1306): *Et assignantur eis auditores* John of Bradford and Richard of Rodney.

32 CP 40/105, m. 9d: *William of Dean parson of Whalton v Robert Burgeys of Whalton* (Trinity 1294): the record notes that *dati sunt ei auditores [...] et partes hinc inde auditoribus illis consenserunt;* CP 40/111, m. 11: *Osbert of Bagestan v Walter Belston* (Hilary 1296): the record notes that *assignantur ei auditores de consensu parcium electi.*

33 CP 40/79, m. 17: *Adam Pykeman v Roger of Mapledurham* (Trinity 1289): here the formula used is *partes consenserunt in auditoribus compoti*; CP 40/89, m. 65: *William Burnel v William of Willoughby* (Easter 1291): here the formula is *de consensu parcium electi sunt auditores*; CP 40/96, m. 64: *Ralph Tailor of Reading v John de Maunt* (Michaelmas 1292): here the formula is that the parties *elegerunt auditores*; CP 40/101, m. 64d: *Robert de Neville v Richard son of Geoffrey Freeman* (Trinity 1293): here the formula is that the auditors are *assensu parcium electis*; CP 40/110, m. 45d: *John de la Chaumbre of Hardingham v John son of Ralph Semere of Hardingham* (Michaelmas 1295): here the parties *elegerunt sibi auditores.*

34 For each party choosing one auditor see CP 40/96, m. 164: *Stephen Rabaz v William of Mowsley* (Michaelmas 1292). For each party choosing two auditors see CP 40/72, m. 50d: *master Jordan of Wimborne archdeacon of Chester v Master William of Wymondham* (Easter 1288) and CP 40/96, m. 301: *Roger Myniot v William le Surreis* (Michaelmas 1292).

35 CP 40/106, m. 27d: *Thomas de Ferrers v Thomas Meverel of Gayton* (Michaelmas 1294): *ex officio curie assignantur auditores.*

36 See BL MS. Additional 31826, *f.* 131*v.* (report of case of 1302).

followed is one whose overriding purpose is to do justice to both parties and therefore lets both parties have a say in the choice of auditors.

A third procedural characteristic of the action of account which can be glimpsed occasionally brings us perhaps closer still to the world of the later Equity courts. This is also something related to the auditing process. One manuscript containing law reports from 1306 records the oath taken by an agent (here a bailiff) before he renders his account before the auditors. It shows that the form of words was 'Hear you this, Justices, that I will truthfully charge myself with the money I received from W. in the village/town of N. in the time I was his bailiff and will render a truthful account and will allege no expenses or payments that are not truthful, so help me God and the Saints.'[37] In other words, the bailiff was being made to render his account on oath. We do not know if the principal (or the lord) was also put on his oath. What we do know is that he might also be questioned by the auditors. This is something we learn from a report of a case of 1300 where we are told something about the process which took place before the auditors.

> The lord charged his bailiff with the sale of pasture. The auditors asked to whom it was sold and for how much and the lord was unwilling to say. Moreover, he charged him with [receiving] fixed rent. The auditors asked from which tenements and from whom it was received and he was not willing to say. He charged him in addition with receiving utensils to the value of forty shillings. He was asked what kind of utensils, whether of brass or wood, and he was unwilling to specify [...].[38]

The procedure of the English Common Law in this period did not normally involve any direct questioning of the parties or any testimony given by them on oath. The process before the auditors (even if not given in court) evidently involved both these things.

One final characteristic of the action of account also struck contemporaries as strange and requiring explanation and led some to provide an explanation that specifically referred to do the court's duty to 'do equity' to both parties. This was that the process of accounting might produce the (evidently unanticipated) result that it was the agent, not the principal,

---

[37] YB 33–35 Edward I, 155: 'Ceo oiez vous justices qe jeo lealment me chargera de deners qe jeo ay receu de W. en la ville de N. del temps qe jeo esteye son bailif e leale acounte renderay e nules mises ne despenses noun verreys ne allegeray, si Dieu moy aide e les Seins.'

[38] BL MS. Additional 37657, *f.* 28*r*.

and thus the defendant and not the plaintiff, who was owed a balance of money. That is the position in at least four early 14th-century cases.[39] In his judgment in a 1302 case, as captured for us in a contemporary law report, Bereford J. said that 'Law requires that right be done to one party and to the other and it has been found that John owes W. 68 shillings by way of surplus *etc.* This court adjudges that W. is quit of the account and he recover the 68s of surplus against John.'[40] The reporter, or perhaps a teacher commenting on the case, who may be the same person, noted also that 'Although at first sight [...] this writ is obtained wholly for the advantage of the plaintiff yet by the words 'reasonable account' which are in the writ equity is to be done to one party and to the other.'[41] In a 1304 case Hengham CJ seems to have gone further. On the basis that if the agent, or bailiff, had been found in arrears to the lord he would have been imprisoned until he had provided satisfaction for the amount owed, he adjudged that the lord or principal who was found in arrears was likewise to be remanded to prison until he had given satisfaction.[42] The formal enrolment of the case, however, only records the recovery and the amercement, but not the imprisonment of the plaintiff. This may, how-

[39] CP 40/134, m. 31: *Master William of Wickham parson of Goldhanger v Robert le Vicarys* (Trinity 1300): after the account was heard it was found that William was indebted to Robert in 36s 0½d which Robert *superexpendit*; followed by failed attempt by lord to charge bailiff with additional items; which failed but judgment was respited until a jury resolved whether or not the bailiff was responsible for two swans; CP 40/129, m. 15d: *John d'Aubigny v John of Gatton of Orpington* (Trinity 1299): after account found that John of Gatton *superexpendit* 68s 11¾d; CP 40/148, m. 69: *Michael le Bret v John of Wicken of Burnham Thorpe* (Trinity 1303): after account auditors attest in court that Michael owes John £4 8s 5¼d; CP 40/153, m. 248d: *Peter of Huntingfield v John de Blauncmouster* (Michaelmas 1305): auditors attest that after all accounted and allowed Peter owes John 21s 11d (but thereupon Peter submits challenges and these go to jury).

[40] *Ber'.* 'Pur ceo qe la ley veut qe dreit seit fet ausibien a la une partie cum a lautre e trove est qe J. ly est tenu en .lxviij. souz etc. de surplusage si agard etc. qe W. seit quites de laconte e qe il recovere ver Jon les .lxviij. etc. de surplus': BL MS. Additional 31826, *f.* 131*v*.

[41] 'Item prima facie licet istud breve seit purchace tut pur le avantage le pleintif tamen par le *racionabilem compotum* qe est en le bref si fra lem equite a la une partie e a lautre.'

[42] This is to be found in three separate reports: those found in BL MS. Additional 31826, *f.* 354*r*. (and *f.* 353*r*.); LI MS. Miscellaneous 738, *f.* 30*r*. and BL MS. Hargrave 375, *f.* 101*v*. The fullest of these is the first, which notes: 'E pur coe qe nous trovum par ceste aconte qe Jon de ky vus avez receu ceste aconte ad plus despendu de iiij livres qe il nad receu e si de tant fu trove en arreres ver vus il demoreit en prisun tant qe il ust de coe fet vostre gre, par quai agard ceste curt qe vus en meme la manere demergez en prisun tant qe vus eez sun gre fet de les iiij livres, dunt vus estis ateint qe vus ly devez par cest aconte e seet en la mercy etc.'

ever, be connected with the king's mandate to send the record of the case to the court of King's Bench, evidently for review.[43]

Conclusions

In this chapter I have explored only some of the ways in which the English Common Law of the later 13th and early 14th centuries can be seen as applying equity or acting equitably or in which its justices talked of themselves in ways that suggest they thought they were acting 'equitably'. I am sure I could have multiplied my examples if I had also gone into a later chronological period, but equally sure that I could not have done so by going earlier. There are other areas which I have not had time to discuss but which are also relevant to my wider topic: evidence for the enforcement of specific performance (later a specialty of the Equity courts) in the action of covenant; the provision of relief against penalties; the employment of quasi-trust mechanisms of limited duration in the use of guardians holding *ad opus*; the development of a regular mechanism in the form of the writ of entry *causa matrimonii prelocuti* to allow women to recover land they had granted to men in anticipation of a marriage that had not then taken place, even though the implied condition was evidenced by no written deed or agreement; and perhaps the extension of statutes and statutory remedies and their deliberate restriction in ways that would later be called the 'equity of the statute'. Hopefully I have shown enough to suggest that the royal justices of the period were able, when they deemed it necessary, to act equitably and use their idea of equity to reach a just result, and in doing so achieved something of the 'equity' of the common law courts in a period before there were separate Equity courts.

43 CP 40/148, m. 69.

CHAPTER THREE

A HOUSE BUILT ON SAND: EQUITY IN EARLY MODERN ENGLISH LAW

D. Ibbetson*

Introduction

One of the most distinctive features of English legal history is the existence of the Court of Chancery, alongside the normal courts of Common law and not bound by their rules and procedures. In the course of the 16th century it came to be said that the Chancellor's jurisdiction was based upon 'equity', replacing the earlier formulation that it was predominantly based on 'conscience'.[1] That said, although the use of the terminology of equity was commonplace before the end of the 16th century, its meaning was wholly unstable, providing no solid theoretical foundation for the work of the Court of Chancery.[2] Recent work has stressed this instability. In his examination of the idea of equity in different contexts, Mark Fortier has shown the breadth of meaning, or meanings, that it had: it was 'a contested concept', with no definable core;[3] even in its usage in legal contexts it is multi-faceted.[4] Focusing more on the language of conscience than of equity, Dennis Klinck has argued that the usage of the word in case-law in the late 16th century is as untheorised as the usage of the word equity;[5] and that even those late-Elizabethan commentators who dealt with the subject produce no clear conclusions.[6] The present chapter does not aim to question any of this. Its purpose is rather to reinforce others'

* I am grateful to Sir John Baker, Mike Macnair and Guido Rossi for comments, advice and assistance.

[1] J.H. Baker, *Introduction to English Legal History*, 4th ed. (London: Butterworths, 2002), ch. 6, especially at 105–108.

[2] See in particular M. Macnair, "Equity and Conscience", *OJLS* 27 (2007), 660–61.

[3] M. Fortier, *The Culture of Equity in Early Modern England* (Aldershot: Ashgate, 2005), quotation at 21.

[4] Fortier, *Culture of Equity*, ch. 2.

[5] D. Klinck, *Conscience, Equity and the Court of Chancery in Early Modern England* (Aldershot: Ashgate, 2010), 80–88.

[6] Klinck, *Conscience*, 88–106.

conclusions by looking more closely at the writings on equity (in its legal context) dating from the late-16th and early-17th centuries, with a view to seeing both how and why there was such a lack of theoretical focus. The case law of the Court of Chancery will be largely ignored, since nowhere in this is there anything even purporting to give a theoretical insight into the nature of the Chancellor's equity; the one exception is the *Earl of Oxford's Case* (1615), which, it is argued, is not really a report of a decision at all, but rather a justificatory essay on the nature of the Chancery's jurisdiction by the Lord Chancellor, Lord Ellesmere.

An additional preliminary point is necessary. From a legal standpoint, the description of a court or tribunal as doing 'equity' did not necessarily imply a positive statement either about the rules and principles which it adopted or about its reasoning processes. When, in the 1570s, London merchants described mercantile courts as 'courts of equitie', it was merely another way of saying that strict law would not be applied.[7] It is in this sense, of courts not hamstrung by Common law rules and processes, that such courts as the Court of Requests could be described as equitable. 'Equity' continued to have this negative aspect for many centuries. Hence, an important aspect of the development of equity in the 16th- and early 17th-century Chancery is the attempt to impose a positive meaning onto 'equity' alongside its essentially negative sense of something that was not Common law.

The English Foundations

Behind the later Elizabethan notion of equity there were two distinct strands which had become substantially intertwined: the idea that statutes should be interpreted according to their 'equity', and the analysis of Christopher St German in his *Doctor and Student*.

Equity and Statutes: The Middle Ages

The idea that a statute might be interpreted according to its 'equity' appeared in England in the latter part of the 14th century and soon became well-established.[8] The word 'equity' here had no overtones of justice or

[7] BL MS. Add. 48020, *f.* 356.

[8] The earliest reference of which I am aware is YB M 48 Edw III *f.* 28 pl. 4 (1374). The terminology was entrenched by the start of the 15th century: YB T 7 Hen IV *f.* 16 pl. 6 (1406); YB P 12 Hen IV *f.* 20 pl.5 (1411). See in particular S.E. Thorne, "The Equity of a Statute and

fairness, a principal sense of the word in the later Middle Ages.[9] A statute giving an action to an executor was held to give one to an administrator too; a statute giving a remedy for the disturbance of 'titles and possessions' was held to apply to the disturbance of a reversionary right; a statute giving a remedy against a gaoler who permitted the escape of a prisoner who was under his custody for arrears of account was held to give a remedy where the prisoner was in custody for a debt.[10] Rather, it connoted the principle underlying a statute, its *ratio*, which justified a slight analogical extension outside its express terms. The core idea was that of similarity: '*equipollens lex est*, for similar cases are adjudged by the equity of the statute'.[11]

Christopher St German's Doctor and Student

St German was more concerned with conscience than with equity; indeed, his *Dialogue in English between a Doctor of Divinity and a Student in the Laws of England* was originally published as *A Dyaloge bytwyxt a Doctour of Dyuynite and a Student in the Lawes of Englande of the Groundes of the Sayd Lawes and of Conscyence*, in Latin *Dialogus de Fundamentis Legum Anglie et de Conscientia*.[12] After an exposition of the grounds of English law, the question is raised how they stand with conscience, focusing on the way in which in an action of debt on a sealed bond the Common law would not allow a defence that the money had been paid already, leaving the hapless debtor who had failed to take a proper acquittance to seek relief in Chancery.[13] The discussion of this is complex, and not helped by

---

Heydon's Case", *ILR* 31 (1936), 208–213, and his edition of *Discourse upon the Exposicion and Understandinge of Statutes with Sir Thomas Egerton's Additions* (San Marino CA: Huntington Library, 1942), 42–51; S. Vogenauer, *Die Auslegung von Gesetzen in England und auf dem Kontinent* (Tübingen: Mohr Siebeck, 2001), 685–691.

9 *Middle English Dictionary*, s.v. 'equity'.

10 YB M 3 Hen VI *f.* 14 pl. 18 (1425); YB T 4 Hen VI *f.* 25 pl. 4 (1426); YB H 15 Edw IV *f.* 18 pl. 8, at *f.* 20 (1476).

11 YB T 7 Hen IV *f.* 16 pl. 6 (1406). For this idea within the classical and medieval tradition in the West, see P.G. Caron, *"Aequitas" Romana, "Misericordia" Patristica ed "Epicheia" Aristotelica nella Dottrina dell' "Aequitas" Canonica* (Milan: Giuffrè, 1971), 2.

12 T.F.T. Plucknett and J.L. Barton ed., *Doctor and Student* (London: Selden Society 91, 1974). The Latin version was published in 1528 (or perhaps 1523), the English in 1530. Page references refer to the Selden Society edition. Fundamental to all later studies of St German is P. Vinogradoff, "Reason and Conscience in Sixteenth Century Jurisprudence", *LQR* 24 (1908), 373.

13 St German, *Doctor and Student*, 76–77 (even-numbered pages represent the Latin, odd-numbered pages the English). For the situation, see J.H. Baker, *Oxford History of the Laws of England* VI (Oxford: Oxford University Press, 2003), 41–42.

its being substantially abbreviated and reordered in the English version by comparison with the Latin, whose logic is easier to follow.[14] For St German, conscience was something distinct from *synderesis*, the natural sense of good and evil, and from *ratio* or reason, the power to deliberate between right and wrong.[15] Its core sense fell to be determined by what he saw as its etymology, the prefix *con* pointing to its being knowledge of one thing *with* another thing.[16] In the present context it was knowledge used in conjunction with the law, so that a default in conscience might arise through ignorance of the law or through a failure to apply it properly.[17] Thirdly, one—but only one—aspect of conscience was the doing of equity in the application of general rules of law to specific cases.[18] In effect, therefore, equity was subordinated to conscience.

It is only after having established that doing equity was an aspect of conscience that St German turned to the explanation of what equity was.[19] At the core of his analysis was the Aristotelian notion of *epieikeia*,[20] already known to English lawyers in the middle of the 15th century[21] but which had come to St German mediated through Jean Gerson and St Thomas Aquinas: the first three sentences of the relevant chapter of *Doctor and Student* are a close paraphrase of a passage from Gerson's *Regulae Morales*, followed by a similarly close copying of a passage from the *Summa Theologica*.[22]

---

14 For the theoretical primacy of the Latin version, see Vinogradoff, "Reason and Conscience", 374.

15 St German, *Doctor and Student*, 78, 79. *Synderesis* is dealt with in ch. 11 (Latin) and ch. 13 (English), 80–83, and reason in ch. 12 (Latin) and ch. 14 (English), 82–87.

16 St German, *Doctor and Student*, 86–87.

17 St German, *Doctor and Student*, 90–91.

18 St German, *Doctor and Student*, 94–95.

19 St German, *Doctor and Student*, 94–107. The discussion of equity constitutes ch. 14 of the Latin edition, ch. 16 of the English. For discussion, see xliv–li.

20 Aristotle, *Nicomachean Ethics*, V.10. I have used the edition of J. Barnes, *The Complete Works of Aristotle* II (Princeton: Princeton University Press, 1984), 1795–96.

21 Sir John Fortescue, *De Natura Legis Naturae*, 1,24 (in *The Works of Sir John Fortescue, Knight* I, ed. T. Fortescue, Lord Clermont (London: privately printed, 1869), 85–86), on which see N. Doe, *Fundamental Authority in Late Medieval English Law* (Cambridge: Cambridge University Press, 1990), 102–03.

22 Gerson, *Regulae Morales* (or *Regulae Mandatorum*), S. 3, in P. Glorieux ed., *Jean Gerson Oeuvres Complètes* IX (Paris: Desclée, 1960–73), 95–6; Aquinas, *Summa Theologica* 2^{a} 2^{ae}, 120.1 (Dominican edition vol. 41, Cambridge: Cambridge University Press, 2006, 278). For Gerson's influence on St German, see Z. Rueger, "Gerson's Concept of Equity and Christopher St German", *History of Political Thought* 3 (1982), 1, esp. at 10–11. The subsequent parts of the chapter bear some relation to Gerson's discussions in *Regulae Morales*, S. 36 and S. 92, in *Oeuvres Complètes* IX, 104 and 116 (reflecting topics discussed by Gerson elsewhere in his works), and to Aquinas, *Summa Theologica* 1^{a} 2^{ae} 96.1.1 (Dominican edition vol. 28, 138–39).

The problem for Aristotle was that laws were inevitably general in their formulation, and consequently did not always respond appropriately to concrete situations: 'and this is the nature of the equitable, a correction of law where it is defective owing to its universality'.[23] The correct thing to do when faced with such a situation, according to Aristotle, was to put oneself in the position of the legislator and say what he would have said had he been present. St German did not go so far as this, but followed Aquinas in delimiting the role of *epieikeia* to situations in which the positive law, if applied literally, would have gone against the common good or involved a conflict with divine law or natural law.[24] Alongside this narrow approach, though, St German incorporated a very different (and perhaps inconsistent) idea, the Canon law-approach that equity was mitigation or tempering of the rigour of the law; in this again he followed Gerson.[25] Finally, St German applied the Aristotelian approach to oaths as well as written laws, denying them strict force according to their letter but rather treating them as implicitly containing exceptions when required by circumstances: a vow not to eat meat might be broken if this was the only way to save one's life.[26]

Only now (in the original Latin) did the student return to the question of the debtor who would be forced by Common law to pay his debt again. This has been described as the 'stock example' of the situation in which the Chancery would intervene to prevent an injustice at Common law,[27] and St German's student gave the stock explanation. It was not the law of England that the debtor who had failed to take an acquittance had to pay

---

[23] Aristotle, *Nicomachean Ethics*, V.10.

[24] St German, *Doctor and Student*, 96–97; Aquinas, *Summa Theologica* 1^{a} 2^{ae} 96.1.1 (Dominican edition vol. 28, 138–39). Aquinas might himself perhaps have been less firm: L.J. Riley, *The History, Nature and Use of EPIKEIA in Moral Theology* (Washington: Catholic University of America Press, 1948), 33–35. Riley's treatment of *epieikeia* (conveniently available at http://www.strobertbellarmine.net/books/Riley-Epikeia.pdf) is a very good introduction to the topic.

[25] St German, *Doctor and Student*, 96–97; Gerson, *Regulae Morales* S. 3 (*Oeuvres Complètes* IX, 96); *De Vita Spirituali Animae*, lect. 5 (*Oeuvres Complètes* III, 189–90). For the Canon law I have relied upon the brief study of P. Fedele, "Equità Canonica", in *Enciclopedia del Diritto* XV (Milan: Giuffrè, 1966), 147–51, and the more elaborate analysis of Caron, *"Aequitas" Romana*, 1–87 (showing the way in which this idea of *benignitas* or *misericordia* was intertwined with the ideas of equity-as-justice and of *epieikeia*). See also the discussion in L. de Luca, "Aequitas Canonica ed Equity Inglese alla Luce del Pensiero di C. Saint German", *Ephemerides Iuris Canonici* 3 (1947), 46.

[26] St German, *Doctor and Student*, 96–97; Gerson, *De Vita Spirituali Animae*, lect. 6 (*Oeuvres Complètes* III, 194–96).

[27] Baker, *Oxford History* VI, 42.

the debt a second time, only a consequence of a procedural rule applied by the Common law courts in order to avoid 'inconvenience'. Hence, following the earlier discussion of equity and asking what the legislator would have done had he thought of this case, the debtor might be helped by equity.[28] 'Can he be helped in the same court?', asks the doctor. 'Not unless there is some subsidiary maxim of law', answers the student, 'but effect can sometimes be given to such an equity in the Chancery by a writ of subpoena'.

As has already been pointed out by others, St German's treatment of equity and conscience was not easily able to deal with his pivotal case of the Chancery's giving relief against bonds.[29] This was not really a case of a generally framed rule having to be moulded in order to fit the circumstances of a particular case; rather it was a situation in which the Common law—perhaps for good reason—refused to give a defence, but where the different processes and rules of proof available in the Chancery allowed the debtor to be relieved.[30] But this was not the theoretical path that St German took. If the Common law courts were acting rightly, then Chancery should not intervene; if they were acting wrongly, then they should alter their own practices rather than leave it to a different court to act.[31] St German's argument could not easily defend the Common law and at the same time justify the intervention of the Chancery.

St German's problem, it is fairly clear, is that he was attempting to deal with the situation which obtained in English law primarily by the use of foreign models which had been developed in very different contexts. The tools in his tool-box were simply not the right ones for the job. However, his use of the language of equity, and the Aristotelian theory underpinning that use, was to be of central importance in the derailing of potential theories about the equity of the Chancery.

---

28 St. German, *Doctor and Student*, 98–100. The English version, at 77–79, is subtly different: where the Latin has *subvenire debet per talem equitatem de qua superius tractasti*, the English version reads 'yet he may be holpen by a sub pena'.

29 G. Behrens, "An Early Tudor Debate on the Relation between Law and Equity", *JLH* 19 (1998), 143.

30 On the centrality of the greater flexibility of the Chancery's rules of proof, in particular its power to examine the defendant on oath and thereby to elicit a judicially relevant confession, see Macnair, "Conscience and Equity", 672–677.

31 Further debate on the point occurred in the anonymous *Replication of a Serjeant at the Laws of England* and St German's *Little Treatise on the Subpoena*: J.A. Guy, *Christopher St German on Chancery and Statute* (London: Selden Society Suppl. 6, 1985), 99–105, 106–126. These works were not published until 1787 and seem not to have had any wide circulation in manuscript; they cannot have had any effect on the later treatments of Equity.

Equity and Statutes in Plowden's Commentaries

Although St German himself regarded his theory of equity as something different from the application of statutes according to their equity as discussed above,[32] there were very clear similarities between the two. A generation later the Aristotelian approach was being used to ground this approach to statutory interpretation. In *Stowel v Lord Zouch* Catlyn CJ used Aristotle to set limits on the power of the courts to extend statutes according to their equity, and hence on the facts of the case refusing any equitable extension:

> And Catlyn said, that Aristotle defines equity thus, *Aequitas est correctio justae legis qua parte defecit quod generatim lata est*. But, he said, this law here is special, and limits a certainty of time in every point, and it is defective in no part as to time, for which reason the time limited shall not be altered or enlarged by equity.[33]

Yet more explicit are the notes of Edmund Plowden to the case of *Eyston v Studd*.[34] Equity, for him, might operate in two ways in the exposition of a statute. On the one hand, as in the 15th century,[35] it might justify the extension of a statute to a case beyond its literal meaning; on the other, and quite differently, equity might warrant reading an exception into the statute. Here the statute in question, the Statute of Chantries of 1547 (Stat 1 Edw VI c 14), if taken literally would have given to the King all parsonages and vicarages, something which (it was said) was not intended. Hence 'equity or *epichaia*' excludes these cases as much as if they had been expressly stated: 'of mere necessity it seems to have a place in the exposition of laws'.[36] This he justified by two references: the first to Aristotle's *Nicomachean Ethics* V.10, quoted from the Latin edition of Perionius,[37] and the second to Gerardus Odonis's commentary on the Ethics.[38]

By the 1570s, therefore, the Aristotelian theory of *epieikeia* was being used to justify two completely distinct aspects of English law. First, as

---

32 St German, *Doctor and Student*, 104–105.

33 *Stowel v Lord Zouch* (1565) Plow. 353, at 375; 75 Eng. Rep. 536, at 569.

34 (1574) Plow. 459, at 465–68; 75 Eng. Rep. 688, at 695–700.

35 *Supra*, 56–57.

36 Plow. 459, at 466; 75 Eng. Rep. 698. The translation here is mine; that in the English Reports ('to be a necessary ingredient in the exposition of all laws') does not quite get the original French right.

37 Perionius, *Aristoteles Ethica* (Heidelberg, 1562), 159. Note the express reference to Perionius at Plow. 465, 75 Eng. Rep. 696.

38 Gerardus Odonis, *Sententia et Expositio cum Quaestionibus super libros Ethicorum Aristotelis cum Textu* (Venice, 1500), *f.* 117.

a result of St German's *Doctor and Student*, it had become linked to the equity of the Court of Chancery; secondly, through *Stowel v Lord Zouch* and Plowden's notes to *Eyston v Studd*, it provided an intellectual underpinning for the 200 year-old interpretation of statutes according to their equity. The latter was plausible, but, as we have seen,[39] the former was not. However, the fact that both of these aspects of English law could be justified by a single theory, rightly or wrongly, made it possible for them to seem no more than different facets of the same legal phenomenon. The very plausibility of the Aristotelian explanation of the principle of statutory interpretation gave it greater credibility as an explanation of the equity of the Chancery. This served only to exacerbate the incoherence of the treatment of equity in the discursive works of the late 16th and early 17th centuries.

Building on the Foundations

In the latter years of the 16th century and the first few years of the 17th century there were a number of works in which the nature of Chancery equity in English law was discussed. A study of these shows the way in which the incoherence in the earlier works remained unresolved. We may divide them into two groups: those which took as their starting point, either explicitly or implicitly, the interpretation of statutes, and generalised from there to the equity of the Chancery;[40] and those which were concerned with the nature of equity, with an explicit or implicit focus on the Chancery.

Statutes and Equity

(i) *Rastell's* Exposition of Termes

John Rastell's *Exposiciones Terminorum*[41] was first published between 1523 and 1525. It was a legal dictionary, explicitly aiming to explain legal terms to 'yong beginners whych intend to be studyentys of the law',[42] yet

[39] *Supra*, 60.

[40] It should be stressed that we are not here concerned with 'the equity of the statute' for its own sake; our concern is with the way in which it affected the understanding of equity in Chancery.

[41] J. Rastell, *Exposiciones Terminorum Legum Anglorum*. No printing date appears. For the work, see J.H. Baker, "John Rastell and the Terms of the Law", in *Collected Papers in English Legal History*, vol. 2, (Cambridge: Cambridge University Press, 2013), 709–721.

[42] *Exposiciones Terminorum*, sig. A2v.

contained no entry for 'equity'. The work was frequently reprinted, but it was not until the edition of 1579 that this lack was remedied.[43] This was the first edition to appear after the second part of Plowden's *Commentaries* (1579), and the definition of equity closely followed the approach of Plowden in his note on *Eyston v Studd* which appeared there.[44] It focused on the interpretation of statutes, repeating without acknowledgment the Aristotelian definition of equity which had been put forward by Catlyn CJ in *Stowel v Lord Zouch* and in its turn quoted by Plowden in his note, and summarising closely the structure of Plowden's treatment: equity both abridges the law and expands it. But while the focus was on the interpretation of statutes, it was not explicitly so limited. The impression given is that the dual function of abridgment and expansion applied generally to equity's relationship with law, not simply to its relationship with statutes. This approach remained in Rastell's work right up to its last edition in 1742.

(ii) *Edward Hake's* Epieikeia

Edward Hake's dialogue *Epieikeia* was written in the latter part of the reign of Queen Elizabeth, and though it was not at the time published it did have some (perhaps limited) circulation.[45] Like Rastell's work, it purported to cover the whole of the ground of equity but did so very much from the standpoint of Plowden's treatment of statutes.

The starting point of the work is promising, asking what it meant for a lawyer to say to his client, 'Yowe have no remedy for this or that at the Common lawe but yowe must seeke your remedy in Equity', signalling that he was concerned with the function of the Court of Chancery.[46] Moreover, Hake further says that the equity of the Chancery is to his mind

---

[43] *An Exposition of Certaine Difficult and Obscure Words, and Terms of the Lawes of this Realme* (1579).

[44] *Supra*, 61–62. The connection between Plowden and Rastell is noted by Fortier, *Culture of Equity*, 65–66, though he reverses the influence. We cannot be sure that Plowden was published before Rastell (the colophon to Plowden's Table of Cases is dated 15 June 1579, but there is no similarly accurate dating for Rastell), but I think it more likely that the simpler text was derived from the more complex rather than vice-versa. Also see Sir Christopher Hatton, *A Treatise concerning Statutes, or Acts of Parliament, and the Exposition Thereof* (London, 1677, but seemingly based on a late 16th-century source), 31–74 (note the reference to *epicaia* and St German at 31–32). It is not clear that Hatton was in fact the author.

[45] Edward Hake, *Epieikeia: A Dialogue on Equity in Three Parts*, ed. D.E.C. Yale (New Haven: Yale University Press, 1953). The dialogue form was clearly influenced by St German's *Doctor and Student*.

[46] Hake, *Epieikeia*, 5.

the 'most speciall and principall' aspect of the subject.[47] However, after a general introductory chapter, the chapter on equity in Common law covers 74 pages in the modern edition while that on the Chancery covers only 26. Given the dominant role of Common law, and especially the application of statutes, in the work, it is unsurprising that the introductory chapter on 'Equity in General' is largely based on Aristotle as interpreted and applied by Plowden: equity operates as a correction to a generally framed law. It is not something separate from the law, but already implicit within it as a 'secreate exception'.[48]

Moving from equity in Common law to the equity of the Chancery, Hake's argument rather falls apart. He tried, perhaps conventionally, to avoid the problem by suggesting that there was very little to say about the Chancery given the recent appearance of two books, by Richard Crompton and William West,[49] but showed himself as being prevailed upon by his interlocutors to continue. But there is nothing he can say about the equity of the Chancery which fits with the theory of his introductory chapter. Chancery equity is not something already within the law by implication or secret exception. Rather, for Hake, it operates when there are collateral circumstances affecting the application of the Common law rule.[50] This was probably an accurate insight into the nature of equity as it was applied in the Chancery, but it bore no relation to the theoretical foundations which he had put down.

(iii) *Thomas Ashe's* Epieikeia

Unlike Hake's work, Ashe's *Epieikeia* was expressly concerned with equity as it applied to statutes; however, its preface *To the Courteous Reader* began with a few pages on equity in general.[51] Superficially learned, this consisted of a few passages from *Doctor and Student* and West's *Symboleography*, interlarded with quotations from Aristotle's *Ethics* (with the commentary of Magirus),[52] Pseusippus, Calepinus, Bracton, Budaeus, 'civilians', St. Cyprian, Cato (seemingly via Coke), Erasmus, Coke, the Bible, Cicero, Lavater's commentary on the Book of Proverbs, Justinian's

[47] Hake, *Epieikeia*, 6.

[48] Hake, *Epieikeia*, 15, 16, 21.

[49] R. Crompton, *L'Authorite et Jurisdiction des Courts* (London, 1594); W. West, *Second Part of the Symboleography* (London, 1594). Crompton had said a good deal about the Chancery but nothing about equity. For West, see *infra*, 66–68.

[50] Hake, *Epieikeia*, 123.

[51] T. Ashe, *Epieikeia* (London, 1609), preface (unpaginated).

[52] J. Magirus, *Corona Virtutum Moralium* (Frankfurt, 1601).

Digests and Institutes, and St Gregory, as well as Plowden and the authors cited by him. Some of the references can be traced into Magirus—Ashe's quote from 'civilians' is attributed to *iurisconsulti* by Magirus[53]—but not all, even of the non-English ones. One quotation by Ashe from Cicero's *De Officiis* which is found in Magirus is continued by him after Magirus's quotation ends,[54] pointing to Ashe having gone to Cicero himself. But the mixture of English and foreign materials, ancient and modern writers, and of legal, theological and philosophical texts, suggests that he used multiple sources; and since he is known to have collected definitions and mottoes of this sort[55] it is not improbable that he had brought them together himself.

Ashe's style of sewing together quotations does not make it easy to follow anything like an argument in his writing, but we may see it as being divided into two aspects. At first he brings together fragments identifying equity with not pressing one's strict rights, with rectitude, with treating all people equally, with justice tempered with mercy. After this, though, he moves into the Aristotelian framework, with fragments saying that one should act according to the spirit of the law rather than its letter and that rules framed generally cannot be applied rigidly to particular cases. This is all in his section on equity in general, and it is only after this that he makes the transition—explicitly—to discussion the equity of statutes. Yet, as with Hake's work, most of the general principles are germane to the question of statutory interpretation rather than to the equity of the Chancery.

In their different ways, Rastell (or, more accurately, the person responsible for the 1579 edition of his work), Hake and Ashe were attempting to treat generally of equity, but took as their starting point the role of equity in statutory interpretation. Refracted through this lens, there was practically nothing of any value they could say about equity as it applied in the Court of Chancery, at least nothing that was consistent with the general principles they were claiming to be uncovering.

53 Ashe, *Epieikeia*, fourth unnumbered page; Magirus, *Corona Virtutum Moralium*, 546.

54 Ashe, *Epieikeia*, sig, Aii; Magirus, *Corona Virtutum Moralium*, 553.

55 See in particular his *Fasciculus Florum* (London, 1617), a collection of sayings culled from Coke's *Reports*.

Equity in General

(i) *William West's* Symboleography

William West's *Symbolaeographia*, or *Symboleography* when titled in English, appeared in two parts, the first in 1590 and the second in 1594.[56] The volumes themselves were largely collections of precedents of documents, drawn in part—perhaps largely—from his practice as an attorney.[57] As well as these, though, there were some sections of a more discursive nature, including one on the Chancery.[58] It has been known for some centuries that the section in the first part dealing with the nature of obligations was drawn from the work of the German jurist Hermann Vulteius.[59] Sections 2 to 37 of the *First Part of the Symboleography*, from the second edition of 1592 onwards, are almost direct translations of paragraphs taken from chapters 26 to 44 of Vulteius's *Jurisprudentiae Romanae a Justiniano Compositae*;[60] the adaptation of Vulteius's text to English law is largely through abbreviation and omission, with hardly any positive alteration—apart from changing the age of majority for contracting from 25 to 21 and the inclusion of a few references to Year Book cases, West's text is almost pure Vulteius. We should not be shocked therefore to find that the section on the Chancery is similarly unoriginal.

The first part of West's discourse on the Chancery, sections 2 to 11, is on the face of it a work of some erudition, with references to Aristotle and Justinian's Digests, Budaeus, Corasius, Oldendorp and Donatus. It is, however, almost completely drawn from the titles *Ius Summum* and *Aequitas* of Simon Schardius's *Lexicon Iuridicum*,[61] translated by West from Latin into English. Schardius himself was heavily dependent on the *Lexicon Iuris* of the German Lutheran Johannes Oldendorp,[62] his entries

[56] References are to the pagination and section numbering in the 1641 edition, which differs from that in the 1594 edition; but the texts are the same.

[57] E. Poole, "West's *Symboleography*: An Elizabethan Formulary", in *Law and Social Change in British History*, ed. J.A. Guy and H. Beale (London: Royal Historical Society, 1984), 96.

[58] West, *Second Part of the Symboleography*, 173–183.

[59] T. Wood, *New Institute of the Imperial or Civil Law* (London, 1704), ix–x; J. Ayliffe, *New Pandect of Roman Civil Law* (London, 1734), xlvii. I am grateful to Mike Macnair for the reference to Wood, and for discussion about West's borrowing from Vulteius.

[60] I have used the 1610 edition of Vulteius, available at babel.hathitrust.org, http://hdl.handle.net/2027/njp.32101066467240. The work was first published in 1590, the same year as the first edition of West.

[61] S. Schardius, *Lexicon Iuridicum* (Basle, 1582).

[62] J. Oldendorp, *Lexicon Iuris* (Frankfurt, 1553).

on *aequitas* largely copying it verbatim.[63] Behind this, in its turn, was Oldendorp's *De Iure et Aequitate Forensis Disputatio*,[64] building on his earlier German work.[65] Underpinning this part of West's treatment, therefore, was Oldendorp's distinctive theory of equity.[66] While Luther himself had seen equity—*aequitas, epieikeia*—as something which might come into play from time to time in exceptional cases, for Oldendorp it was integral to legal interpretation: *all* laws had to be interpreted through equity, since in every instance human judgement was necessary to apply the general rule to the concrete case. Equity and law were therefore not distinct, but inseparably joined.

West's use of Schardius's treatment of equity breaks off after the first paragraph of section 11, moving seamlessly on to a borrowing—duly acknowledged—from *Doctor and Student*.[67] But, as we have seen, St German's analysis of equity was rather different, applicable only when the positive law was in conflict with the law of God or the law of nature.[68] Hence, we might reasonably think it was somewhat tendentious to begin the borrowing from *Doctor and Student* by saying that St German was writing 'to the like effect' as what had been said until that point. West may have been aware of this difficulty: at one point he makes an otherwise incomprehensible alteration in his translation from Schardius. Where Schardius had written that the material cause of equity was '*ius naturae, ius civile, boni mores*', West writes that it was 'the law of nature, *the law of nations*, and good manners' (emphasis added).[69] In theoretical terms, the reference to the law of nations does not make a great deal of sense, since this would never have been a source of any principle of equity. However, it did avoid the otherwise enormous problem of seeing the positive law of the state as a source of equity—something that was central

---

63 We can rule out the possibility that West used Oldendorp directly, since he follows Schardius in referring explicitly to Oldendorp where the latter does so.

64 J. Oldendorp, *De Iure et Aequitate Forensis Disputatio* (Cologne, 1541).

65 J. Oldendorp, *Wat Byllich unn Recht Ys* (Rostock, 1529), in *Quellenbuch zur Geschichte der Deutschen Rechtswissenschaft*, ed. E. Wolf (Frankfurt: Klostermann, 1949), 51. Its inclusion in Wolf's collection, alongside pieces by Savigny and Jhering among others, testifies to the importance of the work in the history of German legal thought.

66 G. Kisch, *Erasmus und die Jurisprudenz seiner Zeit* (Basle: Helbing & Lichtenhahn, 1960), 227–259; J. Witte, *Law and Protestantism* (Cambridge: Cambridge University Press, 2002), 154–168; H. Berman, *Law and Revolution, II: The Impact of the Protestant Reformation on the Western Legal Tradition* (Cambridge, Mass: Belknap Press, 2003), 90–94.

67 West, *Second Part of the Symboleography*, 176–176*v*.

68 *Supra*, 59.

69 Schardius, *Lexicon Iuridicum*, col. 145, identical to Oldendorp, *Lexicon Iuris*, 28. West, *Second Part of the Symboleography*, S. 6.

to Oldendorp's understanding, but quite at odds with St German, and (of course) quite at odds with West's apparent purpose of writing about the Court of Chancery.

After a very brief section dealing with conscience, the rest of West's discussion is impeccably English; its focus is on the Chancery, its sources the Year Books and the early 16th-century *Diversite de Courtes*. The contrast between the treatment of equity and the treatment of the Chancery is very marked. Equity is clearly seen as an essential feature of the Chancery, but West's use of a foreign dictionary to describe it suggests that he had no clear idea what it was.

(ii) On Equitie

The anonymous author of a short tract on equity,[70] seemingly dating from the late 16th century, agreed about the difficulty of identifying what equity was: 'There is nothinge more usual than the name of equitie and scarce any thing more obscure and difficult then the matter it selfe.' His response, like that of West, was to look abroad, turning explicitly to the writings of civil and canon lawyers, and giving express citations to Duarenus, Oldendorp, Covarruvias, Baldus and Zasius as well as to the Digests and Cicero. The only English source used, and that not explicitly, would seem to be *Doctor and Student*. The perceived similarity between Roman law and its derivatives and English law is underscored by the presence of English-oriented headings opposite purely Roman text: 'Chancery Commission against the Roman', 'Chancery power', and 'Chancery', for example, in a single paragraph dealing with the difference between *stricti iuris* and *bonae fidei iudicia* in Roman law.[71] The tract is not polished, so we should not expect to see any well-developed argument in it. What is significant, though, is its location of equity *between* positive law and natural law: '[B]y tempering the rigor of the one with the sanctity of the other, upon consideration of all due circumstances to frame out of both a moderate just and conscionable censure.'[72] This middle course we may identify with what the author of the tract calls 'civil' equity, by contrast with 'natural' equity. Whereas natural equity consists of very general principles known to all men, civil equity is known only to those 'wise, learned and experienced in civil affairs'; and while it should not directly conflict

[70] Cambridge University Library MS. Gg 2.31 *f.* 12–17.
[71] At *f.* 13–13*v*.
[72] At *f.* 12*v*.

with natural equity, it is not to be identified with it.[73] This approach was derived directly, and almost literally, from Duarenus, the mid-century French humanist.[74]

A similar duality exists between equity and conscience: conscience is identified with the canonists' internal forum, which cannot mislead provided it is properly understood, whereas equity is identified with the external forum, where judges may err through their application of presumption and probability—that is to say, because of the need to discover the facts. The unpolished nature of the text means that we do not find in it anything approaching a coherent argument, but underpinning it we may see three pairs of interconnected ideas:

Stricti iuris actions in Roman Law	Bonae fidei actions in Roman Law
Strict law	Equity
Common law courts	Chancery

The use of the category of 'civil' equity, known only to the wise, learned and experienced, provided a justification for marking out equity as something to be applied by professionals—presumably professional lawyers—rather than being left to the natural understanding of all human beings. Still, though, there were two principal unanswered questions. What exactly was equity, once separated from natural and divine law? And why need there be a separate court to apply it?

(iii) *William Lambarde's* Archeion

The small tract *On Equitie* is in a collection associated with Sir Thomas Egerton, Lord Keeper between 1596 and 1603 and (as Lord Ellesmere) Lord Chancellor between 1603 and 1616.[75] A second work associated with Egerton is the *Archeion* of William Lambarde, antiquarian, Master

---

73 At *f.* 14.

74 *In Primam Partem Pandectarum sive Digestorum Methodica Enarratio*, titles *De Pactis* and *De Iudiciis* (in *Opera Omnia* (Lyons 1584), 54, 211). There is an explicit reference to him as providing some resolution to the problem, at *f.* 15. For Duarenus's approach to equity see V. Piano Mortari, "Aequitas e Ius nell' Umanesimo Giuridico Francese", in *Atti della Accademia Nazionale dei Lincei, Memorie della Classe di Scienze Morali, Storiche e Filologiche*, series IX vol. IX (Rome, 1997), 142, at 184–87.

75 For this collection, which exists in a number of copies (though normally not containing this item), see P.L. Ward, "William Lambarde's Collections on Chancery", *HLB* 7 (1953), 271; J.H. Baker, *Catalogue of English Legal Manuscripts in Cambridge University Library* (Woodbridge: Boydell and Brewer, 1996), 265–75. For Lambarde's reliance on Bodin in his section on Chancery, see Ian Williams, "Developing a Prerogative Theory for the Authority of the Chancery: the French Connection" (forthcoming).

in Chancery, and the person responsible for bringing together Egerton's collection of Chancery materials.[76] *Archeion* was only published posthumously in 1635 (twice, the first time in a pirated edition), but its creation can be traced back to the 1570s and the author's dedicatory epistle to Sir Robert Cecil is dated 1591.[77] The manuscript tradition of the work is complex, and there are marked differences between the two printed editions; but although the section on equity and the Court of Chancery shows variation over time, some parts having seemingly been added after Egerton's appointment as Lord Keeper in 1596, the core of the ideas expressed there was probably fixed by 1591.[78]

The heart of Lambarde's treatment is unequivocally Aristotelian: written laws cannot be framed to deal with all eventualities, so equity is needed as a corrective to fit cases to circumstances.[79] There is nothing here that goes beyond what had been said by St German or Plowden, though Lambarde's section is closer to Aristotle's text than are St German's or Plowden's; in particular, here we find the use of the Greek *epieikeia* and not simply a bastardised Latin form of it, as well as a reference to the so-called Lesbian rule, a rule of lead which would bend to any shape by contrast with the rigid rule of iron or steel. It is possible therefore that Lambarde was working directly from Aristotle, and not simply reproducing the already commonplace ideas.

The treatment of equity in *Archeion* is closely in the tradition of that in *Doctor and Student*. There is no hint of Plowden's discussion of equity in statutory interpretation, though it is highly likely that Lambarde would have been aware of it. Rather, it is concerned with the use of equity alongside the Common law and as a corrective to it. As well, the headings of this section of the work seem to show a hardening of the equation of equity with the work of the Chancery. In the 1591 version of the manuscript it is *The Chauncerie Court*; after the alterations made after Egerton's appointment it has become *The Chancery Court for Equity*, and by the time of the (second) printed version of 1635 it had mutated into *The Court of Equitie, or Chancerie*.[80] Similarly, the post-1596 version of the text has sub-headings

---

76 *Supra*, 69, fnt. 75.

77 I have used the edition of C.H. McIlwain and P.L. Ward (Cambridge Mass.: Harvard University Press, 1957), based on the edition of 1635 by 'TL' with references to the Frere printing of 1635. In order to ease the lot of the reader who may not have access to the modern edition, I also give references to the pagination of the TL edition, in square brackets.

78 McIlwain and Ward, *Lambarde's Archeion*, 145–176, especially at 152–6.

79 McIlwain and Ward, *Lambarde's Archeion*, 43 [69–70].

80 McIlwain and Ward, *Lambarde's Archeion*, 37 [58], with n. 6.

not found in the earlier version, *Necessity of a Court of Equitie* and *Use of a Courte of Equitye*.[81] But while the headings testify to an increasing crystallisation of the identity of the Chancery and equity, the idea is clearly present in the text in its 1591 form. This is implicit in the way in which the discussion of equity is dominant in the section of *Archeion* on the Court of Chancery, but in addition there are many places where the argument slips from the Chancery to equity and vice versa. To take just one example, a sentence dealing with the antiquity of the Chancery moves on to speak of the lack of evidence before the reign of Henry IV of causes in equity before the Chancellor.[82]

There are two major points at which Lambarde departs from St German's model. The first lies in his argument that in every 'well-policied' state there was a need for an officer equivalent to the Chancellor.[83] Whereas for St German the separation between the Chancery and the courts of common law was simply a fact, for Lambarde it was a necessity. Secondly, whereas *Doctor and Student* had treated equity as a means of ensuring that positive law did not transgress natural or divine law,[84] *Archeion* stresses its function as a means of softening the rigour of positive law, though saying that it should only be used in 'few or singular cases', 'rare and extraordinary matters'.[85] Nonetheless, despite this difference, it retains the incoherence of *Doctor and Student* in its reproduction of Aristotle's theory of the need for a mechanism to apply general rules to specific cases, while at the same time treating equity as a device to mitigate the common law. Since the latter is for Lambarde the principal function of equity and the Chancery, it follows that the incorporation of the Aristotelian theory was redundant at best and misguided at worst. Moreover, without the justification based in natural and divine law, it was not clear where the legitimacy of equitable intervention came from. In a section omitted from some manuscripts he seems to face up to this in asking whether there should be fixed rules of equity;[86] but no answer to the question is given.

---

81 McIlwain and Ward, *Lambarde's Archeion*, 43, with n. 52 and n. 53.

82 McIlwain and Ward, *Lambarde's Archeion*, 42 [67].

83 McIlwain and Ward, *Lambarde's Archeion*, 40 [65] (not in the 1591 version of the text).

84 *Supra*, 59.

85 McIlwain and Ward, *Lambarde's Archeion*, 44 [71].

86 McIlwain and Ward, *Lambarde's Archeion*, 46–47 [74–76].

(iv) *Samuel Daniel's Epistle to the Lord Keeper*
Also associated with Egerton is a poetic epistle by Samuel Daniel, whose patron Egerton was.[87] This was published in 1603,[88] though a reference to the Chancery's 'provident injunctions' (line 155) might point to its having been written in 1597–8, when the legitimacy of granting injunctions against the enforcement of Common law judgments was a much-debated question.[89]

A conventionally laudatory address to a patron is perhaps not the natural place to look for discussion of abstract ideas, but Daniel's poem is more about equity than it is about Egerton.[90] Its core idea is unoriginally Aristotelian, that equity does not depend on a strict ('stern and unaffable', line 133) adherence to written law but is rather moulded to the circumstances of the case (lines 121–136); and, in line with the narrow approach of St German rather than the broad one derived from Oldendorp,[91] it should operate by reference to the law (a 'gentle relaxation' of it, line 140) rather than by applying unconstrained principles of justice or fairness (lines 137–144).

It is possible that Daniel had access to a version of *Archeion* when he was writing the poem.[92] His Aristotelian stanzas bear some resemblance to Lambarde's treatment of *epieikeia*; and his stanzas on the moderating force of equity (lines 137–144) follow closely Lambarde's argument that equity should only rarely operate against the common law and that the common law should be allowed to retain its 'just honour'.[93]

---

[87] C. Seronsy, *Samuel Daniel* (New York: Twayne Publishers, 1967), 107–109; J. Pitcher, "Samuel Daniel's Gift of Books to Lord Chancellor Egerton", *Medieval and Renaissance Drama in England* 17 (2005), 216. The principal direct evidence for Egerton's patronage of Daniel is a letter, probably of 1602, for the genuineness of which see J. Pitcher, "Samuel Daniel's Letter to Sir Thomas Egerton", *HLQ* 47 (1984), 55.

[88] S. Daniel, *A panegyrike congratulatorie deliuered to the Kings most excellent Maiestie at Burleigh Harrington in Rutlandshire*, sig. C, 'To Sir Tho: Egerton Knight, Lord Keeper of the Great Seale of England'. There is a modern edition in G. Hiller and P. Groves ed., *Samuel Daniel: Selected Poetry and A Defense of Rhyme* (Asheville, NC: Pegasus Press, 1998), 156–165.

[89] J.P. Dawson, "Coke and Ellesmere Disinterred: The Attack on the Chancery in 1616", *ILR* 36 (1941) 127, 134–5.

[90] Seronsy, *Samuel Daniel*, 93–4.

[91] *Supra*, 59 and 67.

[92] Daniel may, perhaps, have borrowed Sir Robert Cotton's copy (now BL MS. Add. 46410). He is known to have used Cotton's manuscripts when writing his *History of England*: M. McKisack, "Samuel Daniel as Historian", *Review of English Studies* 23 (1947), 226, 231 n.5. Daniel's unfavourable views of the law and lawyers are in part derived from Montaigne (*Essays* III, no. 13).

[93] McIlwain and Ward, *Lambarde's Archeion*, 44–45 [71–73].

Alongside this, however, there are ideas which parallel those in *On Equitie*. Equity is described as the isthmus between the two oceans of 'rigor' and 'confused uncertainty' (lines 4–5), an image which Daniel had used elsewhere in his works as a metaphor for something standing between two otherwise warring groups.[94] It is therefore not to be identified with the tract's principles of 'natural' equity, which would equate to the ocean of 'confused uncertainty', but rather with its 'civil' equity.[95] Equity must have some such meaning if the poem is to work as a panegyric to Egerton—it would hardly be a matter for praise if he was simply applying the natural reason that was the God-given possession of every man—but that is not quite the point. What is important in the developing interpretation of equity in the last decade of the reign of Elizabeth is that the distinction between the general ideas of right and wrong and the technical criteria for 'equitable' decision-making is sufficiently well-rooted that it can be found in a poem written by a well-connected non-lawyer.

The second feature, presenting a parallel both with *On Equitie* and *Archeion*, is the identification of equity with the Court of Chancery. Nowhere in the poem is the Chancery mentioned. Instead, Egerton is addressed as the 'Great Keeper of the state of equity' (line 58),[96] his virtues sit on 'this seat of equity' which has been ordained as a 'sanctuary, whereunto / Th'oppressed might fly' (lines 117–20). Hence the antinomies found in *On Equitie* between equity and strict law, and between the Court of Chancery and the Common law courts, are compacted into a single antinomy between equity and the common law together with its courts. Hence the barbarous French, the subtleties of pleading and the delaying processes of the common law can be contrasted with the purity and simplicity of equity (lines 41–56, 65–72). As in the tract, there is no hint that there might be any court of equity other than the Chancery.

Daniel's poem is of little independent worth in understanding the development of the theory of equity at the end of the 16th century, but taken in conjunction with *Archeion* and *On Equitie* it is a valuable piece of evidence of the way in which a certain set of ideas about equity and its relation to Common law were becoming fixed in the circle around Sir Thomas Egerton, the Lord Keeper of the Great Seal. In particular, although Aristotle continued to be an explicit point of reference, his theory of *epieikeia* had

94 Pitcher, "Samuel Daniel's Gift of Books", 217–8. The image is taken from Lucan, *Pharsalia* 1, 101–103.

95 *Supra*, 68–69.

96 Contrasted with the 'state of law' (line 77).

little or no explanatory force. Instead, equity as it was practised in the Court of Chancery was seen as operating at the periphery of the Common law, in some unspecified way preventing it from doing injustice.

The Earl of Oxford's Case

The Earl of Oxford's Case[97] is commonly taken to be the decision in which the legitimacy of Chancery intervention to set at nought judgments at Common law—and hence the practical primacy of Chancery and equity over Common law—was established. I have argued elsewhere that the reported 'decision' was not in truth a decision at all, but rather a set-piece justification of Chancery practice put together by Lord Ellesmere (formerly Sir Thomas Egerton), the Lord Chancellor, and that the true source of the Chancery's predominance was the political act of King James I in resolving that it should be so.[98] More significant than its precise legal status, perhaps, is that while legal decisions normally represent judicial responses to arguments put to them, there is nothing to suggest that Ellesmere had heard any arguments at all on this point. We may realistically treat it as a text coming from Ellesmere himself.

Fortier has read the text this way, revealing the various roots of the ideas of equity and conscience within it, drawn out of theology, philosophy, political theory and law.[99] For him this diversity of sources 'fosters the power of equity, fosters a culture of equity'.[100] There is no reason to dissent from this; we should rather see it too as a facet of the legal discussions of the late 16th and early 17th centuries, underpinning the power of the idea of equity there.

For all its intellectual resonances, there is nothing about equity in Ellesmere's argument that cannot be traced back to *Doctor and Student* and which would not have been familiar to anyone acquainted with the legal thinking of the previous three decades, in particular that which was crystallising in the Egerton circle in the 1590s. The Chancery is always open, and not bound by the law terms, the periods in which Common law

97 (1615) 1 Chan. Rep. 1; 21 Eng. Rep. 485.

98 D. Ibbetson, "The Earl of Oxford's Case (1615)", in *Landmark Cases in Equity*, ed. C. Mitchell and P. Mitchell (Oxford: Hart, 2012), 1, 27–29. The Chancery records, which are very full, show nothing but routine appearances occurring through Michaelmas Term 1615, the period to which the reported *Earl of Oxford's Case* is attributed.

99 Fortier, *Culture of Equity*, 4–8.

100 Ibid., 8.

business could be done.[101] Equity is always ready to render every man his due. It is impossible to frame a general law to apply properly to all particular acts. The function of the Chancellor is to correct consciences for frauds, breaches of trust, wrongs and oppression. He should soften the rigour of the law. Equity and Law work together to achieve justice.[102] Equity can be done at Common law as well as in the Chancery, provided that there is a Common law process available to fit the circumstances. Perhaps the most striking thing about Ellesmere's reasoning here is just how theoretically unsophisticated it is, little more than a collection of standard points which could be said to justify equitable intervention, and in particular the intervention of the Chancery.

Many of these elements are also found in a discourse defending Chancery jurisdiction, written by the lawyer Anthony Ben.[103] Although his arguments on the function of equity are largely commonplace, his discourse brings out a further aspect which should not be ignored, the rhetorical function of the language of 'equity'.[104] Taking the example of Common law judgments obtained by an attorney's fraud or negligence, Ben asks whether the equity of these should not be examined by the Court of Chancery.[105] 'Equity' here can mean little more than 'justice', and of course it was easy to slip into the assertion that the law should be just. The rhetorical step involved here is important, for whilst it might have been easy to accept that equity (in this broad sense) be done, without that step it would have been less easy to accept that the Chancery should have the power to determine whether judgments had been properly given at Common law.

The King's intervention, on the side of equity and the Chancery, made any further argument unnecessary. Ellesmere's 'speech' in *The Earl of Oxford's Case* circulated widely in manuscript, and was later put into print. Whatever its analytical qualities, and even if it remained largely unread, it could be treated as providing the intellectual base for the jurisdiction of

101 For these points, see 1 Chan. Rep. 1, at 6–11; 21 Eng. Rep. 485, at 486–7.

102 See Egerton's speech to the new serjeants at law in 1614, in J.H. Baker, *The Order of Serjeants at Law* (London: Selden Society Suppl. 5, 1984), 327.

103 BL MS. Lansd. 174*f.* 205. For this piece and its context, see J.H. Baker, "The Common Lawyers and the Chancery: 1616" *Irish Jurist NS* 4 (1969), 368, at 382.

104 This can already be seen in the *Earl of Oxford's Case*, if not quite so transparently: G. Watt, *Equity Stirring* (Oxford: Hart, 2009), 71–72.

105 BL MS. Lansd. 174, *f.* 208*v*.

the Chancery in equity, relieving later English lawyers of the necessity of grounding this purely upon the political fact of a royal decision.[106]

Conclusions

Quoting Maitland, Hamilton Bryson has rightly pointed to the incoherence of the idea of 'equity' found in the early modern period:

> 'Equity is that body of rules which is administered only by those courts which are known as courts of equity.' This circular definition is admittedly unsatisfactory, but it is the best that I can find and certainly better than any that I can create.[107]

The present chapter provides several reasons for this confusion. First, as a matter of history, the Court of Chancery had developed without concern for any underlying theoretical framework. In attempting to provide a framework St German was inevitably faced with the problem of imposing a theory on what was an essentially ragged practice. 'Equity' was perhaps not ideal as an interpretative tool; conscience may have been better, though it too would have had its own problems of forcing complex practice into a single mould.

Secondly, within the law, 'equity' had two wholly distinct functions: to allow the application of statutes beyond their literal meaning, and to formulate the basis of the intervention of the Chancery (and other courts) against the rules of the Common law. These two functions were not properly separated. In particular, Aristotle's *epieikeia*, which provided a workable theoretical basis for statutory extension and limitation, was used by writers from St German onwards to explain the working of the Chancery. Once the two separate functions of equity were run together, after the publication of the second part of Plowden's *Commentaries* in 1579, all coherence was lost.

Thirdly, those writers whose works we have examined were largely content to reproduce what had been written before and to supplement this by the uncritical addition of foreign materials. But the nature of

[106] I have argued elsewhere that the power of an (apparently) authoritative decision can sometimes lie in the very incoherence of its underpinning arguments, allowing later lawyers to accept its conclusions without the risk of its reasoning being picked apart: D. Ibbetson, "Coggs v Barnard (1703)", in *Landmark Cases in the Law of Contract*, ed. C. Mitchell and P. Mitchell (Oxford: Hart, 2008), 1.

[107] W.H. Bryson, *Cases Concerning Equity* I (London: Selden Society 117, 2000), xviii.

equity was contested territory across the Channel just as much as it was in England, so that the incorporation of foreign fragments into English texts served only to add to the confusion. It is hard to avoid the impression that these writers believed that there was a single notion of equity—*aequitas, epieikeia*—whose essence could be uncovered if only one looked hard enough.

The consequence was that, after *The Earl of Oxford's Case* and the forced settlement of the dispute between the Common law courts and the Chancery, English law was left with little more than a set of situations in which Chancery intervention was recognised to be available,[108] explicable in terms of 'equity', but with no theorised basis to say what this equity was.

---

108 For these, see Bryson, *Cases Concerning Equity* I, xxii–xxxii.

CHAPTER FOUR

ARBITRARY CHANCELLORS AND THE PROBLEM OF PREDICTABILITY

M. Macnair

Introduction

Our common project is a comparison between Roman *ius praetorium* and English Equity. My particular theme is as follows. Roman law experienced concerns about arbitrary decision-making by the praetors. Since English Equity came into being much more recently, we have much better evidence both for actual arbitrary decision-making by Chancellors, and for concerns about arbitrary decision-making by Chancellors. The remedies adopted, however, are profoundly different. The Romans made the praetorian Edict more like the XII Tables, that is to say more like a code. The development of English law, in contrast, made Equity more like the Common law: a system based on the *communis opinio* of a narrow group of advocates (in the case of modern Chancery equity, the specialist *Chancery* bar), expressed in the heavy use of precedent and case reporting, modified by *particularistic* statutes, and governed by collegiate courts of review or (in modern times) appeal.[1] The eventual upshot is that modern 'Chancery bar equity' is perhaps the *least* 'equitable', in the Aristotelian *epieikeia* sense of 'flexible', branch of English law.

[1] The fundamental characterisation of the Common law here as a system of *communis opinio* of a narrow professional group follows A.W.B. Simpson, "The Common Law and Legal Theory" in *Oxford Essays in Jurisprudence*, 2nd series, ed. A. Simpson (Oxford: Clarendon, 1973); some historical supporting evidence in J.H. Baker, *The Law's Two Bodies* (Oxford: Oxford University Press, 2001), though Baker does not quite reach the point of drawing Simpson's legal-theoretical conclusions. The assessment of the role of English statutes as *particularistic* interventions in the system is a commonplace, and is, in fact, already visible in the Statute of Merton of 1236 and throughout the later Middle Ages in the statutes in [Record Commissioners] *Statutes of the Realm* I (London: George Eyre and Andrew Strahan, 1810). Collegiate courts were, of course, a common feature of the medieval and early modern European legal systems, and the single judge was thus a peculiarity of the English Chancery and some (not by any means all) of the other courts of equity, albeit shared with the episcopal courts. As will appear below, it was a visibly problematic feature of the Chancery.

Arbitrary Praetors

This point must be extremely brief. There is evidence of concerns about arbitrary decision-making by praetors in the late Roman republic, which were expressed (and attempted to be remedied) by the *Lex Cornelia de iurisdictione* of 67 BC, which is reported to have required praetors to comply with their edicts issued on taking up office. There is a possible connection with the ancient Roman historians' reports of projects of codification (or perhaps re-codification) in the period of the ascendancy of Pompey in the late 50s BC and in that of Caesar in 48–44 BC. About the same time, juristic commentary on the Edict reportedly appeared: in effect, this implies that the *Lex Cornelia* had at least sufficient effect in stabilising Edicts and making them more statute-like to make commentary worthwhile.[2] After the fall of the Republic the information available on this issue becomes much less, but it is trite according to the textbooks, though disputed in the literature, that the emperor Hadrian promulgated a codified form of the Edict, drafted by the jurist Julian, *circa* 130.[3] After this point 'equity' in the *epieikeia* sense in Roman law would have to take the form of juristic interpretations or of *actiones utiles* or *in factum*.[4] My point here

[2] On the *lex Cornelia*, see: A. Watson, *Law making in the Later Roman Republic* (Oxford: Clarendon, 1974), 93–94; R.A. Bauman, *Lawyers in Roman Transitional Politics: A Study of the Roman Jurists* (Munich: Beck, 1985), 22, 121; B. Frier, *The Rise of the Roman Jurists: Studies in Cicero's Pro Caecina* (Princeton, NJ: Princeton University Press, 1985), 74–76. On the Pompeian and Caesarian 'codification projects': Bauman, *Lawyers*, 78–85, Frier, *Jurists*, 264–265.

[3] Recent skeptical discussion, with discussion of the extensive literature, by K. Tuori, "Hadrian's Perpetual Edict: Ancient Sources and Modern Ideals in the Making of a Historical Tradition", *JLH* 27 (2006), 219–237. Also see W. Zwalve, "Einige Bemerkungen zur Constitutio Tanta/Dedooken § 18", *TvR* 51 (1983) 139–145.

[4] There are persistent temptations to translate these expressions into English as 'action on the case' or 'equitable action', which point in different and equally misleading directions. E.g. T.L. Mears, *The Institutes of Gaius and Justinian* (London: Stevens, 1882), 504–505, gives 'equitable actions' for *utiles actiones* and 'action on the case' for *actio in factum*; S.P. Scott, *The Civil Law* (Cincinnati: Central Trust, 1932) at http://www.constitution.org/sps/sps02_j1-4.htm, Inst. 4,3,16, has 'equitable actions' for *utiles actiones*, but leaves *actio in factum* untranslated; F. de Zulueta, *The Institutes of Gaius* (Oxford: Clarendon, 1946), 227 gives 'actions on the case' for *utiles actiones*; P. Birks and G. McLeod, *Justinian's Institutes* (London: Duckworth, 1987), 127 give 'actions based on the policy of the statute' for *utiles actiones*, but fall back on 'action on the case' for *actio in factum*; on the other hand T. Sandars, *The Institutes of Justinian* (London: John W. Parker, 1853), 517 left both Latin expressions untranslated, as did R.W. Lee, *The Elements of Roman Law with a translation of the Institutes of Justinian*, 4th ed. (London: Sweet & Maxwell, 1956), 401. J.A.C. Thomas, *The Institutes of Justinian* (Cape Town: Juta, 1975), 272, gives 'extension actions' for *utiles actiones* and 'an action on the facts of the case' for *actio in factum*. This last most successfully avoids misleading analogies.

is not in any sense to explore these issues, which belong to the Romanists, but solely that the *Lex Cornelia* and the eventual codification by Julian attempted to prevent arbitrary decision-making by praetors by turning the *ius praetorium* or *honorarium*, in the shape of the Edict, into a code of the same sort as the XII Tables; and that this is, as will appear below, a contrast to the development of English Chancery equity.

Arbitrary Chancellors

As noted, the evidence for concern about arbitrary decision-making is a lot denser for English Equity than for the praetors. I will subdivide the heading of 'arbitrary Chancellors' into two parts: evidence of *concern about the potential* for arbitrary decision-making, and evidence of *actual* arbitrary decision-making. There are, however, two preliminary points to be made: the first about 'Equity' as *distinct from ius honorarium*, the second about the chronology of Chancery equity.

The first point is that *ius honorarium* meant law contained in the Edicts of magistrates, primarily of the urban praetor, and the much shorter Edict of the aediles.[5] These two Edicts covered distinct topics reflecting distinct subject matter jurisdictions. In contrast, Equity, in the pre-1875 English sense referring to Courts of Equity as distinct from broader senses, is a broadly common body of principles and procedures applied in a substantial range of courts: the Chancery, the Equity side of the Exchequer, the Requests, the Councils in the North and in Wales, the London Mayor's Court and similar local courts of Equity, and so on.[6] Conversely, courts with a sharply distinct subject matter jurisdiction (like the Court of Wards or the Star Chamber) though using procedures like those of the Courts of Equity, were not generally characterised as 'Courts of Equity' or their doctrines as branches of Equity.

[5] Gaius 1,6; Inst. 1,2,7; D. 1,2,2,11 (Pomponius); the provincial Edict, which appears from the fragments of Gaius's commentary to have been modelled on the Edict of the urban praetor, can be set aside.

[6] A more extended, though still summary, list with references in M.R. Macnair, *The Law of Proof in Early Modern Equity*, Comparative studies in continental and Anglo-American legal history, vol. 20 (Berlin: Duncker & Humblot, 1999), 30. Complaints of arbitrary decision-making are not exclusive to the Chancery; but we have much better evidence for the Chancery than for any other equity jurisdiction.

The second point is that the early history of Chancery falls, as far as can be seen, into a series of distinct periods.[7] In the early 15th century what was involved is arguably a form of administrative review of judicial action, or the Chancellor as an ombudsman for judicial maladministration. In the mid-15th century, the Chancery became staffed by civilians and canonists at the levels of the Chancellor, Master of the Rolls and other Masters, though the bar seems to have consisted of common lawyers. At this period, the common lawyers began to think that what happened in Chancery in 'conscience'—what would later be called Equity—was worth reporting (though a lot less frequently and consistently than they reported what happened in Common Pleas). With the appointment of Cardinal Wolsey as Chancellor in 1515, it seems that this development towards a court applying an identifiable body of legal doctrine was largely aborted and the Chancery (and Star Chamber) became, in effect, a form of 'Alternative Dispute Resolution': the Chancellor would entertain a wide variety of claims, but send most of them to compulsory arbitration by local lay worthies, 'commissioners to hear and determine'. This seems, though only Wolsey's immediate successor Sir Thomas More and the Elizabethan Chancery have been studied in depth, to have continued down to the appointment of Sir Thomas Egerton as Master of the Rolls in 1594. In this period, common lawyers did report some cases in Chancery; but what they reported was overwhelmingly not issues of 'Conscience' or 'Equity', but issues of Common law which happened to be discussed in proceedings in Chancery. Christopher St German's *Doctor and Student* and *Little Treatise concerning writs of subpoena*, dating to the 1520s and 30s, are based on precedents from the pre-1515 period (and in this respect constitute an implicit polemic against Wolsey's approach).[8]

Egerton as Master of the Rolls and later Lord Keeper (1596) and Lord Chancellor (1603–17) very clearly set out to regularise Chancery Equity. His subordinates and contemporaries excavated St German and precedents from the late 15th century reports, as well as the more recent records of the court, to try to give shape to the jurisdiction; and he himself added a large number of rulings, which were fairly extensively reported in manuscript; some of these reports later appeared in print. It is reasonably

[7] What follows summarises M.R. Macnair, "Equity and Conscience", *OJLS* 27 (2007), 659–681 at 670–71, with references there.

[8] See also J. Guy, "Thomas More and Christopher St German: The Battle of the Books", and "Law, Equity and Conscience in Henrician Juristic Thought", in *Reassessing the Henrician Age*, ed. A. Fox & J. Guy, (Oxford: Blackwell, 1986), ch. 5 and 8.

clear that though the late 15th century 'Court of Conscience' informed the nature of the Equity which Egerton and his colleagues created, it is only from the time of Egerton that one can really plausibly speak of Chancery Equity as *ius praetorium* or identify any individual Chancellor's conduct as arbitrary *relative to any body of legal doctrine* other than the common law. My evidence of concerns about arbitrary decision-making, and of the basis of these concerns in practice, therefore mostly come from 'after Egerton'. The point is the *persistence* of these issues.

(a) *The Perception of Arbitrariness*

The most famous example of the perception of arbitrariness in Equity comes from John Selden's *Table Talk*, said sometime in Selden's life (1584–1654) but first published in 1689:

> Equity is a Roguish thing: for Law we have a measure, know what to trust to; Equity is according to the Conscience of him that is Chancellor, and as that is larger or narrower, so is Equity. 'Tis all one as if they should make the Standard for the measure we call a Foot, a Chancellor's Foot; what an uncertain Measure would be this. One Chancellor has a long Foot, another a short Foot, a Third an indifferent Foot: 'Tis the same thing in the Chancellor's Conscience.

This famous quotation is immediately preceded by another less famous:

> EQUITY in Law, is the same that the Spirit is in Religion, what every one pleases to make it. Sometimes they go according to Conscience, sometimes according to Law, sometimes according to the Rule of Court.[9]

Concern about the arbitrary or potentially arbitrary character of Equity jurisdiction was, in fact, a recurring theme of what may be called, as Cromartie does, 'constitutionalist' arguments in England from the 16th century and down into the 18th.[10] The ex-judge Sir Robert Atkyns in polemics arguing for Chancery reform in the 1690s was, like Selden, concerned about the doctrinal instability produced by the single judge system:

---

9 *Table-Talk, Being the Discourses of John Selden Esq. [...]* (London: E. Smith, 1689), 18.

10 A.D.T. Cromartie, *The Constitutionalist Revolution: An Essay on the History of England* (Cambridge: Cambridge University Press, 2006), especially ch. 2 and 7; Christopher W. Brooks, *Law, Politics and Society in Early Modern England* (Cambridge: Cambridge University Press, 2008), especially 142–152; M. Fortier, *The Culture of Equity in Early Modern England* (Aldershot: Ashgate, 2005), especially ch. 2. I have argued for the persistence of these arguments into the late Stuart period in M.R. Macnair, "Common Law and Statutory Imitations of Equitable Relief under the Later Stuarts", in *Communities and Courts in Britain 1150–1900*, ed. C. Brooks & M. Lobban (London: Hambledon, 1997), ch. 8 at 116–118.

> Now let us take Notice of the ill Effects that have arisen from the Exercise of this Equitable Jurisdiction [...]. *Secondly*, the Judgment and Determination of Causes in Chancery, depend upon the sole Opinion and Conscience of one single Person, whose Power therein (as some of our Books and Modern Authors presume to affirm) is Absolute and Arbitrary [...]. The Chancellor's Judgment is not guided always by certain and known rules, so that no foresight can fence and provide against it. We are not fore-warn'd, and therefore cannot be fore-arm'd.[11]

A charge of arbitrary judicial decision-making was made in the impeachment of Thomas Parker, Lord Chancellor and first Earl of Macclesfield, in 1725, but besides showing the persistence of the concern, this was entwined with genuine misconduct and I will deal with it under that head. Lord Hardwicke, in a 1759 letter to the Scots judge Lord Kames in response to the latter's treatise on equity, argued for the constitutional importance of keeping Law and Equity separate:

> I agree that, in considering this point upon different principles, there is room for different determinations. [...] All the arguments drawn from the ease and convenience of the suitors, the preventing vexation and delay, and saving of expense, seem to conclude for uniting them in the same court. [...] On the other hand, the arguments drawn from the necessity, or utility, of preserving the rules of law entire, and not leaving it in the power of judges to new-mould and vary those rules at discretion, by insensibly blending law and equity together, hold for keeping them divided. These reasons regard the constitution of the government, and have always appeared to me to outweigh the others; inasmuch as what is of general and public consequence, ought to be preferred to private or particular convenience. [...] My Lord Bacon says, *Si fiat commixtio jurisdictionum, arbitrium tandem legem trahet*, and I think I have in some instances seen that effect produced. No wonder then, that a people jealous of their liberties, and fond of their laws, and therefore desirous to bind the hands of their judges by stated rules, should lean against so dangerous an institution. Besides the tendency it would have to make the judges of the common law law-makers in matters of property, I think, in time, it would have an effect of the like kind upon cases of crime, which affect life and liberty [...]. If this had been allowed in England, the common law would have sunk long ago, and everything been restored into the *arbitrium boni viri*.[12]

---

11 *An Enquiry into the Jurisdiction of the Chancery in Causes of Equity* (London, 1695), 32–33.

12 Hardwicke to Kames, June 30 1759, Philip C. Yorke, *The Life and Correspondence of Philip Yorke, Earl of Hardwicke* II (Cambridge: Cambridge University Press, 1913), 550–555, at 553; quoted and discussed in W.S. Holdsworth, *A History of English Law* XII (London: Methuen, 1938), 600–601.

The issue reappeared in arguments about the constitutionality of equity jurisdiction in the early United States.[13] In England it was still alive in 1818 when Lord Eldon, after the better part of 18 years as Chancellor, felt it necessary to remark—almost as famously as Selden's original—that:

> I cannot agree that the doctrines of this Court are to be changed with every succeeding Judge. Nothing would inflict on me greater pain in quitting this place, than the recollection that I had done anything to justify the reproach that the equity of this Court varies like the Chancellor's foot.[14]

These long-lasting concerns were not unfounded.

(b) *Arbitrary Decision-Making*

The evidence will inevitably consist of a series of examples of decision-making which either was on its face arbitrary by common legal standards, or was found or admitted to be so. The point of the catalogue is merely to show persistence of the issue. My first example is an outlier from 1535, *Docwra v Prior of the Hospitallers*. The former Prior of the Hospitallers had let a property belonging to his order to one of his own relatives, with what is now called a 'break clause' allowing the lessor to determine the lease under certain circumstances. After the original lessor's death, his successor in the office claimed to exercise the break clause. In the draft 'articles of impeachment' of Wolsey produced in 1529, he was charged with issuing a sequestration in this case *ex parte* before a subpoena had been issued to summon the defendant.[15] After Wolsey's dismissal, the Prior obtained a decree in Chancery against the lessee from More LC in 1529. The lessee's widow reopened the case in 1535, and it was heard before Audley LC, Cromwell MR (who was also Secretary of State and the King's principal minister at this date) and Fitzherbert J. During argument, Serjeant Dinshill, counsel for the Prior, ventured to suggest that the Court should regard itself as bound by its own prior decision in the same case:

---

[13] Discussion with references (from a 'reactionary' standpoint) in G.L. McDowell, *Equity and the Constitution* (Chicago, IL: University of Chicago Press, 1982), ch. 2, and (in relation to the Field Code, 'fusion' in New York, and Story), ch. 4. Holdsworth, *HEL* XII, 601 quotes *Federalist* No. 83 (http://www.constitution.org/fed/federa83.htm) defending the separation of law and equity on 'Hardwickian' grounds.

[14] *Gee v Pritchard* (1818) 2 Swanst. 402, at 414; 36 Eng. Rep. 670, at 674.

[15] J. Galt, *The Life and Administration of Cardinal Wolsey* (London: T. Cadell & W. Davies, 1812), appendix, Book VII, cxcviii–ccx, Art. 42 at ccviii–ccix. The status and significance of this document is discussed by P. Gwyn, *The King's Cardinal* (London: Barrie & Jenkins, 1990), 593–594 and 617–618.

> It seems a judgment given by decree here should not be reversed; because there is no more than one judge, the Chancellor. And if each decree that is made here could be reversed in the same court, there would be an incessant confusion in all causes. [...] And our decree is an absolute decree without any *quousque*. And it is similar to a definitive sentence given in an ecclesiastical court, which cannot be corrected in the same court, but should be corrected by appeal to a higher court, which is in their law like a writ of error in our law.

Cromwell MR's response to this argument was a simple prohibition on arguing the point:

> THE SECRETARY interrupted him, and said, do not speak further about the authority of this court.

The prior decision was, in fact, reversed.[16]

The next example is Francis Bacon, Lord Verulam, Lord Chancellor 1617–21. Bacon was impeached for taking bribes as Chancellor; and admitted that he had taken bribes, but argued that his judgment was not affected by them.[17] The plausibility of this argument is diminished by the fact that though Bacon was an eminent counsel before he became Chancellor, and though reporting of cases in Equity had begun under Egerton, the lawyers seem to have thought Bacon's decisions sitting alone as Chancellor were

16 *Docwra v Prior of St John of Jerusalem* (1535) YB T 27 Hen VIII *f.* 14b pl. 6; YB M 27 Hen VIII *f.* 28b pl. 16, this passage at T 27 Hen VIII *f.* 16b: '*Deinshil* Al' contrary & semble un iugement done per decree icy ne serra reverse, car il nest forsque un iuge, cestassavoir le chaunceller. Et si chescun decre qui est fait icy serra reverse in mesme le court, ils serrra un incessant confusion in toutes causes, [& le Chaunceler ad power de tener le matter devant luy, & sil ad power, donques quand il fait decre, il nad pouvoir de reverser ceo luy mesme,] & nostre decre fuit un absolute decre sanz ascun *quousque &c.* et est moult semblable a un definitif sentence done en lespiritual court, le quel ne poit estre redresse en mesme la court, mes serra redresse per appellacion a un Court pluis hault le quele est en lour ley come un bre derrour est en nostre ley. *Le Secretary* luy enterrupt, & dit, ne parles pluis del auctoritie de cest Court [per qui il ne voloit, mes in effect come devaunt.]' (square brackets indicate ellipses in translation in the text). The final part of the report in MT at *f.* 38b pl. 16 is unclear: it looks, from its content and lack of context, like a fragment of the earlier report, containing the 'argument' (judgment) of Cromwell MR, which has been displaced in the reporter's papers or in typesetting from TT into MT. But reversal of the decree is confirmed in *Letters and Papers Henry VIII*, 28 June. R.O. 936, http://www.british-history.ac.uk/report.asp?compid=42661.

17 L. Jardine & A. Stewart, *Hostage to Fortune: the troubled life of Francis Bacon* (London: Phoenix, 1999), 451–462.

not worth reporting.[18] His corruption was notorious,[19] and his purported legal reasoning therefore presumptively unrelated to his decisions.

We now jump forward to the Restoration. Heneage Finch, Lord Nottingham, Lord Keeper 1673–76 and Chancellor 1676–81, has a good reputation among legal historians, and, indeed, a reputation for stabilising equity doctrine. A case which is routinely cited in modern books for this proposition is *Coke v Fountaine* (1676), a case on presumed trusts in which Nottingham said that

> if the Chancery do once take liberty to construe a trust by implication of law, or to presume a trust, unnecessarily, a way is opened to the Lord Chancellor to construe or presume any man in England out of his estate; and so at last every case in court will become *casus pro amico*

and—

> With such a conscience as is only *naturalis et interna* this Court has nothing to do; the conscience by which I am to proceed is merely *civilis et politica* and tied to certain measures; and it is infinitely better for the public that a trust, security, or agreement, which is wholly secret, should miscarry, than that men should lose their estates by the mere fancy and imagination of a chancellor.[20]

In spite of these striking expressions, contemporary reporters did not report Lord Nottingham's judgment quoted here, though they reported many other parts of the same litigation: it was unearthed in the early

[18] M.R. Macnair, "The Nature and Function of the Early Chancery Reports", in *Law Reporting in Britain*, ed. C. Stebbings (London: Hambledon, 1995), 125–126; corroborated by the reports put in print in *Cases Concerning Equity*, ed. W. Bryson (London: Selden Society vols. 117–118, 2000–2001). The lawyers did not report Bacon's successor, Bishop Williams, either; but he was not a lawyer. Going beyond looking simply at the Chancery series of reports, searching in the *English Reports* CD-ROM for 'Chancery' or 'Cancellaria' between 1617 and 1625 produces 108 hits (there are 1884 hits for the dates alone); this includes one case in 1617, *Case Concerning Payment of Tythes in London*, Calthrop 54; 80 Eng. Rep. 672, in which Bacon sat with other senior judges under a special commission; one case on charities just after Egerton's death referred to Hobart CJ and Tanfield CB, *Collison's Case* (1617) Hob. 136; 80 Eng. Rep. 286; and one case in 1625 before Coventry's appointment accidentally picked up by the compiler of *Reports in Chancery*, *Pool v Pool* (1625) 1 Chan. Rep. 18; 21 Eng. Rep. 494 (I deduce the early date from the D&O book reference in the report, 1 Car *f.* 4, which pretty much has to be between James I's death on 27 March and Coventry's appointment as Lord Keeper on 1 November). The other 105 hits are references to writs issued out of Chancery or to proceedings in the Petty Bag. This effective silence pretty much shouts at us.

[19] Jardine and Stewart, *Hostage to Fortune*, 433–437 provide evidence of Bacon's loss of reputation *before* 1621.

[20] *Coke v Fountaine* (1676) 73 SS 362, at 365 and 371; 3 Swanst. 585, at 591 and 600–601; 36 Eng. Rep. 984, at 987 and 990.

19th century from Nottingham's own manuscript. And on close examination it turns out that Nottingham's rhetoric is deceptive. The real party in interest in the case was Nottingham's cabinet colleague the Earl of Danby, who had taken over the finances of the nominal claimant, his son-in-law. And Nottingham's decision flatly broke the Chancery's own procedural rules as restated in his own *Practice*, and considerably bent his own previously stated doctrines on presumed trusts, in order to produce a result favourable to Danby. Even the part of the decision which is ostensibly against the claimant in fact assists claims which were being made in parallel litigation in the equity side of the Exchequer against the same defendant.[21]

Nottingham's successor, Francis North, Lord Guilford, Lord Keeper 1682–85, also has a good reputation in the historiography, in this case because of the existence of a near-contemporary biography by his brother Roger North.[22] On taking over as Lord Keeper, North issued a *de facto* invitation to litigants disappointed by Nottingham to reopen their cases. The result can be seen in the court's records, as cases which had apparently reached final decision reappear in the contemporary name indexes of parties, and the length of the court's decree and order books expands by between 30 and 50 per cent.[23] In one remarkable case North ruled—reversing Nottingham—that a trustee who had expressly covenanted to let the trust property at the best rent obtainable, but had not let it at all, could not be liable for more than he had actually received. This statement led counsel on both sides to settle the case in the face of the court to prevent the ruling becoming a precedent.[24]

---

21 More detail in M.R. Macnair, "*Coke v Fountaine* (1676)", in *Landmark Cases in Equity*, ed. C. Mitchell & P. Mitchell (Oxford: Hart 2012).

22 M. Chan, ed., *The Life of the Lord Keeper North by Roger North* (Lampeter: Edwin Mellen, 1995). The book was published in a heavily edited version by Roger North's son Montagu in 1742 as part of *Lives of the Norths*, and in this form informed subsequent judgments of North. The most recent account, P.D. Halliday, in *Oxford Dictionary of National Biography*, ed. H.C.G. Matthew, B.H. Harrison and L. Goldman (Oxford: Oxford University Press, 2004; hereafter cited as *ODNB*), *s.n. North, Francis* is more cagey about Roger's claims of Francis's impartiality, and does not venture any judgment on North's competence as Lord Keeper.

23 G.W. Keeton, *Lord Chancellor Jeffreys and the Stuart Cause* (London: Macdonald, 1965), ch. 18 discusses the effects on Jeffreys's work as Chancellor. The indexes are at TNA PRO IND1/1640–1652; the Decree & Order books increase in length sharply from C33/261 (1683–1684).

24 *Palmer v Jones* (1682) 1 Vern. 144; 23 Eng. Rep. 376. Lord Nottingham's decision is at (1678) 79 SS 649 No. 824, very briefly noted. Lord Nottingham states the rules applied in his decision at *Prolegomena* ch. 4, par. 1–3, 18, in *Lord Nottingham's 'Manual of Chancery*

Slightly lower down the Chancery hierarchy, Sir John Trevor, Master of the Rolls 1685–88, Commissioner of the Great Seal 1690–93, and Master of the Rolls again 1693–1717, was sacked as Speaker of the House of Commons in 1695 for accepting a large bribe to influence the progress of legislation. Since the Mastership of the Rolls was a venal office which Trevor held under a grant for life, he was able to retire to the Rolls (he died intestate in 1717 leaving a large fortune).[25]

A year after Trevor's death, Thomas Parker, first Earl of Macclesfield, became Lord Chancellor. Macclesfield was impeached in 1725 for corruption in the form of auctioning the Masterships in Chancery (junior judicial posts); the Masters would recoup the costs by investing litigants' money paid into court in the stock market, on their own account. The 1720 crash of the 'South Sea Bubble' exposed the practice. Macclesfield was, in fact, correct to claim in his defence that selling the Masterships was a traditional perquisite of the Chancellor, though he seems to have run the price up above normal levels (perhaps understandably during a financial bubble). In Art. 21 of the articles of impeachment he was charged that he 'did, in an illegal and arbitrary manner, extend the power and authority of Lord Chancellor and of the Court of Chancery, beyond their lawful and just bounds; and did arbitrarily and illegally assume to himself, as Lord Chancellor, and by colour of his office, an unjust and unlimited power of dispensing with, suspending, and controlling, the statutes of this realm [...]'. The substance of the charge concerned a single unreported

Practice' and 'Prolegomena of Chancery and Equity', ed. D.E.C. Yale (Cambridge: Cambridge University Press, 1965), 196–197, 200. By ill luck the law student Thomas Vernon reported it (cited at the beginning of this note), and when his reports were printed in 1726 (*Cases Argued and Adjudged in the High Court of Chancery, published from the Manuscripts of Thomas Vernon* (London: Tonson, 1726–1728; in the *English Reports* at 23 Eng. Rep. 260 *seq.*) it gave rise to temporary confusion about the rule. There are other reports from 1683–1685 (in the sets of printed reports noted below) in which the reporter notes either that counsel were markedly surprised by North's ruling, or that it was reversed by Jeffreys.

25 K. Ellis, *ODNB, s.n. Trevor, Sir John (c. 1637–1717)* finds 'no evidence to suggest that he was anything other than impartial in legal affairs', but does not either here or in her "'The squint from the chair': speaker Sir John Trevor, (*c.* 1637–1717)", *Parliamentary History* 17 (1998), 198–214 examine his judicial decisions in depth. Ellis has him 'reputed to have died worth £60,000'; the best report of the litigation which followed his death, *Trevor v Trevor* (1719) 1 Eq. Ca. Ab. 387, at 388; 21 Eng. Rep. 1122, at 1123, makes the total value of property *not previously settled* in Trevor's estate £70,000, £108m in 2009 money using average earnings as the inflator (http://www.measuringworth.com/ppoweruk/). While some of the assets had been inherited, and these values date from near the high point of the 1720 bubble, it is not *prima facie* plausible that all this wealth was the proceeds of Trevor's private practice before 1685.

case, *Tyssen v Tyssen* (1718). This was a dispute about the management of an infant's estate between the mother, who was testamentary guardian under the father's will, and the uncle on the father's side, who was remainderman under the will in the event of the infant's death before reaching his majority. On the uncle's application Macclesfield had made an order appointing a receiver of rents of the estate, over the opposition of the widow. It was contended that this order was both unprecedented, and inconsistent with the provisions of the Tenures Abolition Act 1660, S. 8, as to the father's power to appoint by will a guardian or guardians of his children. When pressed with the absence of precedent Macclesfield allegedly said 'that then he would make a precedent in that instance'. The underlying grievance which probably led to the inclusion of this charge in the impeachment was that the receiver Macclesfield had appointed embezzled the funds and died insolvent in 1722. This made the case appear to be another example of his appointing improper persons, which was an aspect of the charges against him relating to the Masters. Macclesfield was able to reply, first, that he had taken security from the uncle against any defalcations by the receiver, and second, that the mother could have appealed the decision to the House of Lords.[26]

For whatever reason, at trial the managers for the Commons (the prosecutors) did not offer any evidence on this charge.[27] It is certainly true that Macclesfield's claim that Chancery had a general supervisory jurisdiction over guardians under the 1660 Act was controversial,[28] and that appointing a receiver on the recommendation of the remainderman who would take if the infant died under age was clearly in principle, if only indirectly, inconsistent with the common law rule which *excluded* from guardian-

[26] The articles of impeachment and Macclesfield's answer in *Cobbett's Parliamentary History* VIII, Art. 21 at 434–435, Macclesfield's answer to this article at 450–452. The Tyssen family is briefly discussed at "Hackney: Manors", T.F.T. Baker ed., *A History of the County of Middlesex* X, *Hackney* (1995), 75–91. URL: http://www.british-history.ac.uk/report.aspx?compid=22707. In *Duke of Beaufort v Berty* (1721) 1 P. Wms. 703; 24 Eng. Rep. 579, where the jurisdiction of the Chancery to interfere with testamentary guardians was also disputed, at 705/580 Lord Macclesfield cited an otherwise unreported case of *Kiffin v Kiffin* in which a receiver was appointed; it is just possible that this is a reporter's or typesetter's error for *Tyssen v Tyssen*, though if so Macclesfield in 1721 exaggerated the facts of the case to strengthen the *a fortiori* quality of the precedent.

[27] *The Trial of Thomas Earl of Macclesfield* (1725) 16 State Trials 767, Mr West for the managers at 1057, Macclesfield's closing speech at 1328.

[28] See the arguments reported in *Duke of Beaufort v Berty* (*supra*, fnt. 26) and *Eyre v Countess of Shaftsbury* (1722, 1725) 2 P. Wms. 103; 24 Eng. Rep. 659.

ship in socage persons who might inherit from the infant.[29] But there was a case for the intervention, and the decision looks high-handed in style rather than corrupt or biased. Macclesfield, in fact, was at least partly a scapegoat for problems with the traditional system of corrupt patronage exposed by the 1720 crash and, as Prof. Julia Rudolph argues, for more general anxieties about the crash and its context.[30] He was a vulnerable scapegoat because the lawyers in the Commons chose not to stand up for him against the proposal to impeach.[31] This in turn was partly because of the marked favouritism he had shown as a judge to his protégé Philip Yorke (later Lord Hardwicke; the relationship was an obstacle to Yorke's rise to the bench after Macclesfield's fall).[32] It is this favouritism, rather than the sale of offices, which points to the continued potential for arbitrariness of the Chancellor's office as a single judge.

More generally, it remains impossible to write the history of Chancery Equity before the 19th century except as a history of the ideas of the individual Chancellors (though there may be an unexplored 'hidden history' of the ideas of the Masters of the Rolls, some of whom, like Trevor, were more long-serving than most Chancellors). It was too easy for a Chancellor to reverse the approach of previous Chancellors. Doctrinal stability could be created only by a long-serving Chancellor who devoted substantial attention to the court (as distinct from his other responsibilities as a cabinet minister): thus Lord Hardwicke in 1737–56, and Lord Eldon in (most of) 1801–27.

In the pre-1641 Courts of Equity, there is also an intimate connection with the foundations of the constitutional order. Were these to be found in law, or in *affective personal lordship*, as Thomas Bisson describes the

29 A very long-established rule: G.D.G. Hall, ed., *The Treatise on the Laws and Customs of England Commonly Called Glanvill* [c. 1189] (Oxford: Clarendon, 1993), vii, 11, at 84–85; T.E. Tomlins, ed., *Lyttleton, his Treatise of Tenures* [1460s] (repr. New York, NY: Russell & Russell, 1970), ii.5 par. 123, at 159–160; W. Blackstone, *Commentaries on the Laws of England* I [1765–1769] (repr. Chicago, IL: University of Chicago Press, 1979), 449–450.

30 Prof. Rudolph brilliantly explores the rhetoric of the trial and its general connections to issues of Enlightenment ideas and concerns about commercialisation in her forthcoming book *Common Law and Enlightenment in England, 1689–1750*. I am indebted to her for giving me sight of the chapter on the Macclesfield impeachment in draft.

31 Though he was able to find defence counsel for the trial in the Lords.

32 *ODNB, s.n. Yorke, Philip, First Earl of Hardwicke.* The charge of favouritism towards Yorke as counsel is in Richard Cooksey, *An essay on the Life and Character of John Lord Somers, also sketches of an Essay on the Life and Character of Philip Yorke, Earl of Hardwicke* (Worcester 1791), 72–73. Though this is late evidence, the point was notorious and is also reflected in modern biographies of Yorke, e.g. *ODNB*.

regimes that emerged in the 1100s,[33] based on relations of personal awe and dependence and on clientage chains? The English bill jurisdiction of the Chancery had been from a very early date associated with the King's *absolute* power as contrasted with his *regulated* power—a conceptual distinction drawn from the canon law in relation to the Papacy (and originating in the theology of divine providence).[34] 'Absolute', contrary to the arguments of some historians,[35] meant in this context what it said: government of men, not of laws.[36] We can see this approach of demanding affective submission based on fear in Chancery in Cromwell's peremptory order to counsel in 1535: 'do not speak further about the authority of this court'.[37] In terms of practical legal implications, three examples will do. In the 1590s the Crown began to operate a discretionary practice in insolvency, in which a successful insolvent petitioner could by petitioning the Queen obtain a 'bill of conformity' to force his creditors to accept a reduced payment without going through formal bankruptcy. This practice was not at all available to all debtors, but only to those very few whose personal access to those around the Queen or King would get their cases referred to the Requests or, later, Chancery. The practice moved into Chancery after prohibitions from the Common law Courts to the Requests; it took the fall of Bacon in 1621 and a statute in 1624 to get rid of it.[38]

Slightly earlier, the Stationers' Company developed a private copyright system on the basis of the monopoly it had been granted for censorship purposes by Mary Tudor, and which had been renewed by Elizabeth I. As long as the company itself could manage arbitrations over copyright issues, there was a degree of predictability. But if a dispute went beyond

---

33 T.N. Bisson, *The Crisis of the Twelfth Century* (Princeton, NJ: Princeton University Press, 2008), drawing out the distinction between affective personal lordship, ultimately based in fear, and political action for the (claimed) common good.

34 E.g. YB T 9 Edw IV *f.* 14 pl. 9; Sir John Fortescue, *De Natura Legibus Naturae* [1460s] in *The Works of Sir John Fortescue*, ed. Thomas Fortescue, Lord Clermont (London: privately printed, 1869), 85–86, translation at 214–215. On the theological and canonist background, K. Pennington, *The Prince and the Law, 1200–1600* (Berkeley, CA: University of California Press, 1993).

35 E.g. G. Burgess, *Absolute Monarchy and the Stuart Constitution* (New Haven, CT: Yale University Press, 1996).

36 Note also that some 'Court' supporting pamphleteers and dramatists argued explicitly *for* government of men, not of laws, in the Exclusion Crisis of 1679–1683: S.J. Owen, *Restoration Theatre and Crisis* (Oxford: Clarendon, 1996), ch. 4.

37 *Supra*, 86, fnt. 16.

38 Smith, "The Error of Young Cyrus: the Bill of Conformity and Jacobean Kingship, 1603–1624", *L&HR* 28 (2010), 307; my interpretation of Smith's evidence is more jaundiced about 'bills of conformity' than his is.

the company, where would it go? It could go to the Privy Council, *and, or* to the Chancery, *and, or* to the Star Chamber, *and, or* to the Court of High Commission. The multiplicity of equitable or prerogative venues, *all* deriving their authority from the 'absolute' power of the Crown, i.e. the Queen or King in person, meant that there is little pattern to the (small number of) decisions; the lack of pattern means that individual decisions must fall to be explained primarily by lobbying and patron-client relations.[39]

The history of local government provides us with a third example in relation to which a limited international comparison is possible. Paul D. Halliday's *Dismembering the Body Politic*[40] is a study of the role of law in relations between central and local politics in England between 1650 and 1730. In Halliday's view legal and political developments in this field over the period were primarily driven by local 'partisan politics'; but Charles II and James II made (different) attempts to reduce the municipalities to a proper sense of their dependence on the King. The result, to the extent that the Privy Council was the decision-making body, was dependence of town governments on lobbying aristocrats with personal access to the King. The endpoint resulting from the Revolution of 1688 was something very different, government primarily by law and through King's Bench.

On the other side of the channel, Michael P. Breen's *Law, City and King*[41] is a study of the same issue over a longer period—1595–1715—in relation to a single locality, Dijon. Here the 18th century endpoint is precisely the dominance of affective patron-client relations in decision-making, through the legal indeterminacy created by the existence beyond the Parlements of multiple jurisdictions—Requêtes, Grand Conseil, *etc.*—which, like English Equity and prerogative courts, took their rise from the absolute as opposed to the regulated power of the Prince, and hence which would in England probably have been called Courts of Equity. This cross-channel difference had substantial political-economic implications, drawn out by the 'new institutionalist' Hilton Root's *The Fountain of Privilege*[42] and by

39 C. Lee, "The role of punitive sanctions in the early development of the right to copy", D.Phil. thesis, Oxford 2010, ch. 2, collects a good deal of evidence. Most of the published literature is either by historians of literature, or of the book, without lawyerly sensitivities; or if by lawyers, by polemicists in favour of intellectual property rights, attempting to show that copyright is by natural law or at Common law by using the regime before the 1711 Act as supporting evidence.

40 Cambridge: Cambridge University Press, 1998.

41 Rochester, NY: University of Rochester Press, 2007.

42 Berkeley, CA: University of California Press, 1994.

Steve Pincus' recent account of the revolution of 1688.[43] But to achieve the end result of 'rule of law' (Pincus) or of Parliament as the 'fountain of privilege' (Root) involved stabilising and limiting the scope of equity.

Stabilising Equity

As I said at the outset, there is no sign of any attempt to codify Equity, unlike the praetor's Edict. Chancellors did issue sets of General Orders, but these were overwhelmingly concerned with procedural issues in the narrow sense; and to the extent to which they expressed substantive rules, they did so on the assumption of an existing body of doctrine which they modified in specific ways. An example is Egerton's 1614 order against bills to stay payment of debts, which Bacon rejected.[44] What happened was, rather, a process of assimilation of Equity to Common law patterns: a collegiate bench; the use of *particularistic* statutes to tinker with a perceived existing body of doctrine; a specialist bar, whose *communis opinio* could define what acceptable Equity was; case reporting and the use of precedents. I have listed these in the order in which they seem to have appeared in the development of the Common law in the Middle Ages;[45] but, with the existing Common law model to work from, the development in Equity seems to have been more or less exactly the reverse: the use of precedent and case reporting, followed by statutory interventions in Equity, followed by the emergence of a Chancery bar, followed (after a

[43] *1688: The first Modern Revolution* (New Haven, CT: Yale University Press, 2009).

[44] General Orders: collected in G.W. Sanders, *Orders of the High Court of Chancery* (London: Maxwell, 1845). Bills to stay payment of debts: Smith (*supra*, 92, fnt. 38), at 325 and fnt. 84. Contrary to Smith's use of the Order, this is, in fact, both narrower than 'conformity' (restricted to debts due by record or deed) and wider than it (does not involve any suggestion of the involvement of other creditors).

[45] Collegiate bench: R.V. Turner, *The English Judiciary in the Age of Glanvill and Bracton, c. 1176–1239* (Cambridge: Cambridge University Press, 1985). Statutes as tinkering: there is possibly a connection to the self-representation of the government of Henry II who represented his activities as reviving the customs of his grandfather Henry I, on which B. O'Brien, "The Becket Conflict and the Invention of the Myth of *Lex Non Scripta*", in *Learning the Law*, ed. J.A. Bush and A.A. Wijffels (London: Hambledon, 1999), ch. 1; the tinkering pattern is already present in *Magna Carta* (J.C. Holt, *Magna Carta*, 2nd ed. (Cambridge: Cambridge University Press, 1992) and pretty clearly settled by the time of Henry III (P. Brand, *Kings, Barons and Justices* (Cambridge: Cambridge University Press, 2003). Legal profession: P. Brand, *Origins of the English Legal Profession* (Oxford: Blackwell, 1992. Reporting: P. Brand, *Introduction* to *Earliest English Law Reports* II (London: Selden Society vol. 123, 2006), xi–xxi.

series of abortive attempts and partial devices) by the emergence in the 19th century of collegiate courts of appeal.

(a) *Precedents and Case Reporting*

The use of precedents and case reporting in Chancery Equity began with Egerton, but did not become permanent or really assimilated to the Common law practice until the 1660s.[46] The beginning with Egerton is obscured by two phenomena. The first is that the earliest *printed* Chancery reports in the *English Reports*, 'Cary' and 'Choyce Cases in Chancery', both printed in 1650, contain 'reports' going back to the 1550s. But these are, in fact, extracts from the Court's records collected by Lambarde in the 1590s.[47] The second is that the Deputy Register Richard Powle took notes of decisions in the Chancery in the 1580s, which have been printed in W.H. Bryson's *Cases Concerning Equity*. But Powle's notes are in their overwhelming preponderance notes of points of *common law* which happened to arise in Chancery proceedings, not of points of equity.[48]

The early Chancery reports take three forms. The first is collections of 'Egertoniana': dicta of Egerton from the bench, heavily concentrated in his early years as Lord Keeper in the last years of Elizabeth and the first years of James. Such 'Egertoniana' form the parts of *Cary* and *Choyce Cases* which are not attributable to Lambarde, but they also exist in various manuscripts including some printed in *Cases Concerning Equity*. The second form is alphabetical indexes by subject to usable precedents in the records of the court. These, again, begin in the 1590s, though they contain retrospective references collected at that time, and the surviving manuscripts are mostly of that period. The form continued to be used down to the 1640s, however, and a late version, much fuller than the existing manuscripts, was put in print in 1649 under the name of the Six Clerk William Tothill, as *Transactions of the High Court of Chancery*. This, too, is in the *English Reports*, though it has little to tell a user who does not have ready access to the D&O books. The third form is retrospective collections of precedents extracted from the D&O books, in chronological order. The first example is Lambarde's collections referred to earlier.

46 What follows summarises M.R. Macnair, "Nature and Function", except as specifically indicated below.

47 Ward, "William Lambarde's Collections on Chancery", *HLB* 7 (1953), 270.

48 Selden Society vol. 117, 172–230. Powle's reports continue to 1600 and there are 11 cases on points of Equity (of 372 cases in total) beginning with no. 142, *Branch v Brewdenell* (1593), 197.

By their appearance, later examples look as though they represent efforts by mid- to later 17th century lawyers to construct a corpus of Equity precedents in the absence of regular reporting by lawyers in court.

All three early forms are characterised by their pretty much exclusive focus on the decision of the court, in contrast to contemporary Common law reports, which, following the practice long established in the Year Books, give substantial or predominant space to the arguments of counsel. There may be a connection between the index form and the practice of formal search for precedents which is found episodically in the reports and records from Egerton on. This feature of the early forms tells us two more fundamental things. The first is that there is not yet a Chancery bar: the views of the 'eminent practisers' do not need to be reported because there are not, as yet, any real specialists in the field. The second is the absolute dependence of the idea of Equity as a body of doctrine on the opinions of the Chancellor. This is also reflected in a point I have already referred to: the silence of the reporters in the time of Francis Bacon. In fact, the pattern is not restricted to Bacon.

The early 'Egertoniana' no doubt reflect a period of enthusiasm for Egerton's project of regularising Chancery. Under James I, these reports begin to tail off. By the end of his career Egerton, who had become under James first Lord Ellesmere and then Viscount Brackley, had become involved in an unsought confrontation with the King's Bench led by Coke CJ, and his new title was parodied as 'Viscount Breaklaw'.[49] From this period there are few Chancery reports. There are, as noted earlier, few from Bacon's time. Unsurprisingly, there are equally few from the time of the non-lawyer Lord Keeper Bishop Williams (1621–25). The printed and manuscript reports begin again with Thomas Coventry, Lord Keeper 1625–37. But Coventry did not attract reporters like those of the 'Egertoniana'. What is available from his time is—beyond the occasional reports in common law series which had been present from the 1460s on—index entries in *Tothill*, and retrospective collections of precedents, probably compiled later.[50] From the Civil War, Commonwealth and Cromwellian

49 J. Bruce, ed., *Liber Famelicus of Sir James Whitelocke* (London: Camden Society vol. 70, 1858), 53.

50 In volume 1 of Chan. Rep.: *Reports of cases taken and adjudged in the court of Chancery, in the reign of King Charles I. and to the 20th year of King Charles II [...]* (London: John Walthoe, 1693); in Eng. Rep. at 21 Eng. Rep. 485 *seq.*; Volume 2 is 1694. The earliest report in this set to look at all like a contemporaneous report is *Crisp v Bluck* (1673/4) 2 Chan. Rep. 88; 21 Eng. Rep. 624; the earliest to be certainly a contemporaneous report is *Howard v*

regime there is equally little: chiefly Lord Commissioner Lisle's manuscripts, probably compiled in 1659, according to Allan J. Busch, the only person to have studied them in depth.[51]

Contemporaneous reporting of Chancery Equity restarted, in effect, in 1660, though reports in this style were not printed until considerably later. The first set printed is *Cases in Chancery*, volume 1 printed in 1697 and volume 2 in 1701, which begins with cases from 1660.[52] Next came volume 3 of *Reports in Chancery*, added in 1716 to two volumes dominated by retrospective extracts from the records which had been printed in 1693 and 1694; this begins in 1661.[53] The 'Grub Street' legal writer William *Nelson* in 1717 printed 'Reports' consisting of imperfect copies of material from the records between 1625 and the 1650s, together with a set of reports running 1662–1673 and another running 1689–93.[54] A set of reports attributed to Richard *Freeman* (1645/6–1710) was published posthumously in 1727 and as the second volume of Freeman's *Reports in Law and Equity* in 1742.[55] These are very badly disordered, but the 'reports proper' begin in 1659, running from there to 1665, and then restart in 1673 (which is probably when Freeman himself began reporting Chancery).[56]

Duke of Norfolk (1682) 2 Chan. Rep. 229; 21 Eng. Rep. 665; but the volume continued heavily dependent on the D&O books to its end.

51 "The John Lisle Chancery Manuscripts: the 'Abridgments'", *JLH* 10 (1989), 317, at 320–321; "The John Lisle Chancery Manuscripts: the 'Pleas and Demurrers'" *JLH* 10 (1989), 327, at 332.

52 *Cases argued and decreed in the High Court of Chancery from the 12th year of King Charles II to the 31st* (London: John Walthoe, 1697); *The Second Part of Cases argued and decreed [...]* (London: John Walthoe, 1701). The third volume, which contains a small number of long cases, was only added in 1745.

53 *The third part of reports of cases, taken and adjudged in the court of Chancery* (London: Walthoe & Walthoe, 1716). For the first two parts *supra*, 96, fnt. 50.

54 *Reports of special cases argued and decreed in the Court of Chancery [...]* (London: B. Lintott *et al.*, 1717). For Nelson see *ODNB, s.n. Nelson, William.*

55 *Cases argued and decreed in the High Court of Chancery, from 1676 to 1706*, By the Honourable Richard Freeman, [...] Revised and published by Thomas Dixon [...] (London: Lintot, 1727); *Reports of cases in law and equity: from 1670 to 1706 [...]* (London: Lintot, 1742).

56 *2 Freeman* begins in 1676 and runs from there to 1695 (at 125). There follow cases from (in this order) 1667, 1670, 1665, 1670; a couple of precedents from the records from 1637 and 1649; a run of cases 1672–1676 (at 136–146); *Earl of Suffolk v Greenvill* (1631) from the records, followed by a report of *Lady Dacres v Chute* (1663) which relied on *Suffolk v Greenvill*; then a run of cases, very inconsistently ordered (or dated), between 1659 and 1665 (at 148–184); then reports in chronological order 1692–1703 (at 185–291). There is an appendix of equity cases in *1 Freeman* which runs 1673–79 (at 301–330) and three cases from the 1690s. Freeman's common law reports start in 1670 and are pretty clearly at this stage student work.

Though there are imperfections in the coverage (as is, of course, true at Common law), from the 1660s Chancery was thus pretty much continuously covered by contemporaneous reports of what was said in court, as distinct from retrospective extracts from the D&O books, though the latter continued to be produced. In spite of the delay before printing (which was normal for Common law reports in this period) these Chancery reports plainly circulated in manuscript, as can be seen from the multiple copies of broadly the same report of individual cases to be found in the reports eventually printed. In this respect, Chancery was now more consistently reported than the Exchequer or the Common Pleas.[57]

(b) *Statutory Tinkering*

As of 1616 the idea of a statute modifying the content of equity would have been nonsense. Equity was a mere principle or value, and one which modified statutes: that was what King James VI and I said, and in any case was the only conception of equity which would fit with the Aristotelian idea.[58]

Statutory tinkering with Chancery Equity has to be discriminated from statutes which were (in form at least) directed against the jurisdiction, whether by prohibition of branches (like the prohibition on 'bills of conformity' in the Bankruptcy Act 1624) or by trying to absorb parts of it into common law (like the Statute of Uses 1536 or parts of Somers' Act 1705); and from statutes which gave jurisdiction to the 'Petty Bag' or Latin side of Chancery through the issuance of commissions, like the early Bankruptcy Acts and the 1601 Statute of Charitable Uses.[59] Neither amounted

[57] Exchequer reports in the *English Reports* cover 1605–1608, 1655–1669, 1714–1741. Common Pleas was regularly reported down to the 1620s and appears in 'King's Bench' series subsequently, but there are significant gaps and without judicial manuscripts (Orlando Bridgeman 1660–1667, Vaughan 1666–1673, Willes 1737–1758) they would be larger.

[58] Fortier, *Culture of Equity* and other literature cited *supra*, 83, fnt. 10; Smith, "Young Cyrus"; G.W. Thomas, "James I, Equity and Lord Keeper Williams", *English Historical Review* 91 (1976), 506–528. It is reasonably clear that the underlying conception of equity (as distinct from Chancery jurisdiction) was shared by common lawyers: N. Doe, *Fundamental Authority in Late Medieval English Law* (Cambridge: Cambridge University Press, 1990); G. Behrens, "An Early Tudor debate on the Relation between Law and Equity", *JLH* 19 (1998), 143, and "Equity in the *Commentaries* of Edmund Plowden", *JLH* 20 (1999), 25.

[59] Bankruptcy Act 1624: Smith, "Young Cyrus", 329 (the mechanism used was to make the application for conformity itself an act of bankruptcy). Statute of Uses: of course, the real motivation here was fiscal, but the *ideology* was one of absorbing a branch of equity into the common law: general discussion in J.H. Baker, *Oxford History of the Laws of England* VI (Oxford: Oxford University Press, 2003; cited as *OHLE*), ch. 35. Parts of Somers' Act (and other acts) in Macnair, "Common Law and statutory imitations", 127–128. Bankruptcy

to statutory tinkering *with the substantive content of Equity doctrine* in a way which assumed there was a body of doctrine to tinker with.

The first steps in this direction seem to have been taken with Bulstrode Whitelocke's failed Chancery reform bill in the last years of the Commonwealth and the Cromwellian Chancery Ordinance of 1655.[60] Any impact the Ordinance may have had was, of course, nullified by the Restoration of 1660. But an aspect of the Cromwellian ordinance resurfaced in the provisions for formalities for trusts of land in the Statute of Frauds 1677.[61] Thereafter, tinkering with equity doctrines became, if not particularly a common feature of law reform legislation, certainly not an impossible one.

(c) *Chancery Bar*

The emergence of a distinct Chancery bar is hard to pin down. Wilfred Prest found a distinct group of Chancery 'leaders' in 1616, but this seems to have been attributable merely to favouritism by Egerton.[62] In David Lemmings' 1680 and 1720 sample years around 70% and 76% of the total bar made some appearances in Chancery, suggesting low levels of specialisation, though there was a lot less overlap among the leaders in each court.[63] As late as 1716 the then law student Dudley Ryder could assert that Chancery work 'depends less upon precedents and more upon good sound reason and sense'.[64] Lemmings finds a more distinct Chancery Bar developed by the mid-18th century, but expresses some uncertainty when it began.[65]

Acts: discussion of the early period and procedure in W.J. Jones, *The Foundations of English Bankruptcy*, vol. 69-III of *Transactions of the American Philosophical Society* (Philadelphia: American Philosophical Society, 1979). Charitable Uses: G. Jones, *History of the Law of Charity 1532–1827* (Cambridge: Cambridge University Press, 1969), ch. 3.

60 Whitelocke's bill: A.J. Busch, "Bulstrode Whitelocke and early Interregnum Chancery Reform", *Albion* 11 (1979), 317–330. Chancery Ordinance: in *Acts and Ordinances of the Interregnum, 1642–1660* II, ed. C.H. Firth and R.S. Rait (London: H.M. Stationery Office, 1911), 949–967, http://www.british-history.ac.uk/report.aspx?compid=56575; mainly on procedure, but S. 30 and 44–56 are on matters of substance and S. 63 provides for an appeal from the Chancery commissioners to a court constituted *ad hoc* by members of the three common law courts together with the Chancery commissioners.

61 Statute of Frauds 1677, S. 7–9. See Macnair, *Law of Proof*, 156–157.

62 *The Rise of the Barristers* (Oxford: Clarendon, 1986), 56–71 and 27–29 (favouritism).

63 *Gentlemen and Barristers* (Oxford: Clarendon, 1990), 141–142 and appendices III–X.

64 Ibid., 117.

65 D. Lemmings, *Professors of the Law* (Oxford: Oxford University Press, 2000), 32–33, 181–184, 301–302; the 1736 comment Lemmings cites at 344–345, that the Chancery was

Roger North reports counsel making a fool of Shaftesbury C by inducing him to make absurd *ex parte* orders *nisi*, which he was then forced to abandon on cause shown, so that 'he began to grow wiser, and found that he, who had not the formes of the court, must gain them by the meanes of the councell and officers'.[66] This anecdote has limited value because Shaftesbury was not a legal practitioner at all. Lord Nottingham on his appointment clearly made a special study of the Chancery in his *Practice* and *Prolegomena*, and North seems to have done the same; indicating that there was some degree of specialist knowledge involved in the 1670s–80s.[67]

Possibly an indicator of *perceptions* can be found in appointments. There is no reason to suppose that Clarendon (1660–68), Bridgeman (1668–71), Shaftesbury (1671–73), Nottingham (1673–82), North (1682–85), Jeffreys (1685–88) or Somers (1693–1700) was a specialist Chancery practitioner before appointment; though the Lords Commissioners of 1689–93 *did* include counsel with large amounts of Chancery experience. On the other hand, Sir Nathan Wright, Lord Keeper 1700–05, was criticised as having insufficient knowledge of Equity for the post, and certainly rather frequently sat with Trevor MR and, or, with judges assistant in his first years in post, indicating that he himself had doubts about his knowledge.[68] More clearly, when Macclesfield was impeached in 1725, the Whig administration faced the problem that they had no one who combined sufficient political seniority and reliability with sufficient Chancery experience to take the post except Yorke, who was excluded by his connection with Macclesfield. They appointed Peter King from the Chief Justiceship of Common Pleas, and King was able to drive a hard bargain in the terms on which he took office. King, like Wright, was accused by contemporaries

---

not a good place for a newly qualified barrister to start work, points to specialisation by that date.

[66] Chan, ed., *Life of North*, 331. In addition to the point in the text, the D&O book entries in the *Coke v Fountaine* litigation show the plaintiffs' counsel repeatedly obtaining *ex parte* orders by false assertions of fact and law, reversed on cause shown, from Bridgeman, Nottingham, North and Jeffreys, all of whom had prior knowledge of Chancery, and from the Barons of the Exchequer sitting in Equity. The problem seems to have been the undue facility of *ex parte* applications in the Equity procedure and the absence of sufficient sanctions against counsel who deceived the court, rather than high levels of specialist knowledge among the bar.

[67] Yale, ed., *Nottingham's 'Practice' and 'Prolegomena'*; Chan, ed., *Life of North*, 322–354, though there is no date given in Roger North's extracts from North's papers, and the text is heavily focussed on the practice without anything on the substance other than some proposals for reform of the doctrine relating to mortgages (345 and 352–353).

[68] *ODNB, s.n. Wright, Sir Nathan.*

of causing delay due to insufficient knowledge of Equity, though he had, in fact, appeared in enough reported Chancery cases for this charge to be implausible in his case. When King was disabled by a stroke in 1733, the only candidates were the Attorney-General (Yorke) and Solicitor-General (Charles Talbot) who by virtue of their offices had priority of audience in Chancery. Talbot, though junior to Yorke, was appointed Chancellor, because having had a more or less *exclusively* Equity practice, he could not be appointed to the vacant Chief Justiceship of King's Bench. By this date, therefore, it is clear that there was understood to be a sharply distinct Chancery bar.[69]

(d) *Collegiate Court*

This last head is a more complex and long-lasting story of partial solutions and failed attempts. It needs further subdivision, as follows: (i) the use of judges assistant; (ii) the appellate jurisdiction of the House of Lords in Equity; (iii) Commissioners of the Great Seal; and (iv) the eventual adoption of the Lords Justices of Appeal in Chancery, the precursors of the modern Court of Appeal. Each of these points, however, can be dealt with briefly.

(i) Judges assistant. Though the Lord Chancellor was a single judge, in cases of difficulty it was not uncommon for the Chancellor to call common law judges to assist him, and, or, to sit together with the Master of the Rolls. The practice can already be seen in the late 15th century and our 1535 case of *Docwra*, cited above, is also an example, as is *Coke v Fountaine*. It certainly continued to the later 18th century, though it disappeared in the early 19th.[70] It was only ever a partial solution to the problem that the Chancellor as a single judge could be arbitrary, since the Chancellor was not bound by the advice of the judges sitting with him.

(ii) Appellate jurisdiction of the House of Lords in Equity. This jurisdiction was created by usurpation by the House of Lords in the 1620s.[71]

---

[69] More detail and references for the King and Talbot appointments in M.R. Macnair, "Lord King and Lord Talbot: an eighteenth century attempt to reduce delay in Chancery and its general lessons", in *The Law's Delay*, ed. C.H. van Rhee (Antwerp: Intersentia, 2004), 181–193 at 186 and 189–190.

[70] There is, in fact, some selection bias in favour of such cases both in the retrospective collections of precedents referred to above, and in the occasional Chancery cases reported in 'common law' series. For disuse, M. Lobban, "Preparing for Fusion: Reforming the Nineteenth-Century Court of Chancery, Part I", *L&HR* 22 (2004), 389–426 at 405 fnt. 50.

[71] J.S. Hart, *Justice upon Petition: the House of Lords and the Reformation of Justice 1621–1675* (London: HarperCollins Academic, 1991), ch. 1.

It was sharply limited until 1688 by the fact that it only operated when Parliament was sitting. From 1689, with regular annual sittings of Parliament, the appellate jurisdiction was regularly used. It was, however, an appeal to the House *as a whole* in which, until the late 18th century, the lay peers normally attended and voted—and did so not infrequently on party lines, as can be seen from recorded votes and protests entered in the Lords' Journal against individual judicial decisions.[72] In the late 18th to early 19th century the lay peers stopped participating in the decision-making, with the result that the appeal became an appeal from the Lord Chancellor to—the Lord Chancellor, with other peers sitting merely to make up a quorum. The common use of the advice of the judges to the House may have moderated this characteristic, but did not eliminate it; the existence of other 'Law Lords', i.e. judges and ex-Chancellors who held peerages, could help, but the actual *supply* of other 'Law Lords' was only routinized in 1875.[73]

(iii) Commissioners of the Great Seal. The seal was commonly put in commission temporarily when a Chancellor died or was sacked without a replacement being immediately contemplated. This happened in 1591–92, 1621, 1700, 1710, 1725, 1756–57, 1770–71, 1783, 1972–93, 1835–36, and 1850.[74] But why not leave the seal in commission permanently, turning the court into a collegiate one? The parliamentary side in the Civil War produced its own Great Seal after the outbreak of war in 1641, which was held by a variety of temporary commissioners down to 1649. The execution of the King, abolition of the House of Lords and creation of the republic in that year led to the commission arrangement being put on a more permanent footing, and the seal was held by commissioners through the Commonwealth and Cromwellian Protectorate.[75] The return of the King naturally brought with it the return of the Lord Chancellor or Keeper. However, in 1688 the experiment of permanent Commissioners of the Great Seal was clearly resumed. We don't know why—though it may have involved

---

72 These can be seen in the *Journals of the House of Lords* (London, 1769–), *passim*. A relatively late example of a case in which the full House divided is *Donaldson v Becket* (1774) 2 Bro. Parl. Cas. 129; 1 Eng. Rep. 837; 4 Burr. 2408; 98 Eng. Rep. 257; *Cobbett's Parliamentary History* XVII, 953.

73 P. Polden, "The Judicial Roles of the House of Lords and Privy Council 1820–1914", in *OHLE* XI, part three, ch. 2, 531–537.

74 This list is taken, for reasons of convenience, from Sir Maurice Powicke and E.B. Fryde ed., *Handbook of British Chronology*, 2nd ed. (London: RHS, 1961), 86–88.

75 The major published work on the Interregnum Chancery Commissioners is that of Busch cited *supra*, 99, fnt. 60.

a reaction to the wildly arbitrary conduct of North as Lord Keeper and the political obloquy affecting Jeffreys as Chancellor. It was, however, abandoned in 1693, and we do know why it was abandoned, because Somers in a letter to William III shortly afterwards explains the point: it was thought necessary to keep the legal patronage in a single hand in order to manage the lawyers and, through them, the House of Commons. The Lord Chancellor or Keeper was thus in this respect a branch of the government Whips' office.[76]

(iv) Lords Justices of Appeal. The eventual adoption of a collegiate bench seems not to have been driven by concerns about certainty, but about delays.[77] By the early 1800s the Chancery machinery was clearly creaking under the strain of the enormous increase of business which had begun in the later 18th century and continued through the 19th. In 1810 Parliament added a Vice-Chancellor who could sit at first instance in parallel with the Master of the Rolls and Lord Chancellor, and in 1841 two more Vice-Chancellors were added; but the Vice-Chancellors, like the Master of the Rolls, were subject to unrestricted appeals to the Chancellor, and this appellate jurisdiction thus became a bottleneck reproducing delay in a different form. In 1851 the result was a new court of Lords Justices of Appeal in Chancery, who could sit either with, or separate from, the Chancellor in appeals. From this point on, as Patrick Polden remarks, 'while there was a rapid turnover of Lord Chancellors, Chancery experienced a period of unusual stability among its other judges'.[78]

The overall effect was that the single judge in Chancery was by the mid-19th century finally subject to control by a collegiate court of appeal: the semi-professionalised House of Lords hearing appeals from the Lord Chancellor, while the Lords Justices were available to hear appeals from the Vice-Chancellors and Master of the Rolls. The regime was finally simplified in 1875 with the adoption of the new, unified structure of a Supreme Court of Justice including a common Court of Appeal.

As I noted at the outset, this history discloses a pattern in which there was no pressure to *codify* Equity, but only, rather, a strong tendency to make

[76] W. Sachse, *Lord Somers: a political portrait* (Manchester: Manchester University Press, 1975), 93. The same point is taken for granted in Lord Cowper's 1716 letter printed by D. Lemmings, "Lord Chancellor Cowper and the Whigs, 1714–16", *Parliamentary History* 9 (1990), 163–174.

[77] What follows summarises the discussion in P. Polden, "The Court of Chancery 1820–1875", in *OHLE* XI, part three, ch. 4, 655–660.

[78] Ibid., at 660.

Equity more like the existing Common law. I should add at this final stage that this cannot be explained through an absence of debate about codification *at all*. The question of codification was posed in political debate in the 1640s–50s: though in the 1650s the lawyers managed to head it off in England, codes in an alphabetical form were, in fact, introduced in the New England colonies.[79] The issue was alive again in the 19th century, though the advocates of full codification were then more politically marginal than they had been in the Commonwealth.[80] The codifiers generally advocated the *unification* of Law and Equity; they did not advocate the separate codification of Equity. In the end, of course, they lost. The legal profession and its ideology of 'Common law' conquered both codification advocates *and* Equity.

[79] For England, D. Veall, *The Popular Movement for Law Reform 1640–1660* (Oxford: Clarendon, 1970) at index entries for 'codification'; B. Worden, *The Rump Parliament* (Cambridge: Cambridge University Press, 1974), ch. 6; A.D.T. Cromartie, *Sir Matthew Hale 1609–1676* (Cambridge: Cambridge University Press, 1995), 70–72. For New England, W.E. Nelson, *The Common Law in Colonial America* I (Oxford: Oxford University Press, 1998), 72–73, 94.

[80] W. Cornish, M. Lobban and K. Smith, "Sources of Law", in *OHLE* XI, part one, ch. 3, 55–59.

PART THREE

SUBSTANTIVE ASPECTS

CHAPTER FIVE

EQUITY'S CONNIVANCE IN THE EVASION OF LEGAL FORMALITIES

J. Cartwright

Introduction

The law prescribes a formality for a transaction. The question is to what extent compliance with the formality requirement is really necessary for the transaction to be given effect in law. We might expect the answer to depend largely on the proper interpretation of the legal provision by which the formality requirement was imposed—either a legislative text or, in a legal system where the judiciary is recognised as having such power to act, an authoritative judicial decision or series of decisions. But a further question may follow: whether, over time, the formality should remain fixed, or whether the law should, for example, relax its insistence on compliance with the formality requirement—and if so, by what mechanism such a change should be effected. If a formality was set by the legislator, then clearly we would expect a later emanation of the legislator to have power to change it, whether by relaxing it or by making it stricter. Or a judicially-imposed formality might be changed either by a later court, or by the legislator. And the scope of the new formality requirement would be similarly determined by the proper interpretation of the new provision.

The more difficult situation, however, is where the formality requirement was originally set by an institution in the legal system which apparently has a higher place in the hierarchy of norms than the institution which purports to change it. In English law, this typically involves a formality set by statute, where the courts have sought to allow a party to escape the consequences of non-compliance with the formality. In Roman law, we are in the realm of formalities set by the *ius civile*, where the praetor allows a case to proceed to trial on the basis of a *formula* which fails to give effect to the strict requirement of compliance with the formality. The way in which such changes are effected will generally depend upon the techniques available within the legal system of the institution making the change. In England, the courts may use techniques of interpretation of the statutory text to discover that the legal formality is not, after all, as strict as had been thought; or they may go beyond the statutory text itself to say that there is a principle operating outside the statute which can be applied in order, in effect, to circumvent the formality requirement. This is a technique which was adopted by Equity. In classical Roman law, the praetor, with his control of the system of litigation, had the ability to deny a case, or to allow a case to proceed to trial, on a legal basis which had the effect of circumventing a formality requirement set by the *ius civile*.

Within private law, formality requirements may be set in relation to contracts, or in relation to property transactions. It is in relation to property that the consequences of (non-)compliance with the formalities will be most acute, since the nature of property transactions is that they are liable to affect third parties. Allowing a transaction to have the effect of transferring property rights may therefore affect not only the relationship between the two parties to the transaction who failed to comply with the requirement, but also the rights of successors to the purported transferee, not only as against third parties, but also as against the original *de facto* transferor who may still claim to have the rights *de iure* on the basis that his transaction did not have legal effect. This is the situation which is considered in this chapter: where the Law (statute, or sometimes the common law, in England; the *ius civile* in Rome) sets a formality requirement for the creation or disposition of a property right, but the administration of justice (by the courts of Equity in England;[1] the praetor in Rome[2]) is carried out on such a basis as to give effect to the property right where the formality requirement has not been complied with—in other words Equity is, in effect, conniving in the evasion of legal formalities.

---

[1] The courts of Equity ceased to exist separately from the common law courts on 1 November 1875 upon the fusion of the jurisdictions into a single Supreme Court of Judicature through the Judicature Acts 1873 and 1875. However, the doctrines discussed in this chapter have their origins in decisions of the old, separate courts of Equity, and they continue to be developed (and, to some extent, new doctrines continue to be devised) by the modern courts, still in the name of 'Equity': e.g. the modern developments in the doctrines of constructive trust (*infra*, 116) and proprietary estoppel (*infra*, 117).

[2] The power of the praetor to innovate was curtailed when Julian supposedly finalised the Edict around 130 AD on the instructions of Hadrian. The discussion in this chapter therefore focuses generally on the law as it was developed by the praetor during the classical period of Roman law under the formulary system and until the Edict was finalised, although the law continued to be applied during the later classical period and even under Justinian, except in so far as later developments directly or indirectly changed it—such as the abolition by Justinian of the distinction between *res mancipi* and *res nec mancipi* which had the effect of abolishing the category of 'bonitary ownership', and limiting the scope of the *actio Publiciana* to protection of the bona fide possessor: B. Nicholas, *An Introduction to Roman Law* (Oxford: Oxford University Press, 1962), 106, 128.

The Role of Formalities in Property Transactions

The use of formality as a condition of validity of a property transaction is known generally in legal systems. Modern writers have rationalised the aims of formalities in various ways; a summary was given by the English Law Commission in 1985 discussing the formality of deeds:[3]

> What then are the aims of the formalities for making a deed? We would suggest that there are three main aims:
>
> (a) cautionary: that is, trying to ensure that the maker does not enter into the transaction without realising what he is doing;
> (b) evidential: providing evidence that the maker did enter into a transaction, and evidence of its terms;
> (c) labelling: making it apparent to third parties what kind of a document it is and what its effect is to be.

The advantages of formality can therefore be to ensure that the parties think before they enter into a transaction (*cautionary*); to provide evidence of the fact of the transaction and its terms (*evidential*); and to imprint the transaction with an authority which marks it out as complete, not only for the parties themselves in the event of a dispute, but also for the purposes of third parties who may need to be able to verify it (*labelling*). But there is inevitably a question of balance in the use of formalities, since they cannot sensibly be used for all property transactions: trade would be slowed down to an unreasonable degree. There is a natural instinct, therefore, to identify transactions which should be singled out for special treatment: where the parties need protection against rash decisions; or the law has good reason to require a special form of transfer because the evidence of ownership is so important; or where the asset is in itself so special that a special form of title (and therefore formality for creation or transfer of title) is called for. It is not surprising that *land* is given a special status in most legal systems—it is the most significant economic and functional asset that an individual can own. But other property transactions may also be singled out, and we can see examples in English law and Roman law.

[3] Law Commission Working Paper no. 93, *Transfer of Land: Formalities for Deeds and Escrows* (London: HMSO, 1985), par. 3.2, cross-referring to T.G. Youdan, "Formalities for trusts of land", *CLJ* 306 (1984), at 314–315 and the articles referred to there at fnt. 42 and 44.

In English law,[4] since 1926[5] the conveyance of land and all interests in land has generally required a *deed*[6]—a formal written instrument, executed and delivered by the grantor as his act, in which he expresses an intention to pass an interest to the grantee. In the modern law, the execution of a deed by an individual involves signature and witnesses.[7] However, if the title to the land is registered, the deed is not sufficient to transfer the legal freehold estate in the land, nor many of the legal interests that can exist in or over land. If the disposition is one which is required to be completed by registration, it does not operate at law until the registration requirements have been satisfied.[8] Formalities are also required for the disposition of property (land or other property) by will: a document in writing, signed by the testator or by some other person in his presence and by his direction, where the signature is made or

[4] For discussion of the formalities required for the creation and transfer of estates and interests in land, see E.H. Burn and J. Cartwright, *Cheshire and Burn's Modern Law of Real Property*, 18th ed. (Oxford: Oxford University Press, 2011), ch. 25.

[5] Law of Property Act 1925, S. 51(1) abolished other forms of transfer which had been possible for freehold estates in possession. The common law required a deed of grant for transfer of incorporeal interests, but until 1845 freehold estates in possession could be transferred by livery of seisin—i.e. by delivery of possession. Between 1845 and 1925 freehold estates could be transferred either by deed or by livery of seisin: Real Property Act 1845, S. 2.

[6] Law of Property Act 1925, S. 52(1). There are exceptions for assents by personal representatives, disclaimers by trustees in bankruptcy, surrenders (e.g. of a leasehold interest to the landlord) by operation of law; the grant of many leases not exceeding three years; certain receipts; vesting orders made by the court, and conveyances taking effect by operation of law.

[7] The history of the particular formality of a deed need not concern us here: it was defined by the Common law, but has been amended in modern law by statute, first to introduce (in the case of a deed executed by an individual) the requirement of signature in addition to sealing: Law of Property Act 1925, S. 73; but more recently to redefine the requirements for a deed executed by an individual, as a written instrument which makes clear on its face that it is intended to be a deed by the person making it (or the parties, in the case of a deed *inter partes*), which is signed by the individual in the presence of a witness (or signed at the direction of the individual in the presence of two witnesses) and delivered as a deed: Law of Property (Miscellaneous Provisions) Act 1989, S. 1. Deeds are therefore now no longer sealed by individuals, but the requirement of a witness to the signature has been introduced. There are different requirements for execution of deeds by different forms of corporation, which still use their seal to execute deeds (although companies registered under the Companies Acts can either use their common seal, or execute a deed through the witnessed signatures of company officers: Companies Act 2006, S. 44). It should be noted that English law does not use the *notarisation* of documents in order to authenticate them.

[8] Land Registration Act 2002, S. 27. The dispositions which are required to be completed by registration include a transfer of the estate, the grant of certain leases (notably, all leases for more than seven years), the express grant or reservation of an easement, and the grant of a legal charge (a mortgage).

acknowledged by the testator in the presence of two or more witnesses present at the same time.[9] And the transfer of title to shares (constituting the transferee a member of the company) generally depends upon the registration of a proper instrument of transfer and the entry of the transferee in the register of members of the company.[10]

In Roman law,[11] certain assets were identified as *res mancipi*, and their transfer required either *mancipatio* or *cessio in iure*. *Cessio* required a procedure before a magistrate,[12] and therefore was even more onerous than *mancipatio* which could be done privately[13]—although not in fact very privately, given that it required the presence of the transferor, the transferee, and at least six other citizens, one of whom acted as *libripens* with bronze scales. As Gaius tells us, a particular verbal formula had to be spoken by the transferee, and a symbolic act performed (striking the scales with a piece of bronze).[14] The particular assets for which this procedure was required were Italic estates and houses, slaves, working animals of the kinds that are commonly saddled or yoked (such as oxen, horses, mules and asses), and rustic praedial servitudes (rights of way and of water).[15] The separation of certain assets as *res mancipi* dated back to the XII Tables, and their common link appears to be that they were all fundamental to a basic agricultural community of that early period. And the formality required in *mancipatio*, rather peculiar to the modern reader, was entirely consistent with the needs of the times: pre-coinage[16] and pre-writing.

These examples show a similar concern in the two legal systems: assets of particular economic or social significance are singled out for special treatment, and are subjected to formalities which are not easy to perform without forethought, and which will provide evidence and publicity. Other assets, which are not subjected to the special formality rules, can be transferred with full legal effect much more freely—typically (at least in the case of corporeal assets) by delivery of possession (*traditio*).

---

9 Wills Act 1837, S. 9, as substituted by Administration of Justice Act 1982.

10 Companies Act 2006, S. 770 and S. 112(2).

11 That is, from the early days and throughout the classical period. However, Justinian abolished the distinction between *res mancipi* and *res nec mancipi*, and all corporeal property became capable of transfer by *traditio*: Nicholas, *An Introduction*, 106, 117.

12 Gaius 2,24.

13 Gaius 2,25.

14 Gaius 1,119, using as the example the *mancipatio* of a slave. Gaius refers to *mancipatio* in this context as *imaginaria quaedam venditio* (as it were, an imaginary sale).

15 Gaius 2,14a–2,17.

16 Gaius 1,122.

However, the balance is to be struck not only in relation to the choice of those assets which are to be subjected to the special formality requirements, but also in relation to how strictly the requirements are applied. If a purpose of the formalities is to protect one or other of the parties, should it be possible for the parties to dispense with the requirements—to disclaim the benefit of the formality rules? But where the purpose is to protect not only the parties, but also third parties who need to rely on the validity of a transfer, perhaps a stricter view needs to be taken. As we shall see, both English law and Roman law have had to respond to such questions.

The Evasion of Formality Requirements in Equity in English Law: Equitable Ownership

As between the parties themselves, it may sometimes not be fatal to the transaction under English law that it has not been effected using the required formality. In principle, the Common law would not recognise and give effect to a property transaction which had not been properly entered into, and so, for example, a conveyance of the freehold estate in land or a lease which ought to have been executed as a deed,[17] but which had not been so executed, did not have its intended effect even as between the parties.[18] Even so, it is not attractive for one of the parties to a transaction (typically, the transferor of the property) to raise against the other the lack of formality as an argument that the transaction was ineffective, and the Common law would sometimes find ways of giving effect to it by analysing it as a different transaction whose effect could be recognised. This arose particularly in the context of leases, where a transaction which failed to create an intended legal lease for lack of a deed—for example, a lease for more than three years—might nonetheless create a different lease which did not require the same formality: a *periodic* tenancy, implied from the payment of rent and the fact that the

---

[17] *Supra*, 110.

[18] *Coatsworth v Johnson* (1886) 54 LT 530 (lease signed but not sealed: entry into possession by intended tenant was at landlord's will only; rent had not been paid so there was no implied periodic tenancy (*infra*, 113, fnt. 19), and the agreement for lease would not, in the circumstances, be protected in Equity under the doctrine of *Walsh v Lonsdale* (*infra*, 118–119)). For cases where a document, not in fact properly executed as a deed, was given effect as such through the (common law) doctrine of estoppel, see *Stromdale & Ball Ltd v Burden* [1952] Ch. 223, at 230; *TCB Ltd v Gray* [1986] Ch. 621, at 634; *Shah v Shah* [2002] QB 35.

landlord had let the tenant into possession.[19] This would mean that the tenant under the periodic tenancy would hold under a lease recognised by the Common law, and would have as against the landlord the rights and duties of a tenant.[20] Even if there was no periodic tenancy, then the agreement to create a lease might at least take effect between the parties as a contract to grant the lease. Similarly, the agreement to create or convey any other interest in the land, which failed to be completed because of the lack of a deed, might at least constitute a contract and be enforceable as such. At Common law this would give the intended transferee only a personal claim to damages for breach of the contract to create or convey the interest, since the common law did not enforce contracts by an order for performance. But it would at least give the protection of a financial remedy—although it should also be noted that the failed transaction could take effect as a contract only if the formality requirements for a *contract* for the creation or conveyance of an interest in land had been complied with.[21]

The Courts of Equity, however, developed a range of doctrines under which the failure to comply with the formalities set by statute or the Common law could be, in effect, circumvented.

There are few formalities in modern English law relating to the formation of contracts,[22] but there have long been statutory requirements of writing in relation to *land* contracts. Before 27 September 1989, a contract for the sale or other disposition of land or an interest in land could be oral or written, but it was generally unenforceable by either party in the absence of a written memorandum, signed by the party being sued upon the contract (or by his agent).[23] The lack of a written memorandum

---

[19] The period of the periodic tenancy is implied from the period by reference to which the rent is paid: for example, entry into possession on payment of a yearly rent creates a tenancy from year to year, which constitutes a valid lease since a lease for a period not exceeding three years need not be by deed nor even in writing: Law of Property Act 1925, S. 52(2)(d) and S. 54(2) (replacing earlier provisions to similar effect in the Statute of Frauds 1677 and the Real Property Act 1845). The lease will be tacitly renewed and may therefore continue for more than three years but each period is only a single year and therefore is not required to be granted by deed.

[20] The periodic tenancy contains such terms of the intended lease as are consistent with a periodic tenancy: *Martin v Smith* (1874) LR 9 Exch. 50.

[21] *Infra*, fnt. 23.

[22] J. Beatson, A. Burrows and J. Cartwright, *Anson's Law of Contract*, 29th ed. (Oxford: Oxford University Press, 2010), ch. 3. The Statute of Frauds 1677 imposed the formality of writing for a range of very significant contracts, but of these only two now remain: land contracts (below) and contracts of guarantee.

[23] Law of Property Act 1925, S. 40, replacing a similar provision in Statute of Frauds 1677, S. 4.

was, however, circumvented in Equity if the party seeking to enforce the contract had done a sufficient act of 'part performance'. The underlying rationale was stated by Lord Reid:[24]

> If one party to an agreement stands by and lets the other party incur expense or prejudice his position on the faith of the agreement being valid he will not then be allowed to turn round and assert that the agreement is unenforceable. Using fraud in its older and less precise sense, that would be fraudulent on his part and it has become proverbial that courts of equity will not permit the statute to be made an instrument of fraud.

This was not seen by the courts as a direct attack on the statute which set the requirement of a written memorandum, but as a separate doctrine, operating outside the statute (quite literally, circumventing it),[25] although it was in due course also acknowledged by the legislature.[26]

Since 27 September 1989, a contract for the sale or other disposition of an interest in land must now generally be *in writing*: that is, writing is now a condition of existence of the contract not merely of its enforceability.[27] But the Law Commission which proposed this reform expected that equitable doctrines would still be able to operate so as to allow a land contract to be given effect, even if the requirement of writing was not complied with.[28]

---

[24] *Steadman v Steadman* [1976] AC 536, at 540.

[25] Ibid. ('There is nothing about part performance in the Statute of Frauds. It is an invention of the Court of Chancery and in deciding any case not clearly covered by authority I think that the equitable nature of the remedy must be kept in mind').

[26] The doctrine of part performance was expressly preserved by the Law of Property Act, S. 40(2) when the requirement of a written memorandum, originally contained in the Statute of Frauds 1677, was re-enacted in S. 40(1) of the 1925 Act. On part performance more generally, see E.H. Burn, *Cheshire & Burn's Modern Law of Real Property*, 14th ed. (London: Butterworths, 1988), 114–119; J. Williams, *The Statute of Frauds Section Four* (Cambridge: Cambridge University Press, 1932), 230–261.

[27] Law of Property (Miscellaneous Provisions) Act 1989, S. 2(1).

[28] Law Commission Report no. 164, *Transfer of Land: Formalities for Contracts for Sale etc of Land* (London: HMSO, 1987), par. 17–20. The 1989 Act contains in S. 2(5) an express exception for resulting, implied or constructive trusts (see further *infra*, 117, fnt. 35), and the courts have also generally accepted that the doctrine of proprietary estoppel (*infra*, 117–118) can be invoked to give, in effect, some force to an agreement relating to land which does not comply with the formalities and so does not constitute a contract at law: *Yaxley v Gotts* [2000] Ch. 162, 174, 191, doubted (obiter) by Lord Scott in *Cobbe v Yeoman's Row Management Ltd* [2008] UKHL 55; [2008] 1 WLR 1752, [29], but this has in turn been qualified, doubted or rejected: *Thorner v Major* [2009] UKHL 18; [2009] 1 WLR 776, [92], [96]; *Brightlingsea Haven Ltd v Morris* [2008] EWHC 1928 (QB); [2009] 2 P & CR 11; *Whittaker v Kinnear* [2011] EWHC 1479 (QB); [2011] 2 P & CR DG 20, [28–30].

In relation to the formality requirements set for the law of property, Equity developed other doctrines which had the effect of allowing a right to be asserted by the party in whose favour it was intended to be created, but where the formality had not been complied with.[29] For example, where a named beneficiary under a will has agreed with the testator to hold property for the benefit of a third party who is not named in the will, therefore providing for a disposition of property on death which does not comply with the Wills Act 1837,[30] the courts have held that the named beneficiary takes under the will, but then immediately holds on trust for the intended third-party beneficiary. Yet this trust operates outside the will and therefore outside the statute:[31]

> A Court of conscience finds a man in the position of an absolute legal owner of a sum of money, which has been bequeathed to him under a valid will, and it declares that, on proof of certain facts relating to the motives and actions of the testator, it will not allow the legal owner to exercise his legal right to do what he will with his own. This seems to be a perfectly normal exercise of general equitable jurisdiction. [...] The testator intends his absolute gift to be employed as he and not as the donee desires; he tells the proposed donee of this intention and, either by express promise or by the tacit promise, which is signified by acquiescence, the proposed donee encourages him to bequeath the money in the faith that his intentions will be carried out. The special circumstance, that the gift is by bequest only makes this rule a special case of the exercise of a general jurisdiction, but in its application to a bequest the doctrine must in principle rest on the assumption that the will has first operated according to its terms. It is because there is no one to whom the law can give relief in the premises, that relief, if any, must be sought in equity. So far, and in the bare case of a legacy absolute on the face of it, I do not see how the statute-law relating to the form of a valid will is concerned at all, and the expressions, in which the doctrine has

[29] See further J. McGhee *et al.*, *Snell's Equity*, 32nd ed. (London: Sweet & Maxwell, 2010), ch. 24 (listing a wide range of circumstances, including those discussed in this chapter, in which trusts arise to enforce an informally expressed intention); J.E. Martin, *Hanbury and Martin, Modern Equity*, 19th ed. (London: Sweet & Maxwell, 2012), ch. 12. Some of the points made in this chapter are also covered in J. Cartwright, "Formality and Informality in Property and Contract", in *Rationalizing Property, Equity and Trusts: Essays in Honour of Edward Burn*, ed. J. Getzler (London: LexisNexis UK, 2003), ch. 3.

[30] *Supra*, 111, fnt. 9.

[31] *Blackwell v Blackwell* [1929] AC 318, at 334–335; this is known as a 'secret trust'—'fully secret' where there is nothing on the face of the will to indicate that there is an intended (secret) beneficiary; 'half secret' where the will discloses that there is to be a third-party beneficiary but without identifying him. For discussion of the idea that the trust operates outside ('dehors') the statute, and the difficulties of determining the theoretical basis of secret trusts, see Martin, *Hanbury and Martin*, 5–013 to 5–016; McGhee *et al.*, *Snell's Equity*, 24–030.

> been habitually described, seem to bear this out. For the prevention of fraud equity fastens on the conscience of the legatee a trust [...].

Similarly, there are cases where legal title to land has been transferred to a person, but on the (informal) basis that a third party will have rights to the land, and the courts decide that the transferee takes the property at Common law, but holds it in Equity on trust for the third party as long as his (the transferee's) conscience would be affected by denying the third party's right to an interest in the land.[32] And where the legal title to land is vested in one person, but on the basis that it would be shared beneficially by that person and another (such as a cohabitee) or is vested jointly at Common law in cohabitees but on the basis that the parties' beneficial shares would not be equal, the courts may decide that the legal owner holds the property on trusts which reflect the parties' common intention (even though there is no document to constitute written evidence of the declaration of a trust of land)[33] as long as the legal owner's conscience is affected. This is shown generally by the fact that the other party has acted to his or her detriment in reliance on the agreement. The valuation of the interest under the trust may be based on the parties' evidenced common intention, but in the absence of such evidence may be based on what the court determines is fair, having regard to the parties' dealings relating to the property.[34] Such cases—typically held to be 'constructive' trusts—may appear to have the effect of avoiding the formality requirements for the creation of property rights in favour of the intended beneficiaries, but certain statutes which set formalities have expressly allowed such

[32] E.g. *Binions v Evans* [1972] Ch. 359 (the claimants, on purchasing a cottage, agreed to allow the defendant, the aged widow of the vendor's former employee, to continue to live in the cottage for the remainder of her life, and in consequence they paid a reduced price for it. The case could now be solved by giving the defendant a (personal) right as a third party under the contract of sale, under the Contracts (Rights of Third Parties) Act 1999); *Lyus v Prowsa Developments Ltd* [1982] 1 WLR 1044 (a purchaser of registered land, who had bought it subject to the plaintiffs' earlier contract to purchase it, was held bound to give effect to the earlier contract even though the plaintiffs had not complied with the normal requirements of the Land Registration Act 1925 to protect their rights by registration against the title to the land: it would be 'fraud' for the purchaser to renege on his positive stipulation in favour of the plaintiffs by relying on the Land Registration Act: the statute 'cannot be used as an instrument of fraud' (at 1054–1055)).

[33] Law of Property Act 1925, S. 53(1)(b).

[34] E.g. *Lloyd's Bank plc v Rosset* [1991] 1 AC 107, at 132 (single legal owner, but no trust found); *Abbott v Abbott* [2007] UKPC 53; [2008] 1 FLR 1451 (single legal owner); *Stack v Dowden* [2007] UKHL 17; [2007] 2 AC 432 (joint owners of legal title); *Jones v Kernott* [2011] UKSC 53; [2012] 1 AC 776 (joint owners).

transactions by excluding from the formality requirements the creation or operation of resulting, implied or constructive trusts.[35]

Two other doctrines deserve particular mention: doctrines developed by the courts of Equity to protect the intended direct recipient of a property transaction against the grantor where the required formality for the creation or transfer of the property rights has not been effected. The first is proprietary estoppel; the other is often known as the doctrine of *Walsh v Lonsdale.*

Under the doctrine of proprietary estoppel an 'equity' arises in favour of a claimant where the defendant has made a representation or promise to him that he has, or shall have, an interest in or a right over the defendant's land, or where the defendant has acquiesced in the claimant's mistaken belief that he has or shall have such an interest or right, provided that (in either case) the claimant has reasonably acted in reliance on the belief that he has or shall have the interest or right.[36] The courts of Equity rested this doctrine on the basis that the defendant could not *in conscience* deny the claim,[37] and the 'equity by estoppel' entitles the claimant to seek a remedy to satisfy it[38]—not necessarily an award of the specific interest or right to which the claimant had been induced to believe that he was entitled, but the courts have sometimes awarded the intended property right as the remedy.[39] Although the general principle is that Equity will not perfect an imperfect *gift*, on the basis that a bare donee does not in principle have a sufficient interest to justify the intervention of Equity,[40]

[35] Law of Property Act 1925, S. 53(2) (such trusts can be an exception to the requirements of writing under S. 53(1) for the creation or disposition of an interest in land or the disposition of an equitable interest or trust, and the requirement of written evidence for a declaration of trust in relation to land); Law of Property (Miscellaneous Provisions) Act 1989, S. 2(5) (exception to the requirement of writing under S. 2(1) for a contract for the sale or other disposition of an interest in land).

[36] Burn and Cartwright, *Cheshire and Burn's*, 906–922, 1014–1017.

[37] *Taylors Fashions Ltd v Liverpool Victoria Trustees Co Ltd* [1982] QB 133, at 151 although, as in other developed equitable doctrines based on the 'conscience' of the defendant, its application is based on principle: *Cobbe v Yeoman's Row Management Ltd* [2008] UKHL 55; [2008] 1 WLR 1752, [46].

[38] *Crabb v Arun District Council* [1976] Ch. 179, at 193 ('the relief appropriate to satisfy' the equity), and 198 ('the minimum equity to do justice to the plaintiff').

[39] E.g. *Pascoe v Turner* [1979] 1 WLR 431 (order to execute conveyance of freehold of property); *Crabb v Arun District Council* (*supra*, fnt. 38) (order to grant an easement). If the claimant's expectations are uncertain, or extravagant, or out of all proportion to the detriment he has suffered, the court may order a lesser (more proportionate) response: *Jennings v Rice* [2002] EWCA Civ 159; [2003] 1 P & CR 8, [50].

[40] *Milroy v Lord* (1862) 4 De G.F. & J. 264, at 274; Martin, *Hanbury and Martin*, ch. 4.

nevertheless where the courts order the creation of the intended right as the remedy for proprietary estoppel, they may sometimes in effect order the perfection of an imperfect gift. However, this is on the basis that the defendant's conscience is affected by the claimant's reliance: the equity arises not simply from the defendant's representation, or promise, or acquiescence, but from that coupled with the claimant's action in (reasonable) reliance.[41]

The doctrine of *Walsh v Lonsdale* is based on contract, and in particular on the view that Equity takes of a contract of which specific performance would be granted if it were sought. The case of *Walsh v Lonsdale*[42] itself involved a contract to create a seven-year lease, where the deed required to create the legal lease had not been executed.[43] It was held that[44]

> The tenant holds under an agreement for a lease. He holds, therefore, under the same terms in equity as if a lease had been granted, it being a case in which both parties admit that relief is capable of being given by specific performance.

Although commonly known in the modern law after the name of this case, which involved a contract to create a lease, the doctrine is general, and has been applied similarly in relation to contracts to create other legal estates or interests. Therefore, a contract to transfer the legal fee simple (the freehold title) already creates an equivalent equitable title;[45] a contract to create a legal easement creates an equitable easement;[46] and a contract to create a legal mortgage creates an equitable mortgage.[47] But in all cases the doctrine depends upon the existence of a contract to create

41 *Pascoe v Turner* (*supra*, 117, fnt. 39), 435–436. For other exceptions to the general reluctance to perfect an imperfect gift, see *Re Rose* [1952] Ch. 499 (intended transfer of shares by way of gift, transfer not yet registered to give transferee title to the shares (*supra*, 111); but donor had done all in his power to effect the transfer by executing the document of transfer and delivering it to donees, so equitable title had already passed); *Mascall v Mascall* (1985) 50 P & CR 119 (transferor of registered land had executed deed of transfer and delivered it and land certificate to the intended transferee: transferee had equitable title, although transfer not registered so legal title had not yet passed; see *supra*, 110, fnt. 8 for the current requirements under Land Registration Act 2002).

42 (1882) 21 Ch. D. 9.

43 The tenant had taken possession, and had paid rent calculated on a yearly basis, so at Common law he held under an implied yearly tenancy: *supra*, 113, fnt. 19. But the remedy sought by the landlord (distress for failure to pay the agreed rent in advance) would be available only if the agreed lease had been entered into.

44 *Supra*, fnt. 42, at 14–15.

45 *Lysaght v Edwards* (1876) 2 Ch. D. 499.

46 *McManus v Cooke* (1887) 35 Ch. D. 681.

47 *Tebb v Hodge* (1869) LR 5 CP 73.

the legal estate or interest,[48] and there being no obstacle to the court making an order of specific performance of the contract.[49] The underlying principle is that Equity gives effect to the defendant's promise to create or transfer a legal estate as if he had already done it: Equity regards as done that which ought to be done.[50]

The various doctrines of Equity discussed above can be relied upon by the intended beneficiary of a contract or property transaction to give him a remedy against the party who purported to create or transfer a right in his favour but who has not fulfilled the relevant formality requirements to give effect to the transaction at Common law. As such, this involves giving effect, to greater or lesser extent, to rights for which statute or the Common law prescribes formality but in the absence of that formality. But as long as the claimant and the defendant are the parties to the original transaction which has failed at Common law, it is not perhaps such a significant undermining of the formality requirements. As we have seen, the approach of Equity is typically to say that the grantor of the right cannot rely on his own failure to comply with the formality requirement as against the grantee of the right whom he has induced to accept the (informal) transaction, where it would be against his conscience to do so. And so, for example, the (reasonable) reliance by the other party gives rise to the equity in his favour: the part performance of a contract which used to require a written memorandum for its enforceability;[51] or the creation of a constructive trust,[52] or an equity arising under the doctrine of proprietary estoppel.[53]

Equitable intervention is more significant, however, if the transaction, had it been effected in accordance with the required formalities, would have changed the property rights of the parties, and the intervention of Equity allows those property rights to be similarly changed—that is, if the effect of these equitable doctrines is to allow third parties to be affected by

---

48 *Supra*, 113–114.

49 *Coatsworth v Johnson* (*supra*, 112, fnt. 18) (tenant under contract for lease who had already broken covenants of the intended lease would not obtain specific performance and so had no lease in Equity).

50 For this maxim of Equity, see Martin, *Hanbury and Martin*, 1–032; McGhee *et al.*, *Snell's Equity*, 5–030.

51 *Steadman v Steadman* [1976] AC 536, at 540, quoted *supra*, 114.

52 *Supra*, 116.

53 *Supra*, 117.

transactions which do not satisfy the formalities required by the Common law for valid property transfers. This raises the question of the nature, or strength, of equitable property rights. Is equitable title to land as good as the legal title? Is an equity under proprietary estoppel where the court may be persuaded to order the grant of an easement as the remedy, as good as a legal easement? Is an interest in a house, or to a company's shares, under a constructive trust as good as legal title?

The short answer is 'No'. The general approach taken by Equity was to treat an equitable interest as having proprietary characteristics—in particular, being capable of binding third parties who come to the property in which the equitable interest subsists—whilst still admitting that equitable title is relatively less secure than legal title.[54] Legal title operates in the nature of a right *in rem*, binding all who come to the property. An equitable interest in property will also bind third parties, but *not* those who later acquire a *legal* interest in the property *for value, without notice* (actual or constructive) of the prior equitable interest. The original reasoning for this was that the courts of Equity act upon the defendant's conscience; and if a later purchaser acquires a (superior) legal interest in the property, without notice of the prior equitable interest, his conscience is clear and his legal title should prevail. However, if he acquires only an equitable (not legal) interest in the land, or if he acquires a legal interest as a donee (not as a purchaser for value), or if he acquires a legal interest for value but with notice of the prior equitable interest, he does not deserve to prevail over the prior equitable interest.[55] This general approach to the relative strength of equitable title to property has been developed in relation to interests in land by the introduction of systems of registration of interests. We need not consider the details here,[56] beyond noting that two systems were introduced: under the first, the title to land remains unregistered, but certain interests in or over the land can be entered in a

---

[54] Maitland argued that 'equitable estates and interests are not *jura in rem* [...] they have come to look very like *jura in rem*; but just for this very reason it is the more necessary for us to observe that they are essentially *jura in personam*, not rights against the world at large, but rights against certain persons': A.H. Chaytor and W.J. Whittaker, *Maitland's Equity* (Cambridge: Cambridge University Press, 1929), 112. Their effect is, however, certainly proprietary; and see criticism of Maitland in McGhee *et al.*, *Snell's Equity*, 5–035.

[55] For a general discussion of the development of the doctrine of the bona fide purchaser, see Burn and Cartwright, *Cheshire and Burn's*, 78–91; Chaytor and Whittaker, *Maitland's Equity*, 112–121; McGhee *et al.*, *Snell's Equity*, 2–005.

[56] See Burn and Cartwright, *Cheshire and Burn's*, 121–146, especially 143–146 for a comparison of the two systems in the modern law; and ch. 27 for a detailed account of conveyancing in unregistered land, and ch. 28 for registered land.

publicly searchable register, and whether a purchaser of the legal title to the land is bound by such an interest depends upon whether the interest has been so registered. Under the second system, the title to the estate in the land itself is registered, and interests in or over the land are then noted on the registration of the title to the land. In both systems there are circumstances where equitable interests may still bind a purchaser of the legal title even if not entered in the register.[57] But the general principle is that registration has now taken the place of the equitable doctrine of notice, although it remains the case that an equitable interest is generally less strong, or more precarious, than a legal estate or interest.

The Evasion of Formality Requirements of the Ius Civile by the Praetor: Bonitary Ownership

In Roman law, the question arose of the effect in law of a mere informal *traditio* where the *ius civile* required the formality of *cessio in iure* or *mancipatio*.[58] This arose no doubt naturally because the strict formality, particularly its archaic features,[59] could be an obstacle to simple everyday transactions such as the delivery of a horse following the (informal)[60] contract of sale. The conservatism of the *ius civile* retained the list of *res mancipi* from an earlier age, and only modernised the formality of *mancipatio* to the extent of making the role of the *libripens* and the bronze symbolic,[61] rather than replacing it with a more modern formality. And if publicity was an objective of the formality, this might be achieved through

[57] In unregistered land, some interests are not in the statutory list of registrable interests, and their enforceability against a purchaser of the legal estate for value still depends on the application of the doctrine of notice, rather than registration; in registered land, an equitable interest must be entered in the register of title of the burdened land if it is to bind a purchaser for value, unless (broadly) it is an interest, not actually known about by the purchaser, which belongs to a person in discoverable actual occupation of the burdened land (an 'overriding interest' under Land Registration Act 2002, sch. 3, par. 2).

[58] For another context in which the praetor intervened to relax formalities, see the so-called 'praetorian will', where a will sealed by a number of witnesses was respected by the praetor in granting the named beneficiary *bonorum possessio*, even if there was no transaction satisfying the requirements of a mancipatory will as required by the *ius civile* to institute an heir: Nicholas, *An Introduction*, 254–255; H.F. Jolowicz and B. Nicholas, *Historical Introduction to the Study of Roman Law*, 3rd ed. (Cambridge: Cambridge University Press, 1972), 248–249.

[59] *Supra*, 111.

[60] Mere consent, with no formality of words or writing: Gaius 3,136.

[61] *Supra*, 111; Nicholas, *An Introduction*, 117.

the presence of eight citizens[62] in a small agricultural society of the 5th century BC, but would hardly do in the late Republic, or the Empire of the classical period. It is not therefore surprising that individuals would resort to the simple *traditio* where *mancipatio* was formally necessary. Whether parties would fail to use the required formality because they rejected the troublesome strictness of *mancipatio*, or because they were ignorant of the law (particularly when it became common practice just to use *traditio* where *mancipatio* ought strictly to have been used) is a matter of speculation and, no doubt, varied from case to case. However, there are risks associated with failing to comply with formalities required by law: and in this context, the transferee who knowingly accepts the transfer of a *res mancipi* by *traditio* runs the risks associated with having not ownership but only possession. How significant a risk this is, however—and whether the recipient of a transfer of a *res mancipi* would be willing to run it—depends upon the protection afforded by the law to possession. The praetor's response, probably in the late Republic,[63] was to acquiesce in the fact that parties who should have used *mancipatio* were using *traditio*. Even so, there are two separate dimensions to consider.

First, as between the parties themselves—and using the example where A has transferred a horse by *traditio* to B. Strictly speaking, ownership (*dominium*)[64] of the horse remains with A in the eyes of the *ius civile*. But as long as the transaction was effected freely, so that there is no challenge by A on the basis of B's fraud or duress, it may seem harsh on B to allow A to stand on his strict legal rights and claim back the horse. This is covered by the praetor developing the *exceptio rei venditae et traditae* to provide B with a defence if A should seek to vindicate the horse. B must show the *traditio* by A, and its *causa* (here, sale).[65] But if that is established, A's *vindicatio* will fail. Although under the *ius civile* B only has possession, that is what counts here. The praetor determines the legal basis on which any case may proceed to trial, and if the praetor protects B's possession over

---

62 The two parties, plus at least six others including the *libripens: supra*, 111.

63 Nicholas, *An Introduction*, 125; Jolowicz and Nicholas, *Historical Introduction*, 265.

64 *Dominium* is here used in the sense of ownership as recognised by the *ius civile*. For the argument that the words *dominus* and *dominium* came to be used at the latest by the time of Paul and Ulpian to refer to the beneficial ownership of the bonitary owner, no less than the full owner, see H. Ankum and E. Pool, "*Rem in bonis meis esse* and *rem in bonis meam esse*: Traces of the Development of Roman Double Ownership" in *New Perspectives in the Roman Law of Property: Essays for Barry Nicholas*, ed. P. Birks (Oxford: Clarendon, 1989), 41.

65 Extended also to gifts, in the use of the *exceptio rei donatae et traditae*, and to other transactions such as exchanges through the use of the *exceptio doli*: D. 44,4,4,31.

A's *dominium*, the technical *dominus* has no power to assert his *dominium* and so as between the parties B is free to act as if he were the owner.

Secondly, as between the parties and third parties. To continue the example, B is in possession of the horse. Does it matter to third parties that he is not technically the *dominus*? Other issues may arise—for example, if the horse causes damage, who should be the one to pay for it?[66] But, as regards claims to the horse itself, a third party has no right to vindicate the horse against B, since he has no title. The real question is whether B can vindicate[67] the horse against a third party who has come by it (whether in good or bad faith), or even against A, the original transferor who still has *dominium* under the *ius civile* and who may have in fact regained possession of it. Here the praetor gives the so-called *actio Publiciana*[68]—B is allowed the *vindicatio*, even though he is not *dominus*, as long as he has possession which (but for the time period not yet having elapsed) is sufficient to establish title on the basis of *usucapio*. His possession does not equal *dominium*; but as long as he is on the way to securing *dominium* through the normal processes of the civil law, he is protected during that period by being allowed to insert into the formula of his *vindicatio* the fiction that the time period has already elapsed. The *actio Publiciana* is a neat trick. It does not involve the creation of a new form of ownership—although we commonly know it as 'bonitary ownership', and Gaius even once called it *dominium in bonis* by contrast with *dominium ex iure Quiritium* (ownership under the *ius civile*).[69] It acknowledges that B may not be *dominus*, but has possession, and that if he can establish all the elements of *usucapio* except for the passage of the time period of uninterrupted possession (one year for movables, two years for immovables), he may have his *vindicatio* on the fiction that that time has

---

[66] Liability for damage (*pauperies*) caused by an animal which was not of a wild species, but had unusual individual wild characteristics, fell on the *dominus* at the time of the action (the action was noxal): D. 9,1,1,7; D. 9,1,1,12; and D. 9,1,1,17, although fault-based liability for failure to control an animal would fall upon the person in fact in control of it: D. 9,1,4–6, and liability under the aediles' edict for damage caused by an animal fell on the person keeping the animal in a place where others pass by: D. 21,1,42.

[67] There may be other possible claims by which B may assert a positive right to the horse: possessory interdicts (also developed by the praetor to protect the possessor: Nicholas, *An Introduction*, 108–109; Jolowicz and Nicholas, *Historical Introduction*, 259–263); and claims in delict for theft of the horse (*infra*, 124, fnt. 73).

[68] D. 6,2 *rubr.*

[69] Gaius alone in the classical period refers to it as double ownership (*duplex dominium: in bonis* and *ex iure Quiritium*): Gaius 1,54; 2,40 ('divisible' *dominium*). The term 'bonitary owner', *despotès bonitários*, was coined by the later Greek writers: Theophilus, *Paraphrasis* 1,5,4; Jolowicz and Nicholas, *Historical Introduction*, 265. See also *supra*, 122, fnt. 64.

already passed. Thus, again, as long as the thing was delivered to him on a lawful cause, such as sale or gift, he is protected. He is not the *dominus ex iure Quiritium*, but his position is as if he had become *dominus*.[70] If it is A, the *dominus ex iure Quiritium* against whom the claim is brought, even if A tries to defeat the *vindicatio* by asserting his ownership under the *ius civile* (by the *exceptio iusti dominii*), B can in turn assert again the fact that A sold (or gifted) the horse to him and on that *causa* delivered it by *traditio* (*replicatio rei venditae/donatae et traditae*).

There are then only two gaps to fill. The first is where B, the 'bonitary owner' who technically has not ownership but (protected) possession, passes the horse on to C. What does C acquire? If the transfer is by *mancipatio*, it cannot transfer *dominium* since B had none. But if this later transfer is also by *traditio*, then C is in the same position vis-a-vis B as was B vis-a-vis A, and similarly protected. C is (let us assume) a *bona fide possessor* and as such is himself protected during the period of usucapion against all except the *dominus*—but here the *dominus*, A, is one who has himself voluntarily parted with the property by *traditio*, and on that account it appears that the *exceptio rei venditae et traditae* will lie by C against A, to complete his protection.[71] The second gap is where A, the *dominus*, having already sold and transferred possession of the horse to B, then transfers *dominium* to D before B has himself acquired *dominium* by *usucapio*. Whether he is A's universal successor or merely the successor in relation to this particular horse, in the eyes of the *ius civile* D is *dominus*, but any claim by which he seeks to assert his rights against B (or B's successors) will also be met by the *exceptio rei venditae et traditae*.[72]

In almost every respect,[73] then, the bonitary owner acquired in practice the benefits of ownership.

---

[70] Gaius 4,36. The other requirements of *usucapio* are that the acquisition was in good faith and the thing has not been stolen or taken by force: Gaius 2,45.

[71] D. 21,3,3 pr.

[72] D. 21,3,3,1.

[73] See F. de Zulueta, *The Institutes of Gaius, Part II* (Oxford: Clarendon, 1952), 67–8: a slave handed by *traditio* by A to B was in B's *potestas*, not A's (Gaius 1,54), and acquired for B. However, he could be made a *civis Romanus libertus* only by A, not by B. For a detailed textual analysis concluding that 'from early classical times legal practice put bonitary ownership almost completely on a par with full (Quiritary plus bonitary) ownership', see Ankum and Pool, "Rem in bonis meis", 33. For a discussion of the protection by the praetor of a creditor who received a pledge from a debtor who was not *dominus* but only bonitary owner, see Ankum and Pool, "Rem in bonis meis", 26–27. References in D. 9,2,11,8 and D. 9,2,17 to the bona fide possessor having an action for damage to property may originally have referred to the bonitary owner: F.H. Lawson, *Negligence in the Civil Law* (Oxford: Clarendon, 1950), 65–66; J. Thomson, "Who could sue on the lex Aquilia?", *LQR* 91

Comparisons

There are certain similarities between the approaches of Roman law and English law in the areas discussed in this chapter. Each system sets up the requirement of a particular formality for the validity of the transfer of certain assets to be recognised in law. Each system has its own reasons for identifying the assets which are subject to the special formality rules, based on policies designed to protect one or other party, or to provide evidence of the transaction or clarity for third parties.[74] But cases emerge in which parties do not in fact respect the formality requirement, and the law has to determine how strictly to apply the rules: whether to deny the validity of the transfer or, in effect, to connive in the evasion of the legal formalities. The failure to comply may be inadvertent (for example, the parties, and in particular the transferee, may not know the law), or it may be deliberate (for example, the transferor may just find it too troublesome to comply, or he may even fail to do so knowing that he will retain rights in the eyes of the law rather than transfer them).

It is not perhaps surprising that the courts of Equity in England, or the praetor in Rome, should have felt uncomfortable in simply applying the strict formality rules, without in some circumstances finding solutions to protect a party to a transaction who would fail to have title because of the failure to comply with the rule. The English courts did not simply reject the formality requirements and give effect to informal transactions as if they were formal: the court of Equity operated on the basis of the parties' *conscience*. And so the transferor was made to give effect to the transaction, even though it had not complied strictly with the requirements set by the Common law or by statute, where he could not in conscience refuse it. The language sometimes shifts to that of *estoppel*: it is the fact that I have led you to believe that you will have the benefit of a contract, or of an interest in property, on which you have relied, that allows you to seek relief from the court, to estop me from relying on the absence of formality to deny giving effect to the transaction.[75] A civil lawyer might think more in terms of a principle based on the prohibition of acting

(1975), 207, at 212–213. The bonitary owner would also have an action for theft of the property based on his interest in its safety: Gaius 3,203; P.F. Girard, *Manuel Elémentaire de Droit Romain*, 8th ed. (Paris: Rousseau, 1929), 379 (the texts refer to the *bona fide possessor* having the action: e.g. Gaius 3,200; but do not discuss the bonitary owner).

[74] *Supra*, 112–124.

[75] *Supra*, 114 (part performance of a contract); 117–118 (proprietary estoppel). See also the doctrine of secret trusts (*supra*, 115, fnt. 31) and constructive trusts (*supra*, 116, fnt. 32)

against one's own previous conduct: *venire contra factum proprium*. Such principles have a common underlying motive for the court to intervene, to stop a party blowing hot and cold,[76] and it does not stretch the imagination to see the same underlying motive for some of the praetor's intervention, perhaps most obviously in developing the *exceptio rei venditae et traditae*.[77]

However, the way in which the courts of Equity and the praetor intervened was fundamentally different. In the particular context discussed in this chapter, the courts of Equity developed what we commonly refer to as 'equitable property rights', 'equitable interests' or 'equitable title', alongside the property rights recognised by the Common law, and the courts of Equity provided remedies to protect this equitable title. But we have seen that these equitable rights are not as secure as legal title. They have proprietary effect, in that they can bind a third party who comes to the property. But they do not do so in the same absolute fashion as the civil lawyer expects a third party to be bound by a right *in rem* attaching to the property. As the courts of Equity devised the general principle, they do not bind a third party who should not *in conscience* be bound by them. The purchaser for value of legal title to the property, without notice of the equitable interest, takes free of it.[78] Even in our modern system of land law, under which the title to land, and to interests in or over land, is generally based on the registration of title and the entry of property interests in the register of title, the same essential distinction between the (superior) legal title and (potentially less secure) equitable interests is maintained.[79]

By contrast, the property rights which the praetor developed, through his provision of remedies to protect what we now call 'bonitary ownership', were altogether more absolute. The bonitary owner was much more fully treated as equal to *dominus ex iure Quiritium*.[80] Not only as against the party who had transferred the property to him without respecting

---

where the defendant who acquires property of which he has led a third party to believe he will respect the claimant's interest is made to do so if his conscience so requires.

76 See B. Fauvarque-Cosson, ed., *La Confiance Légitime et l'Estoppel* (Paris: Société de Législation Comparée, 2007), 11.

77 *Supra*, 122.

78 *Supra*, 120.

79 *Supra*, 120–121: registration is the modern substitute for notice.

80 *Supra*, 124, fnt. 73. See also De Zulueta, *The Institutes*, 66 (the civil law owner 'was in no sense a trustee for' the bonitary owner).

the formality required by the *ius civile*, but also against third parties, he could behave as an owner and receive the protection of both claims and defences which would give him the same rights to vindicate the property and resist claims to the property as if the formality requirements had been complied with. And more than this: his protected status under the *actio Publiciana* was only, in principle, temporary since he was on the way to becoming *dominus ex iure Quiritium* by the operation of *usucapio*.[81] The praetor in effect gave the party who was on the way to acquiring ownership the same protection during the period of *usucapio* as if he had already completed the time.[82]

The reason for the difference, however, is not difficult to find.[83] The courts of Equity, in devising the remedies before the fusion of the jurisdictions of Common law and Equity, were acting as a supplementary jurisdiction. But the fusion of the jurisdictions in the Judicature Acts 1873 and 1875[84] did not change the fundamental balance between the Common law and Equity. The continuing development of the doctrines of Equity since then has maintained the dual nature of property rights, under which legal estates and interests in property maintain superiority over equitable interests. Although the courts of Equity recognised rights which, in substance, 'mirror' the equivalent Common law rights, they remain in the mirror, liable to be wiped out by a superior legal title. The praetor however, was not charged with a secondary or merely supplementary jurisdiction. He had the sole control over the process of litigation in the classical period: he set the remedies, and if he designed a remedy which contradicted the *ius civile*, then the praetorian law applied. At first sight the roles of Equity and the praetor might seem similar, designed 'to support, supplement and correct the Common law'.[85] But in relation to property rights at least, the 'equitable' rights which were created by the English courts of Equity remain much more of a 'supplement' to the Common law than those of the praetor in Rome.

---

[81] *Supra*, 123.

[82] W.W. Buckland and A.D. McNair, *Roman Law and Common Law*, 2nd ed., ed. F.H. Lawson (Cambridge: Cambridge University Press, 1952), 64; Gaius 2,41.

[83] See also H.J. Wolff, *Roman Law, An Historical Introduction* (Norman: University of Oklahoma Press, 1951), 79.

[84] *Supra*, 108, fnt. 1.

[85] D. 1,1,7,1.

CHAPTER SIX

IUS HONORARIUM, EQUITY AND REAL SECURITY: PARALLEL LINES OF LEGAL DEVELOPMENT

H.L.E. Verhagen

Introduction

There is no other Roman legal institution where the formative effect of legal practice can be so clearly observed as the right of pledge (*pignus*).[1] For instance, the non-possessory pledge (*hypotheca*),[2] the creditor's right to sell the pledged assets,[3] the creditor's obligation to pay any surplus of the enforcement proceeds back to the debtor,[4] the creation of multiple security rights over the same assets,[5] the charging of receivables,[6] the lessor's pledge on goods brought onto the leased property (*invecta et illata*)[7] and the general pledge[8] all find their origin in transactional practices. The law of *pignus* was largely developed through transactional practices which were recognised by the *ius honorarium*. A similar observation can be made for the English law of charges, where the role of transactional lawyers and the courts of Equity also played a formative role in the development of law.

---

[1] M. Kaser, *Ausgewählte Schriften* II (Naples: Jovene, 1976), 171–219 (= "Ueber mehrfache Verpfändung im römischen Recht", in *Studi in onore di Giuseppe Grosso* I (Turin: Giappichelli, 1968), 29–76). See also M. Kaser, *Studien zum römischen Pfandrecht* (Naples: Jovene, 1982), 218.

[2] See *infra*, 132–133. In this chapter, with respect to Roman law the terms '*pignus*' and 'pledge' will be used as the generic term for possessory and non-possessory pledges, while the term '*hypotheca*' will be used specifically for non-possessory pledges.

[3] Kaser, *Studien zum römischen Pfandrecht*, 72–78. See also H.L.E. Verhagen, "Das Verfallpfand im frühklassischen römischen Recht. Dingliche Sicherheit im Archiv der Sulpizier", *TvR* 79 (2011), 32–40.

[4] Kaser, *Studien zum römischen Pfandrecht*, 75–78; Verhagen, "Das Verfallpfand", 40–45.

[5] Kaser, *Ausgewählte Schriften* II, 201–205.

[6] M. Kaser, "Zum 'pignus nominis' ", *IVRA: rivista internationale di diritto romano e antico* 20 (1969), 172–190.

[7] M. Kaser and R. Knütel, *Römisches Privatrecht. Ein Studienbuch*, 19th ed. (Munich: Beck, 2008), 165; P. Du Plessis, "The Interdictum de Migrando revisited", *Revue Internationale des Droits de l'Antiquité* 54 (2007), 232–235.

[8] See *infra*, 135–139.

There are other interesting common patterns of development in Roman law and English law. In respect of two subjects, in particular, it is apparent that law was developing in parallel. The first subject is the evolution of ownership-based security. In both legal systems the most valuable assets—*res mancipi* in Rome and land in England—were transferred in full ownership to the creditor. The parallel development which we can identify here is that the debtor's rights were reinforced, eventually resulting in what one could call a proprietary 'equitable' interest. Moreover, if one compares the Roman and English rules on the enforcement of security, one can see that in substance their evolution again follows similar patterns, resulting in an increased protection of the debtor. An important formal difference, however, is that in English law the rules protecting the debtor find their origin in Equity, while in Roman law they are rather part of the *ius civile* (*usureceptio, bona fides*) or the product of the imperial chancery.

In this chapter I will discuss these three (more or less) parallel lines of legal development: first the *ius honorarium* and Equity as mechanisms for absorbing transactional practices into the law of charge-based security, then the evolution of the debtor's equitable interest in case of ownership-based security and finally the impact of Equity on the enforcement of security.[9] My own research was focused on classical Roman law, but each time I have compared my results with those found by others (in particular Nolan and Armour) for English law.[10] Using English law as an object of comparison was particularly interesting, not only because like Roman law (*ius civile* / *ius honorarium*) it has a stratified structure (Common law / Equity), but also because we can follow—as in Roman law—the development of security almost from its embryonic beginning to its mature state. The question to what extent the English law of security was actually influenced by Roman law is outside the scope of this chapter. The fact

---

9 There are other interesting similarities between the Roman and English law of security, but they are less specifically connected with *ius honorarium* or Equity. See W.W. Buckland and A.D. McNair, *Roman Law & Common Law. A Comparison in Outline*, 2nd ed. F.H. Lawson (Cambridge: Cambridge University Press, 1952), 314–324; H.D. Hazeltine, "The Roman Fiducia cum Creditore and the English Mortgage", General Preface to R.W. Turner, *The Equity of Redemption* (Cambridge: Cambridge University Press, 1931), vii–lxiii. See also W.J. Zwalve and B. Sirks, *Grundzüge der europäischen Privatrechtsgeschichte* (Cologne/Vienna: Böhlau, 2012), 489–519.

10 My research on Roman law has resulted in another publication, which contains a much more detailed analysis on the Roman law of *pignus*: H.L.E. Verhagen, "The Evolution of Pignus in Classical Roman Law", *TvR* 81 (2013), 51–79. Parts of the following argument are adapted from this article.

that the patterns of development are similar would suggest that this influence was anything but pervasive. One would expect that if English lawyers and judges consciously adopted the Roman *pignus* or *fiducia*, they would have adopted the mature forms of these institutions, rather than take the whole evolutionary path again.[11] However, this does not rule out the fact that certain details of English law were influenced by Roman law or its continental descendants.[12]

Charge-Based Security

Roman Law

(i) *Changing the* formula *of the* actio Serviana

A decisive factor for the evolution of Roman law as an autonomous system was the role played by the praetor in instructing the judges as to how to arrive at their decisions. These instructions, which were documented and passed on in the edicts of the praetor, were cast in the form of what the German sociologist (and lawyer) Niklas Luhmann calls 'conditional programmes'.[13] In its most basic form a legal conditional programme reads as follows: 'if conditions x1, x2 and x3 occur the judge shall condemn the defendant to C1.' Luhmann mentions the Roman *formula* as the archetype of a conditional programme. The concept of the conditional programme is 'one of the great evolutionary achievements of social development'.[14] It is through its conditional programmes that the legal system responds to demands from society (e.g. economy, politics, religion), without compromising its separate identity. Although they may borrow the values from other systems, the filters included in the conditional programmes (the conditions x1, x2 and x3) themselves determine whether (and which) legal consequences should be attached to certain fact patterns. This 'operative closure' of the Roman legal system resulted in an increasing complexity, requiring the existence of a corresponding

---

[11] Hazeltine, "The Roman Fiducia", xxiv–xxv, xxvii. In terms of evolutionary theory, the similarities are analogous (due to similar selection pressures) rather than homologous (due to a common history). See M. Blute, *Darwinian Sociocultural Evolution* (Cambridge: Cambridge University Press, 2010), 54.

[12] Hazeltine, "The Roman Fiducia", ix–xi, mentions the influence of the Roman *hypotheca*.

[13] N. Luhmann, *Law as a Social System* (Oxford: Oxford University Press, 2004; transl. of *Das Recht der Gesellschaft* (Frankurt am Main: Suhrkamp, 1993)), 196–210.

[14] Luhmann, *Law as a Social System*, 197.

expertise: the jurists. The jurists developed legal knowledge (jurisprudence), resulting 'in abstractions, which rendered the law and its self-referential concepts independent of plain facts and made a law-centered evolution possible'.[15] According to Bruce Frier the achievement of the late Republican jurists was to create 'a law of markedly liberal temper, freed from archaism and oriented to the needs of commerce'.[16] The jurists had developed from mere 'expert witnesses' on the content of the law to the 'effective determiners of law'.[17] They carried out this function in all stages of the legal process. They would advise the parties in drafting contracts, security documents and other transactions.[18] They would assist the praetor in drafting the edict and later the emperor in issuing rescripts. In individual litigation they would advise the litigating parties in choosing the proper action and other remedies (exceptions, replications), the praetor in granting these actions and remedies and the *iudex* in applying the actions and remedies to the case at hand.

One of the most significant examples of how the Roman legal system responded to demands from the economy, by the praetor adapting an existing *formula*, is the creation and gradual extension of the *actio Serviana* in response to new transactional practices. In all likelihood the right of *pignus* originated in the early *ius civile* as a form of possessory security.[19] It is often held in modern literature that the non-possessory pledge was only first recognized by the 2nd-century jurist Julian.[20] It seems, however,

[15] Luhmann, *Law as a Social System*, 249. In a similar sense, B.W. Frier, "Autonomy of Law and the Origins of the Legal Profession", *Cardozo Law Review* 11 (1989–1990), 259–286. See now also A. Schiavone, *The Invention of Law in the West* (Cambridge Mass./London: Belknap press, 2012; transl. of *Ius. L'invenzione del diritto in Occidente* (Turin: Einaudi, 2005)).

[16] Frier, "Autonomy of Law", 275.

[17] Ibid., 279–280.

[18] For the role of legal experts in drafting the documents (including security documentation) contained in the archive of the Sulpicii (1st century AD) see J.G. Wolf, "Der neue pompejanische Urkundenfund", *ZSS* 118 (2001), 131. This article is now included in J.G. Wolf, *Aus dem neuen pompejanischen Urkundenfund, Gesammelte Aufsätze* (Berlin: Duncker & Humblot, 2010), 104–155.

[19] The great majority of modern authors accept this: see G. Krämer, *Das besitzlose Pfandrecht, Entwicklungen in der römischen Republik und im frühen Prinzipat* (Cologne/Vienna: Böhlau, 2007), 121, with further references. An important exception is Schanbacher, who argues that the Roman *pignus* could already from its beginning be created merely by contract. As such it was a 'Fremdkörper' in the world of Roman law and must have been a legal transplant from Greece. D. Schanbacher, "Zu Ursprung und Entwicklung des römischen Pfandrechts", *ZSS* 123 (2006), 49–70.

[20] Krämer, *Das besitzlose Pfandrecht*, 37, whose own opinion is that the non-possessory pledge was recognised much earlier. See also M. Kaser, *Das römische Privatrecht I: Das altrömische, das vorklassische und klassische Recht*, 2nd ed. (Munich: Beck, 1971), 457.

that *pignus* already could exist as a non-possessory security right (*hypotheca*) much earlier than Julian. First of all, there is the lessor's pledge on goods brought onto the leased property (*invecta et illata*), which can be regarded as an intermediate form between a possessory and a non-possessory pledge.[21] Moreover, in the Digests there are several fragments from before Julian which seem to concern non-possessory security. One example is D. 13,7,30, in which Paul restates the opinion of the jurist Alfenus Varus (1st century BC) on what appears to have been a non-possessory pledge of a raft.[22] Finally, the archive of the Sulpicii provides epigraphic evidence of a transactional practice of creating non-possessory pledges already in the first half of the 1st century AD.[23] In view of the careful consideration given to legal issues in the Sulpicii documents, it would seem unlikely that the parties would have purported to create a non-possessory pledge if such a pledge would have been invalid.[24]

There is a tendency in modern literature to also allocate the origin of the *actio Serviana*—as an action to recover pledged assets from third persons—to the time of Julian.[25] The main argument is that there are no sources mentioning the *actio Serviana* from before Julian. Wubbe notes that, as the number of surviving fragments dating from before Julian is relatively small, it appears risky to attach too much value to statistical data of this kind.[26] According to Wubbe the *actio Serviana* is closely related to the *actio Publiciana* and was introduced around the same time in the 1st century BC, during the transition period from the *legisactio*-procedure to the *formula*-procedure.[27]

---

21 Krämer, *Das besitzlose Pfandrecht*, 197.

22 Ibid., 211–248. Another example, important according to Krämer (but in my view more problematic) is D. 13,7,18,3 (Paulus), referring to the opinion of Cassius (1st century BC): see ibid., 249–275.

23 TPN 43, 44, 86 / TPSulp. 45, 51, 52.

24 See Krämer, *Das besitzlose Pfandrecht*, 300–338; Verhagen, "Das Verfallpfand", 28.

25 See e.g. M. Braukmann, *Pignus: Das Pfandrecht unter dem Einfluß der vorklassischen und klassischen Tradition der römischen Rechtswissenschaft* (Göttingen: Wallstein, 2008), 56–62 with further references. The *actio Serviana* could also be instituted against the pledgor himself, in particular when in case of a *hypotheca* the creditor intended to enforce the pledge by selling the pledged property.

26 F.B.J. Wubbe, *Ius vigilantibus scriptum. Ausgewählte Schriften*, ed. P. Pichonnaz (Freiburg: Universitätsverlag Freiburg Schweiz, 2003), 219 (= F.B.J. Wubbe and P. Pichonnaz, "L'action Servienne dans l'Edit du Préteur", in *Mélanges à la mémoire de André Magdelain*, ed. M. Humbert and Y. Thomas (Paris: Editions Panthéon-Assas, 1998), 361–382).

27 The alternative explanation is that the praetor Servius Sulpicius Rufus strengthened the transactional practice of pledging *invecta et illata* by creating a new action with which the pledged assets could be recovered from third parties: the *actio Serviana*. Subsequent praetors have extended the *actio Serviana* to possessory and non-possessory pledges in

As a result of the extension to non-possessory pledges, the *formula* of the *actio Serviana* did not include the condition that the pledged property should have been in the possession of the creditor, but instead referred to the pledge agreement (*conventio pignoris*).[28] The first condition listed in the *intentio* of the *formula* of the *actio Serviana*, or in the *actio in factum* (*actio utilis*) derived from it, referred to the pledge agreement: '*inter A^m A^m et Lucium Titium convenisse, ut ea res qua de agitur A^o A^o pignori esset propter pecuniam debitam.*'[29] The pledge agreement was made a central component of the *formula* of the *actio Serviana*, which enabled the praetor to sanction new transactional practices which were included in the *conventio pignoris*.

An example which illustrates how the *formula* of the *actio Serviana* allowed the praetor to respond to new transactional practices is the pledging of claims (*pignus nominis*). When the economic need arose to enable debtors to use contractual debts owed to them as collateral, the praetor at some stage became willing to grant an *actio in factum* (or *actio utilis*) to a creditor to whom contractual debts had been pledged. The cause of action (the *factum*) of this *actio in factum* was, like that of the *actio Serviana* itself, the pledge agreement, so that any admissible form of property defined in the pledge agreement could be made the object of the action.[30] This action was modelled after the *actio Serviana* (but also included elements of the action on the original debt) and with it the pledged debt could be enforced by the pledgee against the debtor thereof.[31]

---

general, first perhaps as *actio quasi Serviana* or *actio hypothecaria* (D. 16,1,13,1, Gaius). See for this account, for instance, F. Schulz, *Classical Roman Law* (Oxford: Clarendon, 1951, repr. 1969), 408–409; Krämer, *Das besitzlose Pfandrecht*, 38–51.

28 The oldest fragment in the Digests mentioning the *conventio (pignoris)* is D. 41,3,33,4–5 (Julianus).

29 See O. Lenel, *Das Edictum perpetuum. Ein Versuch zu seiner Wiederherstellung*, 3rd ed. (Leipzig: B. Tauchnitz, 1927), 493. Aulus Agerius ('A^m A^m') is the creditor / pledgee and Lucius Titius is the pledgor. Only a creditor could be a pledgee. See J.C. Out, *Vormen van Accessoriëteit. Een Romanistische studie over het verschijnsel accessoriëteit bij het goederenrechtelijke zekerheidrecht* (Nijmegen: Gerard Noodt Institute, 2005), 86–87, referring to D. 20,1,33 (Tryphoninus). However, the capacities of debtor and pledgor did not necessarily have to coincide: a pledge could be granted exclusively for someone else's obligations (D. 20,1,5,2, Marcianus).

30 Kaser, *Studien zum römischen Pfandrecht*, 181–182. C. 8,16(17),4 (Alexander) provides a description of this.

31 See Kaser, "Zum 'pignus nominis'", *passim*; W. Selb, "Formulare Analogien in 'actiones utiles' und 'actiones in *factum*' am Beispiel Julians", in *Studi in onore di Arnoldo Biscardi* III (Milan: Cisalpino-Goliardica, 1982), 335.

The *formula* of the *actio Serviana* required that the pledged assets were *in bonis* of the pledgor, at the time the pledge agreement was entered into (*in bonis Lucii Titii, tunc cum conveniebat*).[32] In other words, the debtor should have Quiritary or praetorian ownership of the pledged objects when the transaction was entered into. This requirement, if strictly adhered to, would prevent the creation of a pledge over a future property. However, the possibility of pledging future property is confirmed by a number of texts in the Digests.[33] Apparently the praetor intervened by granting an *actio utilis* (or *actio in factum*) to the creditor, which was modelled after the *actio Serviana*, but which did not include the condition that the pledged assets were *in bonis* of the debtor at the time of the conclusion of the *conventio pignoris*. This condition must have been modified, to the effect that property which was *in bonis debitoris* after the conclusion of the pledge agreement could also be included.

This evolutionary sequence created the building blocks from which a Roman 'floating charge' could be constructed: first the non-possessory pledge, next the pledge over receivables and finally the pledge over future property.

(ii) *The Roman 'floating charge'*

In comparative law the floating charge, a security interest over a changing fund of assets, is often regarded as a unique Common law institution.[34] It is true that, with some limited exceptions (such as the French 'gage sur fonds de commerce'), the present civil law systems do not have a floating charge.[35] However, classical Roman law did, which is another remarkable example of what Pringsheim called the 'inner relationship' between

32 On the requirement that the property should be *in bonis* of the pledgor, see H. Ankum and E. Pool, "Rem in Bonis Meis Esse and Rem in Bonis Meam Esse: Traces of the development of Roman Double Ownership", in *New Perspectives in the Roman Law of Property: Essays for Barry Nicholas*, P. Birks ed. (Oxford: Clarendon, 1989), 16–29, 32 and 41.

33 D. 13,7,41 (Paulus); D. 20,1,1 pr. (Papinianus); D. 20,1,16,7 (Marcianus); D. 20,1,22 (Modestinus); D. 20,4,7,1 (Ulpianus). Fragments on general pledges can also be used as evidence for the possibility of pledging future property, such as D. 20,1,15,1 (Gaius, discussed *infra*) and D. 20,1,34,2 (Scaevola, discussed *infra*).

34 See e.g. E.M. Kieninger, "Introduction", in *Security Rights in Movable Property in European Private Law*, E.M. Kieninger ed. (Cambridge: Cambridge University Press, 2004), 13.

35 Medieval continental indigenous systems of (customary) law did have something similar to the floating charge. Moreover, the general pledge was permitted as an institution of the *ius commune*. It was only with the great codifications of the 19th century that a pledge over a fund of assets was no longer permitted. See W. Zwalve, "A Labyrinth of Creditors: a Short Introduction to the History of Security Interests in Goods", in *Security Rights in Movable Property*, Kieninger ed., 42–44.

English and Roman law.[36] An interesting fragment is D. 20,1,15,1, because it expressly refers to transactional practices. In his commentary on the *formula hypothecaria* Gaius writes:

> D. 20,1,15,1: When it is said that the creditor should prove that, when he made the agreement, the thing was in the debtor's estate, this applies to that agreement that has been especially made, not to the clause commonly inserted in deeds that beside the property specially hypothecated, the debtor's remaining assets, both those which he now has and those which he will afterwards acquire, will be liable in the same manner as if these things were especially charged.[37]

The Gaius fragment demonstrates that in Gaius' time a transactional practice existed of combining specific and general security. The text says that these clauses were inserted 'daily' (*cottidie*). There are many other fragments in which the possibility of pledging all one's present and future assets is acknowledged.[38] The praetor would allow a description of the pledge agreement referred to in the *intentio* of the *formula* of the *actio Serviana* (= *actio hypothecaria*) to be based on the clauses discussed by Gaius. The reference in the *formula* to *in bonis* [*debitoris*] would have been changed as well, as appears from D. 20,1,15,1. Again, it can be observed that at some stage the praetor responded to this new transactional practice of creating general pledges by extending the existing remedies for *pignus* and *hypotheca* to creditors to whom such wide-ranging security had been granted.

---

[36] F. Pringsheim, "The inner Relationship between English and Roman Law", *CLJ* 5 (1935), 347–365. For a comparison of the Roman general pledge and the English floating charge, see Buckland and McNair, *Roman Law & Common Law*, 322.

[37] Gaius, *libro singulari ad formulam hypothecariam. Quod dicitur creditorem probare debere, cum conveniebat, rem in bonis debitoris fuisse, ad eam conventionem pertinet, quae specialiter facta est, non ad illam, quae cottidie inseri solet cautionibus, ut specialiter rebus hypothecae nomine datis cetera etiam bona teneantur debitoris, quae nunc habet et quae postea adquisierit, perinde atque si specialiter hae res fuissent obligatae.* On this text see: H. Wagner, *Voraussetzungen, Vorstufen und Anfänge der römischen Generalverpfändung* (Marburg: N.G. Elwert, 1968), 64–71; R. Mentxaka, *La pignoracion de colectividades en el derecho romano clasico* (Bilbao: Universidad del País Vasco, 1986), 280–285. English translations of all Digests texts in this chapter are taken from A. Watson, ed., *The Digest of Justinian*, 4 vols. (Philadelphia: University of Pennsylvania Press, 1998), and adapted where I preferred a different translation.

[38] D. 40,9,29 pr. (Gaius); D. 20,1,34,2 (Scaevola); D. 20,1,1 pr. (Papinianus); D. 20,1,29 pr. (Paulus); D. 20,4,7,1 (Ulpianus); D. 40,8,6 (Marcianus); C. 8,16(17),1 (Severus and Antoninus); C. 8,16(17),4 (Alexander); C. 8,17(18),6 (Valerianus and Gallienus); C. 8,13(14),17 (Diocletianus and Maximianus). For a discussion of these and other fragments, see Mentxaka, *Pignoracion*, 279–350.

Much has been written about D. 20,1,15,1, among other things about its implication for the burden of proof for the creditor in relation to the debtor's ownership of the pledged assets, which appears to be the central problem of this text.[39] In this chapter, I will discuss two aspects of the Gaius fragment that are more interesting from a comparative perspective. First, what exactly was the relationship between the special pledge and the general pledge? Second, what exactly was the nature of the general pledge? As we will see, the issues are much the same as those concerning the English floating charge.

(iii) *General and Special Pledges Combined*

There are several possible explanations for the combination of a special and a general pledge in the clauses discussed by Gaius. The most plausible interpretation has been forwarded by Wubbe. He notes that someone who pledges his whole patrimony can freely dispose of individual assets, without the pledge attaching to these assets.[40] The general pledge would be a 'floating' charge, in the sense that it vested only in the assets which from time to time were within the debtor's patrimony. This is different for those assets that have been charged with a special pledge. These assets may not be disposed of freely and will remain subject to the pledge if the pledged assets are nevertheless transferred to third parties.

The purpose of this transactional practice of combining a special pledge with a general pledge over the debtor's present and future remaining assets could have been to create a residual preferential position for the secured creditor in respect of the other creditors, providing additional protection in case the proceeds of the assets specifically pledged would not be sufficient to discharge the secured debt. In this interpretation the situation was similar to that described in a recent book on the English law of security: 'the single floating charge has been superseded in fact by a combination of separate fixed charges over as many different assets as can support a fixed charge, together with a residual floating charge that sweeps up all assets that escape the row of fixed charges'.[41]

In this respect two interesting texts are discussed by Du Plessis, dealing with a contractual clause pursuant to which a tenant pledges present and

---

39 Wagner, *Voraussetzungen*, 64–71; Mentxaka, *Pignoracion*, 280–285.

40 Wubbe, *Ius vigilantibus scriptum*, 172. Wubbe's view has met with considerable opposition: most elaborately, see Wagner, *Voraussetzungen*, 100–125.

41 H. Beale *et al.*, *The Law of Personal Property Security* (Oxford: Oxford University Press, 2007), par. 1.13.

future assets to his landlord, which 'created nothing more than a floating charge'.[42] One of these texts is:

> D. 20,2,9: There is a difference between assets charged for rent and those which are held as pledge pursuant to an express agreement; we cannot free slaves charged with an [express] pledge, but we can free slaves living on rented premises, until we are locked out for non-payment of rent: after that we cannot effectively free slaves detained by way of pledge.[43]

This text deals with a situation where a 'fixed charge' is created in combination with a 'floating charge' over the *invecta et illata*. The debtor cannot dispose of assets subject to the fixed charge, but can dispose of assets subject to the 'floating charge'. However, the debtor's authority to dispose of the latter category of assets terminates when there is a payment default (non-payment of rent). This whole arrangement is very similar to a modern security package under English law, consisting of fixed and floating charges, where payment default leads to crystallization of the floating charge.

(iv) *Pledge Over a Fund of Assets*

From an economic perspective, differentiation between general and specific pledges would certainly have been the most efficient solution. If a general pledge would in all respects have had exactly the same consequences as a special pledge, the debtor would only have been able to dispose of assets in the ordinary course of business with the pledge continuing to attach to them. Given the fact that Roman law did not protect a *bona fide* purchaser against a pledge unknown to him, this could have paralyzed the debtor's business.[44] But is there other support for Wubbe's theory that the general pledge did not attach to the pledged assets when they were disposed of by the debtor? One interesting and relevant fragment is from Scaevola:

---

[42] P. Du Plessis, "The Interdictum de Migrando revisited", 229. The other text is D. 2,2,6 (Ulpianus).

[43] Paulus, *libro singulari de officio praefecti vigilum. Est differentia obligatorum propter pensionem et eorum, quae ex conventione manifesta<ri> pignoris nomine tenentur, quod manumittere mancipia obligata pignori non possumus, inhabitantes autem manumittimus, scilicet antequam pensionis nomine percludamur: tunc enim pignoris nomine retenta mancipia non liberabimus [...].*

[44] In a similar sense, with respect to the pledge of a *taberna* (see *infra*), E.A. Daubermann, *Die Sachgesamtheit als Gegenstand des klassischen römischen Rechts* (Frankfurt am Main: Lang, 1993), 121.

> D. 20,1,34 pr.: When a debtor pledged a shop to the creditor, the question was put whether this was invalid or whether by 'shop' the merchandise in the shop was to be taken as charged. And if he sold goods from time to time, bought others, brought them into the shop, and then died, could the creditor institute the *actio hypothecaria* for all that was then on the premises, in view of the turnover of stock? Scaevola replied: what was in the shop at the debtor's death was subject to the pledge.[45]

According to Scaevola, there appears to be nothing to invalidate the pledge, such as a lack of identifiability, as Scaevola concludes that the pledging of a shop (*taberna*) meant that the merchandise which was present in the *taberna* at the time of the shopkeeper's death, was subject to the pledge.[46] In modern terminology this pledge created a security interest on circulating assets, a 'floating' charge. The text clearly indicates that the pledge was vested in the specific assets as they were from time to time stored in the shop. Accordingly, the most plausible interpretation of this fragment is that newly purchased merchandise would replace sold merchandise as collateral, and that consequently the latter category could be transferred free of pledge.

English Law

In English law, there are several forms of real security which can be created over movable assets. The ownership of movables can be conveyed to the creditor, in which case a 'chattel mortgage' will be created.[47] When possession is to remain with the debtor this is—somewhat confusingly—called a 'bill of sale' (which needs to be registered in order to be effective against the debtor's other creditors).[48] Movables can also be pledged, in which case ownership remains with the debtor and the creditor acquires

---

45 Scaevola *libro vicesimo septimo Digestorum. Cum tabernam debitor creditori pignori dederit, quaesitum est, utrum eo facto nihil egerit an tabernae appellatione merces, quae in ea erant, obligasse videatur? Et si eas merces per tempora distraxerit et alias comparaverit easque in eam tabernam intulerit et decesserit, an omnia quae ibi deprehenduntur creditor hypothecaria actione petere possit, cum et mercium species mutatae sint et res aliae illatae? Respondit: ea, quae mortis tempore debitoris in taberna inventa sunt, pignori obligata esse videntur.*

46 On this fragment, see also Mentxaka, *Pignoracion*, 207–214; F. Sturm, "Die Digestenexegese", in *Die rechtsgeschichtliche Exegese: römisches Recht, deutsches Recht, Kirchenrecht*, ed. H. Schlosser, F. Sturm and H. Weber, 2nd ed. (Munich: Beck, 1993), 26–54; Daubermann, *Die Sachgesamtheit*, 116–126.

47 L.D. Smith, "Security", in *English Private Law*, ed. A. Burrows, 2nd ed. (Oxford: Oxford University Press, 2007), par. 5.74.

48 Beale *et al.*, *Personal Property Security*, par. 9.53.

(in civil law terminology) a limited real right in the pledged assets.[49] A pledge requires the transfer of possession of the pledged assets.[50] For this reason, the security interest which is most frequently used in practice is the so-called 'equitable charge', which is, as the term indicates, a creation of Equity. An equitable charge over movables is a non-possessory security interest. Where the Common law did not recognise the disposition over future assets, but insisted on a fresh conveyance when the asset came into existence, Equity treated these assets as being automatically transferred or charged once they originated.[51] Moreover, where the Common law did not recognise an assignment by way of mortgage of receivables, again, Equity permitted a security assignment or charge of receivables. Equity's recognition of non-possessory security over future and intangible assets paved the way for 'one of equity's most subtle creations' (Goode): the floating charge.[52]

In 2004 two interesting publications appeared on the history of the floating charge, one by Nolan and the other by Armour.[53] They both describe the process of the early development of the floating charge in terms of 'an iterative relationship between transactional lawyers drafting loan agreements and judges called upon to enforce them'.[54] The impetus for the present day floating charge was a specifically mandated statutory charge. In the first half of the 19th century companies were created by a special Act of Parliament. Such an Act often gave the company the power to create security over its 'undertaking'. This allowed the company to grant security over its present and future assets, with the right to alienate the assets free of charge. When under the Companies Act 1862 companies could be incorporated by registration, this statutory charge was not made available. Nevertheless, in practice, indentures were also executed by registered companies, in which they purported to pledge the 'undertaking' of the company. This raised two crucial questions. The first concerned the range of assets that were charged. Initially, this was confined by the courts

49 Smith, "Security", in *English Private Law*, par. 5.66.

50 Ibid., par. 5.66.

51 *Tailby v Official Receiver* (1888) 13 AC 523.

52 R. Goode, "The Exodus of the Floating Charge", in *Corporate and Commercial Law: Modern Developments*, ed. R.R. Pennington, D. Feldman and F. Meisel (London: Lloyd's of London Press, 1996), 193–203.

53 R.C. Nolan, "Property in a Fund", *LQR* 120 (2004), 108–136; J. Armour, "The Chequered History of the Floating Charge", *Griffith Law Review* 13 (2004), 25–56.

54 Armour, "Chequered History", 28.

to the company's present assets,[55] but the Court of Appeal in Chancery later extended this to include the company's future assets.[56] The second crucial issue concerned the chargor's power to dispose of its assets free of charge. This question arose in connection with the company directors' duties: if the charge was a fixed charge (without the power to dispose), granting a charge over all of the company's assets would paralyze the business and could thus constitute a breach of the directors' duty. With this in mind, transactional lawyers drafted the security documentation to expressly reserve various powers for the company to be able to dispose of its assets in the ordinary course of business. These transactional practices were recognised by the courts and thus the modern floating charge was born.[57]

Comparison

If we look at the laws of charge-based security of Rome and England, we can discern distinct parallel lines of legal development. In both legal systems these lines are drawn by 'an iterative relationship' between transactional lawyers drafting security documents and judicial authorities (the praetor in Rome and Chancery in England) prepared to enforce them.[58] For English law Armour describes this as follows:

> [T]he development of the law was driven, at least in part, by innovation on the part of transactional lawyers that was 'encoded' and 'replicated' through precedents by the judiciary.[59]

In essence, this is the same kind of evolutionary process that caused the Roman pledge to develop from a possessory pledge over a single tangible asset into a non-possessory security interest over all the present and future, tangible and intangible assets of a debtor.[60] In order to reach

---

55 *In re New Clydach Sheet and Bar Iron Co.* (1868) LR 6 Eq. 514.

56 *In re Panama, New Zealand, and Australian Royal Mail Co.* (1870) LR 5 Ch. App. 318.

57 Nolan, "Property in a Fund", 109.

58 Adapted from Armour, "Chequered History", 28.

59 Armour, "Chequered History", 30. In a similar sense, for English law, Nolan, "Property in a Fund", 109 and, for Roman and English law, Hazeltine, "The Roman *Fiducia*", xxv.

60 A general pledge did extend to the pledgor's receivables. For instance, C. 8,16(17),4 (Alexander, 225): *Nomen quoque debitoris pignerari et generaliter et specialiter posse pridem placuit.* 'The claim against a debtor can be pledged as well, both generally and specifically, as has already earlier been accepted.' The Scaevola fragment on the pledge of a *taberna* demonstrates that the Roman 'floating charge' could also be created over a class of assets rather than over all the debtor's present and future assets.

this destination, the same obstacles had to be overcome: the objection against non-possessory pledges, pledges over contractual claims and security over future assets and the requirement of identifiability of the objects of security.[61]

Both the English floating charge and the Roman general pledge can be regarded as a security interest over a *fund of assets*. Nolan's definition of an English floating charge is:

> The floating charge is a charge over a fund of assets, in the sense that the chargee has an immediate security interest in identified assets owned by the chargor, which is nevertheless subject to, and restricted by, the superior but limited power of the chargor (as owner) to manage and alienate those assets free of the chargee's interest. In addition, the chargee will almost invariably have security in identifiable future assets if, as and when acquired by the chargor.[62]

This definition could also be used to describe the Roman general pledge. Moreover, the most plausible interpretation of both the Roman general pledge and the English floating charge appears to be that the security interest is not vested in the fund as such, but in the specific assets comprised therein from time to time.[63] Nevertheless, there are also important differences between the Roman general pledge and the English floating charge. The most significant difference is that the origin and evolution of the English floating charge is closely connected with company law, yet there is no similar connection in Roman law, which did not have a company law. Despite the differences, one can conclude that in both Rome and England, charge-based security is largely the product of the *ius honorarium* and Equity respectively, and both had similar 'manufacturing processes'.

---

[61] For the English floating charge, see Goode, "The Exodus of the Floating Charge", 195.

[62] R.C. Nolan, "Property in a Fund", 117.

[63] So for Roman law Sturm, "Die Digestenexegese", 38–44; Daubermann, *Die Sachgesamtheit*, 124–126, who points out that when the present and future merchandise would have been treated as one *res*, the pledge of D. 20,1,34 pr. would also have extended to merchandise arriving at the shop after the shopkeeper's death. In the same sense for English law, Nolan, "Property in a Fund", 130. Nolan observes (at 136): 'There no need to reify the fund, to treat it (rather than its component parts) as the object of property.'

Ownership-Based Security: The 'Equitable' Interest of the Debtor

Roman Law

(i) Fiducia cum creditore

Under Roman law *res mancipi* were transferred as security to a creditor by way of *fiducia cum creditore*. The debtor would—through a *mancipatio*—transfer land, slaves or cattle as collateral to a creditor.[64] As a consequence of the *mancipatio*, the creditor acquired *dominium ex iure Quiritium* (civilian ownership) of the object of *fiducia*. Based on this civilian ownership, the creditor had the legal power to make a testamentary disposition of the property, sell and transfer it, liberate slaves *etc.*[65] The debtor was left with merely a personal claim for reconveyance (*remancipatio*) of the property after the secured debt had been paid: the *actio fiduciae*. From the perspective of property law, the debtor's position was therefore fundamentally different from that in case of *pignus*. In the latter case, the debtor remained the civilian owner of the charged property: the creditor merely acquired a limited right *in rem*, which automatically expired when the secured debt was discharged.[66]

(ii) Actio fiduciae

In the accompanying *pactum fiduciae* it would normally be expressly agreed that the creditor would retransfer the collateral if and when the secured debt was discharged. We have an example of a clause to this effect from actual practice. The first sentence of the *pactum fiduciae* accompanying the *Mancipatio Pompeiana* (AD 61) provides as follows:

---

64 A transfer in court by way of *in iure cessio* was also possible, though it is likely to have been relatively rare. Gaius (2,25) explains why: 'what we can do through our own acts in the presence of friends, there is no necessity for us to do with greater difficulty before the praetor, or the governor of the province.' The epigraphic sources all concern a *fiducia cum creditore* with a *mancipatio*. See also G. Noordraven, *Die Fiduzia im römischen Recht* (Amsterdam: Gieben, 1999), 154–155. My hypothesis is that orginally *res mancipi* were always provided as collateral by way of *fiducia* and *res nec mancipi* by way of *pignus*. During the classical period, however, this changed and *res mancipi* could also be charged by way of *pignus* (*hypotheca*). Verhagen, "Das Verfallpfand", 8–9 with further references.

65 D. 17,1,27,1 (Gaius); D. 17,1,30 (Julianus); D. 40,1,13 (Pomponius) and other fragments mentioned by Noordraven on the liberation of slaves. According to Noordraven there are no surviving fragments on the sale of objects of *fiducia*, other than by way of enforcement. Noordraven, *Die Fiduzia*, 164.

66 E.g. D. 20,6,6 pr. (Ulpianus).

> *FIRA* III, no. 91, 293: Those *mancipia* which today you have sold to me thus, let them be restored to you or your heir when that previous money, which today I gave to you as *mutuum* for the two *mancipia* is all paid back to me or my heir or when it returns to or comes by *usus*.[67]

One would think that the fiduciary nature of the *fiducia cum creditore* entailed that even in the absence of such a clause in the *pactum fiduciae* the creditor would have a duty to redeliver (remancipate) the object of *fiducia* upon discharge of the secured debt. The reference to redelivery in the accompanying *pactum fiduciae* may have served only to specify the modalities of the redelivery.

Originally, the *mancipatio* by way of *fiducia* was a transfer by a person to a friend, so that the latter could manage the first's property in his absence. In this early stage it is likely that there was no actionable agreement at all: the fiduciary owner was under a moral duty, and not under a legally enforceable obligation, to remancipate the object of *fiducia*.[68] At a later stage fiduciary transfers to creditors also took place, and it is probably at this time that the praetor would grant an action for redelivery of the object after the debt had been discharged. It is clear that this *actio fiduciae* was not based on the ancient *ius civile* (i.e. the Law of the XII Tables, its interpretation by the jurists or further legislation). The basis for this action would have been the *fides*, which was recognized in the Republic as a non-statutory source of liability, beside the *ius civile* and the *ius honorarium*.[69] In other words, although the *actio fiduciae* may not have originated in the *ius honorarium*, it was a creation by the praetor.

---

[67] *[Quae mancipia hodie mihi ven]didi[sti, ita tibi heridive tuo (?) restituentur, ut antea pecunia quam] m[u]t[uam] pro duobu[s mancipiis tibi hodie (?) dedi, o]mnis mihi <h>ere[dive meo solvatur vel ad me ut rede]at usu ve[ni]at.* Translation taken from E.A. Meyer, *Legitimacy and Law in the Roman World, Tabulae in Roman Belief and Practice* (Cambridge: Cambridge University Press, 2004, 141. The *pactum fiduciae* of the *Formula Baetica* (1st–2nd century AD) provides that after repayment of the debt the object of *fiducia* shall be 'liberated' (*liberataque esset*). *FIRA* III, no. 92, 295. Tab. Herc. 66,6,1–3 is evidence of a remancipation of three slaves which were the object of a *fiducia cum creditore*: *Remancupatio mancipior(um) trium|ab M. Nonio [Cra]sso|M. Nonio Fusco*. See A. Biscardi, *Appunti sulle garanzie reali in diritto romano* (Milan: Cisalpino-Goliardica, 1976), 260 (includes the edition of the text by V. Arangio Ruiz and G. Pugliese Carratelli, "Tabulae Herculanenses IV", *La parola del passato* 34 (1954), 64).

[68] According to Noordraven, there was no remedy available to the debtor in the *legisactio*-procedure: the *actio fiduciae* was only recognised in the *formula*-procedure. Noordraven, *Die Fiduzia*, 297.

[69] Kaser, *Studien zum römischen Pfandrecht*, 100–101.

In classical law this *actio fiduciae* became a *bonae fidei iudicium* and as such part of the *ius civile*.[70]

(iii) *Debtor as 'true owner'*

Although as a consequence of the *mancipatio* the creditor acquired civilian ownership, the debtor retained certain rights and liabilities in respect of the object of *fiducia*.[71] This reflects that the debtor was not only socially regarded as the true owner,[72] but also that, to some extent, the law treated the debtor as though he remained the owner of the object of *fiducia*. When the debtor was praetorian owner, the *usucapio* would continue after *mancipatio* to the creditor.[73] When the object was stolen, the debtor was entitled to institute the *actio furti*, unless the creditor had his own interest in instituting this action.[74] If a slave, who had been fiduciarily transferred, committed a delict, the praetorian noxal action, which must normally be instituted against the owner of the slave, should still be instituted against the debtor.[75] Significantly, in several fragments dealing with noxal liability the debtor is still referred to as the '*dominus*' of the object of *fiducia*.[76] After the debt had been discharged the debtor could repossess the property against the creditor's will without committing theft (*furtum*).[77] This indicates that in some respects the debtor was already regarded as the rightful title holder to the property, even before the property had been remancipated. Although, as we have seen, the creditor could on his death dispose of the object of *fiducia* by way of *legatum per vindicationem*, Papinian says that in a legacy of all of someone's furniture, silverware accepted by way of *fiducia* shall not be included in the legacy, in particular when

---

70 According to Wieacker, Kaser and others all *bonae fidei iudicia* originated in the *ius honorarium*. F. Wieacker, *Römische Rechtsgeschichte. Quellenkunde, Rechtsbildung, Jurisprudenz und Rechtsliteratur* I (Munich: Beck, 1988), 457–458; Kaser and Knütel, *Römisches Privatrecht*, par. 2.13.

71 See Noordraven, *Die Fiduzia*, 166–185. See also S. Romeo, "Fiducia auctionibus vendunda nelle Tabelle Pompeiane. Procedure e modalità di redazione delle testationes nelle auctiones puteolane del 61 d.C.", *Polis: studi interdisciplinari sul mondo antico* 2 (2006), 216–221.

72 Certainly when the object of *fiducia* remained with the debtor in fact, which is likely to have been the case normally. Noordraven, *Die Fiduzia*, 166 and 177.

73 D. 41,2,36 (Julianus). Ibid., 182–185.

74 Ibid., 207–215, with further references to the Digests and secondary literature.

75 D. 9,4,22 (Paulus). Although the text speaks of *depositum* and *commodatum*, Noordraven has demonstrated that originally it must have dealt with *fiducia*. Ibid., 178–179.

76 E.g. D. 9,4,22 (Paulus). Ibid., 180, 202 and 213, with further examples.

77 Gaius 3,201.

the debtor did not allow the creditor to use the silver and it had been set aside by the creditor with a view to his duty to redeliver it.[78] The motivation given in the text (which speaks of *pignus*, but actually deals with *fiducia*)[79] is: 'because he [the creditor] legated his own furniture' (*quia supellectilem suam legavit*). This is thought to be an interpolation, because the silverware is also owned by the creditor and therefore also belongs to 'his own furniture'.[80] I am not so sure, however, as we have seen that in fragments dealing with noxal liability, the debtor is still referred to as *dominus* of the object of *fiducia*. In other words, it may very well be that the silverware, though formally owned by the creditor, was not regarded as part of the creditor's 'own furniture' for the purpose of the legacy. The Papinian fragment demonstrates, in any case, that the fiduciary nature of the creditor's ownership entailed special consequences: the object of *fiducia* was presumed not to be part of the legacy.

The debtor could still sell the object of *fiducia*, or promise it as a dowry (*dos*). This in itself is not extraordinary: anyone can make a contractual promise to transfer an object, even when the object is not (or no longer) owned by him or her. But when Roman law accepts that the debtor can make a valid legacy in favour of one of his heirs (*legatum per praeceptionem*) of objects fiduciarily transferred by him, this does indicate that the debtor still had some sort of conditional proprietary interest in the object of *fiducia*. In these cases, Gaius says, the common heirs are obliged to redeem the collateral, so that the legatee can take the object as his own. It should also be noted, however, that Gaius does mention this as an example of a legacy that can be made of someone else's property (*aliena res*).[81]

---

[78] D. 33,10,9,2 (Papinianus).

[79] Noordraven, *Die Fiduzia*, 10 and 162–165. This is a peculiar text, as *fiducia* is normally associated with *res mancipi*, which obviously does not include silverware. The transfer to the creditor may have been by way of *in iure cessio* (which could also be used for *res nec mancipi*), perhaps as part of a larger collection of assets. It is conceivable that this text constitutes evidence of the fact that in the 2nd century AD *res mancipi* were sometimes fiduciarily transferred through a *traditio*. Wubbe notes that although a *traditio fiduciae causae* would theoretically appear to have been possible, there is no trace of it either in the writings of the jurists or in the epigraphic souces. Wubbe, *Ius vigilantibus scriptum*, 237. D. 33,10,9,2 may, however, be the exception.

[80] Ibid., 162–164.

[81] Gaius 2,220. Wubbe, *Ius vigilantibus scriptum*, 173–176.

(iv) Usureceptio fiduciae

Perhaps the most remarkable manifestation of the proprietary nature of the debtor's interest is the so-called *usureceptio fiduciae*. This is, however, not an institution of the *ius honorarium* but of the *ius civile*. Under this special form of *usucapio* the debtor in possession of the object of *fiducia* regained civil ownership of it after one year, also in respect of land (where the general *usucapio* term was two years).[82] The debtor could rely on *usureceptio*, even if he took away the object of *fiducia* without the creditor's permission and even if the debt had not yet been discharged. Under the general rules for *usucapio* this would not be possible, because he would be regarded as lacking good faith (*bona fides*) and the property would be *res furtiva*. Also, the absence of *iusta causa* apparently did not prevent the debtor from acquiring *dominium* after one year, even though there was no agreement between the creditor and the debtor that ownership should return to the latter before discharge. All in all, *usureceptio* would seem to have made the *fiducia cum creditore* a very weak form of real security.

The unpaid creditor's position, however, was not as bad as it may seem. When the object of *fiducia* was kept under his physical control, this would prevent the debtor from acquiring possession: without possession no *usureceptio*. If nevertheless the debtor managed to take the object of *fiducia* from him, the creditor still had one year to recover it with a *rei vindicatio*. Most importantly, Gaius says that *usureceptio* only takes place when, during the time the secured debt has not yet been discharged, the debtor neither rents the property from the creditor nor holds it as bailee (*precarium*).[83] Apparently it was felt that in case of a non-possessory *fiducia* the creditor should not, before the debt was discharged, lose ownership as a consequence of the 'lighter' *usureceptio*-rules.[84] When the secured debt was discharged, the *locatio conductio* or *precarium* would automatically terminate, which would only then trigger the *usureceptio* mechanism.[85] Here, *usureceptio* could even have the advantage for the creditor of dispensing with the necessity of a formal remancipation. For the majority of cases, therefore, *usureceptio* is not as odd as it is often

82 According to Gaius 2,59: 'this species of *usucapio* is called *usureceptio*, because we regain that what we once had by way of *usucapio*' (*Quae species usucapionis dicitur usureceptio, quia id quod aliquando habuimus, recipimus per usucapionem*).

83 Gaius 2,60.

84 Kaser, *Studien zum römischen Pfandrecht*, 169–170.

85 Kaser, *Studien zum römischen Pfandrecht*, 43; Wubbe, *Ius vigilantibus scriptum*, 9. The situation is very similar to a *traditio brevi manu* and is perhaps even identical to it.

professed to be. The creditor could prevent *usureceptio* from taking place by allowing the debtor to use the object of *fiducia* pursuant to *locatio conductio* or *precarium*. The debtor would, after discharge of the secured debt, automatically re-acquire civilian ownership of the collateral after one year. During that year the debtor would be in the position of a praetorian owner and would have the *actio Publiciana* (or an analogous action) at his disposal for recovering the property from third parties.[86]

One feature of *usureceptio* that *is* peculiar, is that, if the debtor had taken away the property from the creditor's premises without the latter's permission, it could lead to loss of ownership at the side of the creditor *before* the secured debt had been discharged. Several explanations have been offered in modern literature for this peculiarity.[87] The most interesting one for our purposes is the explanation put forward by Wubbe. In terms not unfamiliar to Anglo-American lawyers, Wubbe observes that Roman law originally neither endorsed an absolute nor a unitary concept of ownership. In archaic law several ownership rights could co-exist simultaneously in respect of the same object.[88] As long as the debt existed, in a conflict between the debtor and the creditor the latter would have the better right. At the same time it must be assumed that the debtor would have been able to recover property from third parties in possession of it without good title. Thus ownership originally was functionally divided: the creditor would acquire a 'security ownership' subject to redemption (and thus temporary), while the debtor retained a right of ownership for the 'remainder'. It is unlikely that at the time of the classical period this division of ownership still persisted, but the *usureceptio* can be regarded as a remnant of it. In the legal institution of *usureceptio* the notion may have survived that the debtor was still the true owner and that when this

---

86 The *formula* of the *actio Publiciana* reads as follows: *Si quem hominem A^s A^s bona fide emit et is ei traditus est [...]*. Lenel, *Edictum perpetuum*, 171. Although some extensions (to other contracts than sale) may have taken place, it is possible that the inclusion of *usureceptio* cases within the scope of the direct action would have gone one step too far. In that event an *actio in factum* or *actio utilis* would have been granted, which was modelled after the *actio Publiciana*.

87 See the overview provided by Wubbe, *Ius vigilantibus scriptum*, 238–239.

88 Ibid., 22–25, 239. Fuenteseca even goes so far as to say that the debtor remained civilian owner and that only the *usus* was temporarily transferred to the creditor. This is, however, irreconcilable with *mancipatio* and *in iure cessio* as modes of transferring civilian ownership. See Krämer, *Das besitzlose Pfandrecht*, 18, fnt. 15, referring to P. Fuenteseca, "Líneas generales de la '*fiducia cum creditore*'", in *Derecho romano de obligaciones*, ed. J. Paricio Serrano (Madrid: Ceura, 1994), 405–406. For archaic law even *pignus* can be analysed in terms of dual ownership: Kaser, *Studien zum römischen Pfandrecht*, 72–73.

coincided with his possession of the object for a considerable time, the law should respond by regarding him as the Quiritary (civilian) owner.

All this provides sufficient reason to say that analytically the *fiducia cum creditore* resulted in the debtor retaining some sort of proprietary interest in the object of *fiducia* transferred to the creditor. Although the latter acquired Quiritary ownership—*dominium*—, the debtor's interest in the object was more than a mere contractual claim for redelivery upon discharge. The *ius honorarium* was only partly responsible for this, mainly by granting the *actio Publiciana* to debtors in the process of regaining Quiritary ownership through *usureceptio*.

(v) *Redemption*

In classical law the debtor only appears to have had a right of redemption—i.e. the right to recover the object of security by satisfying the secured debt—by the end of the classical period. The Codex Justinianus contains a rescript by emperor Gordian III, which provides that an enforcement sale is invalid when the creditor refused to accept the money offered by the debtor before the sale took place. This text must be interpreted as granting the debtor the right of redemption.[89] Although this rescript deals with *pignus* only, it is plausible that the same would apply to *fiducia*, in particular on the basis of the *bona fides*.[90] In case of an actual enforcement sale to a purchaser, the debtor could only exercise the right of redemption against the purchaser if such a right of redemption had been agreed between the creditor and the purchaser.[91] This also appears from the rescript by Gordian, which unequivocally states that the enforcement sale cannot be revoked if the money was offered to the creditor after the creditor has exercised his power of sale.[92]

Finally, the Codex Justinianus contains a regulation by Justinian himself, which refers to an 'ancient law' pursuant to which the debtor still had one year to redeem the property after default.[93] This may have reflected the law of the postclassical period. The Justinianic enactment itself only

---

[89] C. 8,27(28),8 (239). The second part of the rescript deals with the case where the debtor offers to pay after the creditor has exercised his power of sale: this can only take place when the debtor has defaulted under the loan. It may be assumed that the first part of the rescript also deals with a situation where the debtor has already defaulted.

[90] Noordraven, *Die Fiduzia*, 259.

[91] D. 13,7,13 pr. (Ulpianus). See Kaser, *Das römische Privatrecht* I, 471.

[92] See also C. 8,19(20),2 (Diocletianus and Maximianus, 293). See W. Felgentraeger, *Antikes Lösungsrecht* (Berlin/Leipzig: De Gruyter, 1933), 23.

[93] C. 8,33(34),3 (530).

allows the creditor to sell the pledged objects two years after a written notification (*denuntiatio*) has been sent to the debtor or a judgment has been rendered against him, thus effectively extending the redemption period to two years. However, when the transaction documents indicated how and when a sale should take place, this prevailed. In other words, even here there was no 'equity of redemption' overriding the contractual terms of the security interest.

English Law

A similar development took place in English law, in respect of the mortgage and the equity of redemption.[94] A mortgage involves the transfer of the property which is being used for the purposes of security.[95] The mortgage is therefore structurally related to the Roman *fiducia cum creditore* rather than to *pignus* and *hypotheca*. The equity of redemption is the right to have transferred back this property upon the discharge of the secured debt.

Under the classical Common law mortgage (in general use until 1926), the debtor conveyed his land outright in fee simple to the creditor, with a covenant for reconveyance if the debt was properly discharged.[96] The debtor's only remedy for breach of this covenant at Common law was a personal action for damages.[97] The Common law courts construed mortgages 'strictly and unsympathetically'.[98] If a payment default occurred,

---

[94] See also Hazeltine, "The Roman *Fiducia*", *passim*; W. Erbe, *Die Fiduzia im römischen Recht* (Weimar: Böhlau, 1940), 78. This chapter will not discuss equitable mortgages, which may exist when an equitable interest (including the equity of redemption!) is mortgaged or when the formalities for creating a legal mortgage have not been satisfied: Smith, "Security", in *English Private Law*, par. 5.15–5.17.

[95] Under the Law of Property Act 1925, S. 85, a conveyance of a legal fee simple by way of mortgage is no longer possible. However, the equity of redemption continues to exist. Smith, "Security", in *English Private Law*, par. 5.11.

[96] Hazeltine stresses that the earliest form of the classical mortgage (the 'Littletonian mortgage'), which was occasionally used as late as the 1840s, was a conditional conveyance, subject to the condition subsequent of payment. Hazeltine, "The Roman *Fiducia*", xxvii–xlvii. This entailed that payment of the secured debt would *ipso facto* terminate the mortgagee's title (at xxxix). Accordingly, in contrast with the *pactum fiduciae*, which was purely contractual, the proviso for redemption, or reconveyance, had 'both proprietary and contractual effects', not only in Equity but also at Common law (at xlvii).

[97] A.W.B. Simpson, *A History of the Land Law*, 2nd ed. (Oxford: Oxford University Press, 1986), 242. For the other forms of mortgages, see ibid., 242–243. Mortgages were not restricted to land, although land was still regarded as the paradigm object at the beginning of the 19th century. W.R. Cornish *et al.*, *The Oxford History of the Laws of England XII: 1820–1914, Private law* (Oxford: Oxford University Press, 2010, cited as *OHLE* XII), 132.

[98] Simpson, *A History of the Land Law*, 243.

the mortgaged land was immediately forfeited to the creditor. This would even be the case where the value of the land grossly exceeded the amount of the debt. Moreover, in contrast with Roman law, forfeiture would not discharge the secured debt: the debtor would remain fully liable. However, from the mid-15th century onwards the Chancellor began to intervene in order to protect the debtor, first in 'peculiarly scandalous cases', later (probably from the 17th century onwards) as a matter of course.[99] Here lies the origin of the equity of redemption. Debtors were allowed to redeem (recover) the property, by payment within a reasonable time of the principal, interest and costs, even when they had defaulted and the land had been forfeited to the creditor under the terms of the mortgage deed. The equity of redemption evolved into 'a peculiar form of property which could be dealt with by the debtor like other forms of equitable property'.[100] At the same time, the creditor was granted a right of foreclosure, pursuant to which he could ask the court to decree that he would acquire absolute title to the mortgaged land, free from the debtor's equity of redemption, if the secured debt was not be paid within a certain period.[101]

Ultimately the mortgagor was simply regarded as the equitable owner of the land.[102] The debtor could dispose of this equitable property interest, by selling it to third parties, leaving it to his heirs, *etc*. Moreover, the equity of redemption could be invoked against third parties who acquired the legal title to the mortgaged property.[103] As a corollary, the creditor's legal title to the mortgaged property was in many respects treated as a security interest.

Comparison

In substance, there are strong similarities between Roman law and English law. The idea behind the equity of redemption is formulated by Simpson as follows:

---

99 Ibid., 244; D. Sugarman and R. Warrington, "Telling Stories: Rights and Wrongs of the Equity of Redemption", in *Property Law. Commentary and Materials*, ed. A. Clarke and P. Kohler (Cambridge: Cambridge University Press, 2005), 673–680, 674.

100 Simpson, *A History of the Land Law*, 245. The expression 'equity of redemption' now refers to this property interest and therefore has a wider meaning than the specific right to redeem. Beale *et al.*, *Personal Property Security*, par. 16.18, fnt. 70.

101 Simpson, ibid., 244; Sugarman and Warrington, "Telling Stories", 674.

102 Simpson, ibid., 245.

103 As to the position of a *bona fide* purchaser from the mortgagee, see Turner, *The Equity of Redemption*, 454–455, who notes that these cases were extremely rare.

> The general theory accepted in Chancery from the seventeenth century onwards was that a mortgage, whatever its outward form, was no more than a security for a debt, and that the mortgagee's rights to the land must be so limited in Chancery as to ensure that he obtained a security and no more.[104]

This is not unlike the treatment which the Roman *fiducia cum creditore* received over the course of the classical period. In both legal systems, although the creditor became the formal owner of the collateral, the debtor had more than a mere personal claim for reconveyance. It is clear, however, that the debtor's interest is far more articulated in English law than in Roman law. While in English law the equity of redemption developed into a full-fledged interest in the property, in Roman law the debtor's interest was never conceived as such. The debtor merely had a bundle of proprietary and personal rights, which analytically can be regarded as amounting to some sort of property interest.[105] Roman law comes closest to 'equitable' ownership in cases where the debtor could rely on *usureceptio*. This particular legal institution demonstrates that, as in English law, the creditor's ownership was rather formal and destined to be temporary. *Usureceptio*, however, was not an institution belonging to the *ius honorarium* but rather to the republican *ius civile*. Moreover under classical Roman law the right of redemption itself was not a matter of *ius honorarium*, but rather of the *bona fides* and late- and post-classical imperial rulings. All these differences should, however, not obscure the parallel lines of legal development by which Roman law and English law, in some respects, came to regard the debtor as the owner of the property.

Enforcement of Security

Roman Law

In respect of the creditor's right of recourse in case of default by the debtor, three (partly overlapping) stages of development can be distinguished, in all likelihood both for *fiducia* and *pignus*.[106] In the *first* stage, which may have lasted well into the 2nd century AD, the credi-

---

104 Simpson, *A History of the Land Law*, 246.

105 Hazeltine, "The Roman *Fiducia*", xlviii: 'Both the *fiducia* and the mortgage, viewed as transactional entities, are in fact bundles of proprietary and personal rights: and in each of these bundles the two classes of rights are intertwined in a complicated and somewhat confusing network.'

106 See also Kaser, *Studien zum römischen Pfandrecht*, 75–78; Noordraven, *Die Fiduzia*, 247.

tor's obligation to remancipate the object of *fiducia* extinguished when the debtor failed to discharge the secured debt in time. In case of *pignus*, the object of the pledge would be forfeited to the creditor as well, who would become its owner. From that point on the creditor could treat the object as his own, even if its value exceeded the amount of the secured debt.[107] It was apparently felt that a debtor who defaulted lost his right to the object of security. During this stage, the contracting parties already started to include an express authorisation in the documentation allowing the creditor to sell the object of security in case of a payment default.[108] From the law's perspective this was not necessary, as the creditor's right of ownership (*pignus* acquired after forfeiture) would already have enabled him to transfer the charged object to a purchaser at auction. In practice, however, such power of sale was always coupled with the provision that any surplus of the proceeds of a sale (*superfluum*) would be paid to the debtor, while the debtor would remain liable for any deficit (*reliquum*).[109] The main purpose of this combination of clauses was probably to prevent forfeiture of the object of security from fully discharging the debt in case the object was worth less than the amount of the debt.[110] Where the sale of objects of security was market practice, such a combination of clauses would also provide protection to the debtor in case the proceeds of a sale were higher than the amount of the secured debt. However, it should be stressed that all this was entirely voluntary: at this stage there was neither a legal obligation to sell nor one to pay the surplus to the debtor.

In the *second* stage, even in the absence of an express clause to that effect, the creditor may have become obliged by law to pay the surplus

107 The only difference was that in case of *fiducia*, ownership would immediately transfer to the creditor, whereas in case of *pignus* this would take place upon the debtor's default.

108 The epigraphic sources as well as the Digests contain contractual provisions granting the creditor the authority (not: imposing the obligation) to sell the collateral: *vendere liceat*. TPN 69 / TPSulp 79 (*pignus*); *FIRA* III, no. 91 (*fiducia*). See also D. 20,1,35 (Labeo); D. 44,3,14,5 (Scaevola); D. 46,1,63 (Scaevola); D. 20,3,3 (Paulus); D. 13,7,4 (Ulpianus); D. 13,7,6 pr. (Pomponius). In the same sense Gaius 2,64 and C. 4,24,4 (Alexander, 223). D. 20,5,4 (Papinianus) speaks of the exercise of a *vendendi pignoris potestas*. For a discussion of this licence to sell, see Verhagen, "Das Verfallpfand", 40–45.

109 TPN 69 / TPSulp 79 (*pignus*); *FIRA* III, no. 91 (*fiducia*). See Verhagen, "Das Verfallpfand", 40–45 (with further references). According to Camodeca TPN 67 / TPSulp 77 is a confirmation by the debtor that he had received the *superfluum* (HS 4,300) which remained after the auction of a slave who had been fiduciarily transferred. G. Camodeca, *Tabulae Pompeianae Sulpiciorum, Edizione critica dell'archivio puteolano dei Sulpicii* (Rome: Quasar, 1999), 176.

110 See Verhagen, "Das Verfallpfand", 40–45. *Contra* Noordraven, *Die Fiduzia*, 246–247.

to the debtor.[111] Exactly when a legal duty to pay the surplus came into being is impossible to indicate, although this may have been rather late. The basis of this obligation may have been the *bona fides*, both in case of *fiducia* and *pignus*.[112] In the Digests there is only one fragment by Ulpian (D. 13,7,24,2) which indicates that the creditor is obliged to pay the *superfluum* to the debtor, and then only after he has received the purchase price from the purchaser.[113] From another fragment (D. 20,1,16,9, Marcian) it can be deduced that a legal duty to pay the surplus existed at the time of emperor Septimius Severus. One would expect that during this stage the creditor would normally take recourse against the collateral by selling it to third parties, for only then would a surplus manifest itself. However, as D. 20,1,16,9 (Marcian, reviewed below) demonstrates, such a sale could also take place to the creditor himself.

In the *third* and final stage the creditor's principal legal remedy had become to sell the object of security. We can derive this from a rescript of 222 by emperor Alexander Severus, which provides in respect of a forfeiture clause that it should be read as referring to the right of enforcement granted to the creditor by general law, i.e. to sell the collateral to third parties.[114] A second rescript from Alexander Severus provides that

---

[111] Kaser, *Studien zum römischen Pfandrecht*, 75–78. Noordraven, *Die Fiduzia*, 247. According to these authors this happened in the 2nd century AD.

[112] The pledgor's contractual action against the pledgee—the *actio pigneraticia* (*directa*)—was originally *in factum concepta* and with it the claimant would claim the return of the object or its value in money. However, it is not entirely clear whether the *superfluum* could be also claimed with this action instead of the pledged object. This is one of the reasons why, according to Kaser, an *actio pigneraticia* with a *formula in ius concepta* and an *ex fide bona* clause came into existence during the course of the classical period. Kaser, *Studien zum römischen Pfandrecht*, 78–80.

[113] According to Noordraven this text deals with *fiducia*. Noordraven, *Die Fiduzia*, 245. Another fragment from the late classical period (or later, if this work is not by Paul) is from the *Pauli Sententiae* (PS 2,13,1): *Debitor distractis fiduciis a creditore de superfluo adversus eum habet actionem* ('When the [objects of] *fiducia* have been sold by the creditor, the debtor has an action against him for the *superfluum*').

[114] C. 8,34(35),1. *Imp. Alexander A. Victorino. Qui pactus est, nisi intra certum tempus pecuniam quam mutuatam accepit solveret, cessurum creditoribus, hypothecae venditionem non contraxit, sed id comprehendit, quod iure suo creditor in adipiscendo pignore habiturus erat. Communi itaque iure creditor hypothecam vendere debet* ('He who has agreed that, unless he should pay the money which he accepted as a loan within a certain time, he would cede to the creditors, has not made a contract of sale of the object of pledge; but this must be understood as only referring to the right which the creditor would (otherwise) have had in taking the pledge. The creditor must accordingly sell the object of pledge in accordance with the general law.') It is likely that the parties purported to effect a *datio in solutum* of the pledged object, but this is regarded in the rescript as an (apparently) invalid sale to the creditor.

if no interested purchasers can be found, the creditor may ask for the emperor's express permission (*impetratio dominii*) to retain ownership of the object of security (C. 8,33(34),1, of 229).[115] The consequence of these rescripts was, according to some modern authors,[116] that at this time forfeiture of the object of security to the creditor, even if expressly provided for by the parties, became invalid. This interpretation is, however, not without problems. Emperor Constantine's prohibition of forfeiture clauses (*leges commissoriae*) is of a much later date (320 or 326). Moreover, there are fragments from the late 2nd century AD which uphold the validity of a conditional sale of the pledged object by the debtor to the creditor, triggered by a default under the loan. One of these texts, D. 20,1,16,9 (Marcianus), expressly states, with reference to a rescript by the emperors Septimius Severus and Caracalla, that the purchase price must then reflect the market value (*iustum pretium*) of the pledged objects. It is certainly possible that this rescript by Septimius Severus and Caracalla, alluded to by Marcian, was already rendered obsolete several decades later by the rescripts of Alexander Severus and again in the next century by Constantine's unequivocal prohibition of forfeiture clauses. But my own interpretation is that forfeiture clauses (in the form of conditional sales) were still valid at the end of the classical period, provided that the collateral was valued at the market price, so that any surplus would go to the debtor.[117]

English Law

It has already been observed that mortgaged property would originally be forfeited to the creditor at law, and Equity intervened by granting the debtor the right to redeem it. As a corollary, Equity granted the creditor the right to request a decree of foreclosure: the English equivalent of the Roman *impetratio dominii*. Such a decree extinguishes the debtor's equity of redemption, so that the creditor will become the absolute owner of the mortgaged property. However, the court has a discretionary power to make an order for sale of the property at the request of any interested party (including the mortgagor). The court will only make such an order

115 This rescript concerned *pignus*, but according to Noordraven D. 13,7,24 pr. (Ulpianus) provides the same for *fiducia*. Noordraven, *Die Fiduzia*, 260.

116 Ibid., 259–262. For a different view see H.L.E. Verhagen, "Die Vereinbarung des Pfandverfalls im ius commune", *Zeitschrift für Europäisches Privatrecht* 19 (2011), 115.

117 Verhagen, "Die Vereinbarung", 122.

if full discharge of the secured debt is guaranteed, for instance by fixing a minimum price for the sale.[118]

It was felt to be a slow, inconvenient and expensive manner of enforcement, amongst other reasons because Chancery allowed debtors generous extensions of time to redeem their property. Transactional lawyers therefore looked for ways to circumvent the process of foreclosure and established the mortgage with a power of sale, which began to be included in mortgage deeds from the end of the 18th century.[119] Although legal commentators at that time argued that this power of sale could only be for an assignment of the secured debt itself, which would have left the debtor's power to redeem intact, judicial decisions soon held otherwise.[120] The power of sale came to be regarded as proprietary, in the sense that it extinguished the equity of redemption.[121] In the 1840s it had already become standard practice to attach a power of sale to mortgages and in 1860 legislation granted the mortgagee a statutory power of sale (which could be excluded by the parties).[122] It was held that the mortgagee held any surplus on trust. Moreover, the mortgagee could not sell to himself.[123]

An important principle developed by Equity in the 19th century is that provisions in mortgages that are 'clogs on the equity of redemption' will be void.[124] There are three types of 'clogs' or 'ties', the most interesting of which is formed by provisions which are inconsistent with or repugnant to the right to redeem and are thus irreconcilable with the nature of a mortgage.[125] Various views have been endorsed by judges as to the scope of this doctrine. Some judges have attributed a relatively wide scope to it and believed that the doctrine served to strictly control the nature of mortgages.[126] Other judges felt that freely bargained commercial transactions must be upheld, so that the doctrine is 'only applicable to the most obvious clogs'.[127] Modern legal writing goes even further and argues that

---

[118] Beale *et al.*, *Personal Property Security*, par. 17.27.

[119] *OHLE* XII, 135.

[120] *Clay v Sharpe* (1802) 18 Ves. Jr. 346; *Corder v Morgan* (1811) 18 Ves. Jr. 344.

[121] *OHLE* XII, 136.

[122] Ibid., 137.

[123] Ibid., 138.

[124] Beale *et al.*, *Personal Property Security*, par. 16.17.

[125] The other two categories of clogs are provisions which are unconscionable and provisions which are in the nature of penalty clauses. Ibid., par. 16.18.

[126] Ibid., par. 16.20, referring to *Noakes v Rice* [1902] AC 24 HL, 32 *per* Lord Macnaghten and 34 *per* Lord Davey and another decision.

[127] Ibid., par. 16.20, referring to *Santley v Wilde* [1899] 2 Ch. 474 CA.

there is much to be said for abolishing the doctrine altogether.[128] Nevertheless, the relatively recent case of *Jones v Morgan* (see below) demonstrates that the doctrine is still part of English law, albeit 'in the limited form set out by the House of Lords in the *Kreglinger* case' (see below).[129]

From a comparative perspective, it is interesting to consider whether a conditional sale of mortgaged property, triggered by default under the secured debt, would constitute a clog. It has been held in the famous *Kreglinger case* that the option granted to the mortgagee to purchase the property is a clog, as it is inconsistent with the right to redeem.[130] In the *Kreglinger case* it has also been held that where an advantage is conferred upon the mortgagee by a separate agreement, it is not a clog. In the more recent case of *Jones v Morgan* the Court of Appeal rejected the argument that an option to purchase the mortgaged property was separate, because it had been granted in an agreement made three years after the mortgage agreement.[131] According to the court this new agreement was a 'refinancing agreement', which was not independent from the mortgage agreement, so that the purchase option was inconsistent with the right to redeem and therefore void. With reluctance (not being a common lawyer), I venture to say that as a matter of English law, a conditional sale of the type contemplated by Marcian will also run a serious risk of being void. The sale has the effect that the mortgagor can no longer recover the mortgaged property and as such would be a clog on the right to redeem. It would seem that if the conditional sale were to be separately documented, this would not save it from voidness, as it only becomes operative on default under the secured debt and is therefore specifically linked to it and may not be substantially separate at all.

Comparison

When we look at the origin of the rules concerned, we can see that in English law the restrictions on the enforcement of security largely find their origin in Equity, while in Roman law they are rather the product of

---

128 Ibid., par. 16.24.

129 Ibid., par. 16.23.

130 *Kreglinger v New Patagonia Meat and Cold Storage Company Ltd* [1914] AC 25 HL, *per* Lord Parker at 51.

131 *Jones v Morgan* [2001] EWCA Civ. 995 CA.

the *ius civile* concept of *bona fides* and the '*ius novum*' (Severan rescipts).[132] When we concentrate on their substance, we may conclude that the evolution of the rules on enforcement of Roman law and English law has taken similar paths. Originally, the object of security would be forfeited to the creditor, while in the last stage the usual way of enforcement would be by a sale to a third party. Forfeiture would no longer be permitted unless with the permission of a judicial authority: the *impetratio dominii* in Roman law and the decree of foreclosure in English law. As the economic historian (and lawyer) Moses Finley observed in a study on land secured credit in classical Athens: '[i]n its earliest form, security is always substitution, a forfeit'. The shift from substitution to collateral (i.e. compulsory sale and a division of proceeds according to the amount of the secured debt and the value of the charged property) is the consequence of a 'profound economic transformation'.[133] According to Finley the cause of this transformation lies outside the law of security and has everything to do with the growing importance of credit. Credit providers are not interested in obtaining ownership of the object of security as such: they want to liquidate it as soon as possible, so as to be able to take recourse against the proceeds in order to satisfy their claims.[134] At the same time, debtors wish to lay their hands on the excess value of the collateral they provided. Thus, rules providing for a compulsory sale of collateral and the return of the *superfluum* to the debtor result in an equilibrium in which the interests of creditors and debtors are more or less balanced. This evolution from substitution to collateral security has taken place both in classical Roman law and English law.

One difference is that English law appears to be more hostile than Roman law with regard to conditional sales of collateral to the creditor. In respect of conditional sales of charged property it may be interesting to note that, although in the *ius commune* and even under the 19th-century codifications, conditional sales as envisaged by Marcian were held to be reconcilable with Constantine's prohibition of forfeiture clauses, the tide turned against them in the 20th century.[135] A conditional transfer of pledged objects which is exclusively triggered by default under the

---

[132] J.P. Coriat, *Le prince législateur: la technique législative des Sévères et les méthodes de creation du droit impérial à la fin du principat* (Rome: École française de Rome, 1997), 169–172.

[133] M.I. Finley, "Land, Debt, and the Man of Property in Classical Athens", *Political Science Quarterly* 68 (1953), 266.

[134] Ibid., 267.

[135] Verhagen, "Die Vereinbarung", 111–113.

secured debt is invalid. Thus the German Reichsgericht held that a sale of pledged property which was conditional upon breach of the loan agreement served to secure the creditor and was therefore invalid. The fact that the purchase price reflected the market value of the property and that the creditor would pay the debtor the difference between the market value and the amount to be paid under the loan could not detract from this.[136] In this respect the Common law and the civil law have converged (unfortunately, I would almost say). There are exceptions, however, such as Italian law, where, in contrast with the 'patto commissorio', 'the patto marciano' (*sic*) is regarded as valid.[137] In 2006 the law of charges of the French Code civil has been overhauled and it now recognizes that forfeiture clauses are valid, provided that the pledged object is valuated by an expert and that the surplus is returned to the debtor (Art. 2348 Cc).[138] This is basically the interpretation by the famous 14th-century commentator Bartolus de Saxoferrato, who held that the conditional sale described by Marcian in D. 20,1,16,9 should be accompanied by an assessment of the purchase price from a judge or an expert designated by the parties.[139]

Conclusion

Looking at the role of Equity in the evolution of real security in English law, one can identify two main functions: protecting the debtor against the harshness of the Common law and adapting the law to the needs of commerce. This is reflected in the response by Equity to transactional practices.

136 Reichsgericht 29 January 1918, *Entscheidungen des Reichsgerichts in Zivilsachen* 92, 101. See D. Schanbacher, "Die Gegenwart der Geschichte in der Rechtsprechung des Bundesgerichtshofs: *BGHZ* 130, 101", in *Iurisprudentia universalis. Festschrift für Theo Mayer-Maly zum 70. Geburtstag*, ed. M.J. Schermaier *et al.* (Cologne: Böhlau, 2002), 657–658.

137 N. Lipari and P. Rescigno, ed., *Diritto civile IV.2: Attuazione e tutela dei diritti. L'attuazione dei diritti* (Milan: Giuffrè, 2009), 212–213.

138 P. Ancel, "La réforme du droit des sûretés en France", in *La réforme du droit privé en France: un modèle pour le droit privé européen?*, ed. V. Sagaert (Brussels: Larcier, 2009), 29–47.

139 Bartolus de Saxoferrato, *In secundam Codicis partem* (ed. Venice, 1585), on C. 8,34(35),3, *f.* 104, at 'quoniam'. *Si pecuniam ad tempus non solves, sit fundus mihi emptus iusto pretio, declarando arbitrio talis et talis, quos et nunc eligimus in arbitratores, ac bonos viros et tene menti* ('If you do not pay the money in time, the land shall have been purchased by me for a just price, at the declared estimation of so and so, who we now elect as arbitrators, as honest men and with a sound judgment'). See Verhagen, "Die Vereinbarung", 131–132.

The first function resulted in Equity tending to strike out certain transactional practices. In Roman law this was largely achieved through *ius civile* concepts (*usureceptio* and *bona fides*) and through imperial intervention. The imperial rescripts practice (the '*ius novum*') in particular took over the role of adapting Roman law to the perceived needs of society after the consolidation of the *edictum perpetuum* when the innovative role of the *ius honorarium* was more or less finished. There is a constitution of emperor Constantine (AD 316), which may very well also reflect late classical law, from which it appears that the emperor's judicial function (*de facto*: that of his chancery) had become not unlike that of Chancery in England: to apply the law and correct it where equity (*aequitas*) required this.[140] In other words, in particular from the Severans onwards, it is the *ius novum* rather than the *ius honorarium* that can be regarded as Equity's Roman counterpart.

With respect to the second function, it can be concluded that Equity and *ius honorarium* really did run parallel courses. In relation to the floating charge and other forms of charge, both Equity and the *ius honorarium* have recognised new transactional practices and thus contributed decisively to the evolution of the law of security. Interactions between the legal system and the economy, mainly through transactional practices, largely took place via the Equity / *ius honorarium* 'stratum' of the legal system. Accordingly, both the Roman and English law of charges are to a large extent the product of the *ius honorarium* and Equity rather than of the *ius civile* and Common law.

[140] C. 1,14,1 (Constantinus): *Inter aequitatem iusque interpositam interpretationem nobis solis et oportet et licet inspicere* ('To solve doubts arising between equity and law must be left solely to us'). See also C.Th. 1,2,3 and Zwalve's contribution to this volume, 18 *seq.*

CHAPTER SEVEN

RESCISSION OF CONTRACTS: WAS ROMAN LAW MORE CONSISTENT THAN ENGLISH LAW?

F. Brandsma

Introduction

The Roman knight Gaius Canius went to Syracuse for a holiday, as he himself said. While there it became known that he desperately wanted to buy a seaside villa. The local banker Pythius heard of this and invited Canius to come and dine at his own seaside villa. Pythius stressed the fact he did not want to sell the house. He merely wanted to let Canius enjoy himself. When Caius came and sat on the porch enjoying the view an enormous fishing fleet appeared and anchored in the bay. Fish after fish was unloaded and laid at the feet of Pythius. It made Canius' mouth water. He had to buy the place, he told Pythius. Of course, Pythius at first refused to sell, but in the end he gave in. Pythius sold the villa to Canius for a not quite inconsiderable price and gave Canius the keys. The next day Canius sat on the porch once again and waited for the fishermen to come and serve him dinner. Of course, nothing happened. He went to his new neighbours and asked them whether it was perhaps a holiday for fishermen. They told him they were very surprised yesterday, because they had never seen these fishing boats before. Only then did Canius realise that he had been tricked into buying the property at a high price. What could be done about it? Nothing, as Gaius Aquilius Gallus had not yet introduced the *actio de dolo malo* and the *exceptio doli*.[1]

It is Cicero who relates this well-known story and one can almost sense the glee with which he does so.[2] This will not have been the first case of fraud committed in the history of mankind, but it was the case which led to the two mentioned praetorian remedies being designed. They were

[1] Whether *actio* and *exceptio* were both created by C. Aquilius Gallus is the subject of debate. See e.g. M. Kaser and K. Hackl, *Das römische Zivilprozessrecht* (Munich: Beck, 1996), par. 35, fnt. 35, with references.

[2] *De officiis* 3,14,58–60.

necessary because with regard to formal contracts liability followed from performing the formalities. The contract of sale, *emptio venditio*, is in itself not formal, but consensual, and gave rise to actions for both parties in which the so-called *clausula bonae fidei*, the clause of good faith, was to be found. It would, of course, not have been in good faith for Pythius to exact the purchase price from Canius. In an *actio venditi*, an action of sale, Canius could not have been held liable, because he was only liable to do what good faith required, *dare facere oportet ex fide bona*. So the purchase price must have been promised in a formal way. The debate among scholars is whether Canius promised to pay the price by way of stipulation, a verbal contract, or by way of a *contractus litteris*, a contract in writing, which one can perhaps compare to a deed.[3] These were valid once the words required were spoken or the debt had been written down. Without any specific remedies the debtor who had performed would not be able to recover what he had given to the creditor, and he would not be able to defend himself against the claim of the creditor, notwithstanding the fraud committed by the creditor. That is where the *actio de dolo* and the *exceptio doli* came in.

Roman Law

The *actio de dolo* was a penal action introduced in the praetorian edict to come to the relief of a debtor who had performed although the contract had been procured by fraud. The *exceptio doli* could be used when the debtor had not yet performed and was being sued by the creditor. This exception was only necessary with regard to *stricti iuris* contracts, contracts of strict law. These were formal, one-sided contracts, in which there was just one debtor and one creditor. They were enforced by the so-called *condictio*, which was an action for a certain amount in which the clause of good faith was not contained. The defendant was liable for the amount specified, but not liable to do what good faith required, *dare facere oportet ex fide bona*, which would have transformed the action into one for an unspecified amount. In case of *bonae fidei* contracts the contracting parties were both creditor and debtor of one another. That meant there had

[3] See e.g. U. von Lübtow, "Die Ursprungsgeschichte der exceptio doli und der actio de dolo malo", in *Eranion in honorem Georgii S. Maridakis* I (Athens: Klissiuni, 1963), 183 *seq.*; W.J. Zwalve, "Sola scriptura, An essay in comparative legal history on 'obligacions' in thirteenth century France and England", *TvR* 80 (2012), 95 *seq.*

to be some kind of equilibrium between the reciprocal obligations. What one party had to perform depended upon what the other had to perform, so good faith came in and some indefiniteness had to be taken for granted. In case of fraud that meant the debtor did not have to use an exception, but could merely state he was not obliged to perform on the basis of the requirements of good faith. The action against him had to be dismissed. But did that also mean the debtor who had already performed could claim the contract was void and could reclaim as being not due what he had delivered, by way of the *condictio indebiti*, or, better still, the *condictio ob turpem causam*? That conclusion seems not to have been drawn. So in the case of executed *bonae fidei* contracts another way of restitution was necessary and the *actio de dolo* could be brought.

As said, the *actio de dolo* was penal in nature. The defrauder could be condemned to the value of the performance rendered to him and this condemnation brought infamy with it. This penalty entailed certain civil disabilities, such as the loss of the right to sue in civil and criminal cases and the loss of eligibility to certain magistracies.[4] The action furthermore contained a *clausula arbitraria*. That meant the judge appointed to adjudicate the matter had to give the defendant an opportunity to return what he had received to the plaintiff. If the defendant complied, he was not condemned and did not receive the stain of infamy. This probably was the way in which restitution was accomplished. It has been the subject of debate whether a separate remedy of *in integrum restitutio* was granted.[5] Traces of it have not been found. It has been suggested that the Byzantine compilers of Justinian's codes are responsible for this, because they would have merged the *in integrum restitutio* on account of fraud into the *actio de dolo*.[6] Oh, these Byzantines. 'The less one knows of them the more

[4] See e.g. M. Kaser and R. Knütel, *Römisches Privatrecht*, 19th ed. (Munich: Beck, 2008), par. 13.13.

[5] In favour: e.g. E. Levy, "Zur nachklassischen in integrum restittutio", *ZSS* 68 (1951), 360 *seq.* and 410 *seq.* Against: A. Wacke, "Kannte das Edikt eine in integrum restitutio propter dolum?", *ZSS* 88 (1971), 105 *seq.*; O. Lenel, *Das Edictum perpetuum*, 3rd ed. (Leipzig: Tauchnitz, 1927), 115 *seq.*; F. Schulz, "Die Lehre vom erzwungenen Rechtsgeschäft im antiken römischen Recht", *ZSS* 43 (1922), 237, fnt. 5; F. Schulz, *Classical Roman Law* (Oxford: Clarendon, 1951), 608; U. von Lübtow, *Der Ediktstitel 'Quod metus causa gestum erit'* (Greifswald: L. Bamberg, 1932), 87 *seq.*; B. Kupisch, *In integrum restitutio und vindicatio utilis bei Eigentumsübertragungen im klassichen römischen Recht* (Berlin: De Gruyter, 1974), 241 *seq.*; A. Hartkamp, "Die Drittwirkung der *in integrum restitutio*", in *Daube Noster. Essays in Legal History for David Daube*, ed. A. Watson (Edinburgh: Scottisch Academic Press, 1974), 131 *seq.*

[6] E.g. O. Karlowa, *Römische Rechtsgeschichte* II (Leipzig: Veit, 1901), 1069; see Kupisch, *In integrum restitutio*, 242, fnt. 5.

easily one thinks of them as monsters of whom anything might well be believed', as Liebs once said.[7] *Communis opinio* nowadays appears to be that the aim of *in integrum restitutio* was realized by the *actio de dolo* and its *clausula arbitraria*.[8]

A specific feature of the *actio de dolo* was that it was not available against third parties who had not perpetrated the fraud.

> C. 4,44,10: Emperors Diocletian and Maximian to Aemilius Severus: Fraud of the purchaser depends upon the nature of his acts, not on the quantity of the price. If such fraud is shown to have been committed, the vendor has no action to recover the property (*vindicatio*) against the person to whom the purchaser transferred ownership, but an action of restitution to his former condition against the person with whom he had made his contract.[9]

In this and some other respects the *actio de dolo* differed from the action which was provided in cases of contracts concluded by way of coercion, force or the threat of force, which for the moment I will collectively call duress. The remedies to relieve debtors who were coerced into contracts by way of force, *vis*, or the fear, *metus*, the force had engendered, were devised about the same time as the remedies against fraud, that is at the beginning of the 1st century BC. From the days of the Gracchus brothers, Rome had seen quite a lot of violence and coercion—not that the Romans were unaccustomed to violence before.[10] The remedies developed in this area were on the one hand a bit harsher, but on the other hand less severe than those concerning fraud. The action which was provided for restitutionary purposes was once again a penal action. It was the *actio quod metus causa* and it led to a condemnation of the coercer to four times the value of the performance coerced. This time the action did not involve infamy. The condemnation *in quadruplum* of itself was sufficient to force the defendant to use the possibility offered by the *clausula arbitraria* to

---

[7] "The History of the Roman *Condictio* up to Justinian", in *The Legal Mind, Essays for Tony Honoré*, ed. N. McCormick and P.B.H. Birks (Oxford: Clarendon, 1986), 182.

[8] See e.g. M. Kaser, *Das römische Privatrecht* I (Munich: Beck, 1971), par. 59 IV 1.

[9] *Impp. Diocletianus et Maximianus Aemilio Severo: Dolus emptoris qualitate facti, non quantitate pretii aestimatur. Quem si fuerit intercessisse probatum, non adversus eum, in quem emptor dominium transtulit, rei vindicatio venditori, sed contra illum cum quo contraxerat in integrum restitutio competit.* F.H. Blume trans., *Annotated Justinian Code*, 2nd ed. T. Kearley (2010), at: https://uwacadweb.uwyo.edu/blume&justinian/default.asp.

[10] See A.W. Lintott, *Violence in Republican Rome* (Oxford: Clarendon, 1968, 2nd ed. 1999), 175 *seq.*; R. Zimmermann, *The Law of Obligations. Roman Foundations of the Civilian Tradition* (Oxford: Clarendon, 1996), 651 *seq.*

prevent condemnation by voluntarily parting with the objects obtained by coercion. It has been suggested infamy was not coupled with the action because many members of the Roman nobility would not have escaped it in those days.[11] The coerced debtor who was sued could avail himself of the *exceptio quod metus causa* if necessary. Once again this was the case with formal contracts, not with *bonae fidei* contracts. These bilateral contracts were unenforceable when concluded under pressure of force. No exception was needed to reach this result. However, the texts do not speak of performance upon the basis of contracts which were null and void and so it seems that specific restitutionary remedies remained necessary also with regard to *bonae fidei* contracts, if performance had already taken place. Whether under classical Roman law restitution was effected by the *actio quod metus causa* itself, or whether a separate *in integrum restitutio* existed, has also been the subject of debate.[12] At least under Justinianic law restitution was realized by the penal action.[13]

We find slightly more, though not a lot, of theory developed by the Roman lawyers with regard to the validity of contracts concluded under duress. *Coactus tamen volui* is the famous phrase used by Paul.[14] Although coerced I have chosen to contract, one could translate. The person under the threat of force still has a choice: to contract or not to contract. Not that the last alternative is appealing in cases of force, but still, a will has been formed, although under peculiar circumstances. This leads to the conclusion that these contracts are valid to begin with, but can be avoided or rescinded by the party coerced. This was true, all agreed, with regard to formal contracts. Was it also true with regard to consensual contracts? Paul seems to have thought so. His maxim explained why these forced contracts were still binding and why special remedies were necessary to avoid them. But Ulpian states in one of the *regulae iuris*: 'Nothing is more contrary to consensus, which is the foundation of *bonae fidei* actions, than violence and intimidation.'[15] Of course, even Ulpian could not deny the

[11] See e.g. Kaser, *Das römische Privatrecht* I, par. 59 III 2b *i.f.*; Zimmermann, *Law of Obligations*, 655 *seq.*, and in general A. Hartkamp, *Der Zwang im römischen Privatrecht* (Amsterdam: Hakkert, 1971), 250 *seq.*

[12] Kupisch, *In integrum restitutio*, 123 *seq.* argues for the *actio quod metus causa* as a way of realizing restitution. He refers, at 124, fnt. 5, to the authors favoring a separate *in integrum restitutio*.

[13] See Kupisch, *In integrum restitutio*, 124, fnt. 6 and 7.

[14] D. 4,2,21,5.

[15] D. 50,17,116 pr.: *nihil consensui tam contrarium est, qui ac bonae fidei iudicia sustinet, quam vis atque metus.*

validity according to the *ius civile* of formal contracts made under duress. He seems to imply, however, that there is no consensus when a *bona fide* contract is coerced. In modern terms one would speak of void contracts as opposed to avoidable contracts.[16] These conclusions were not drawn by the Roman lawyers. They were thinking in terms of the remedies provided and the actions and exceptions granted; the forms of action, to speak in the terms of the common lawyer. Hartkamp has argued Ulpian considered these contracts to be null and void.[17] His evidence is, however, circumstantial. A text would have to be found in which the remedy of the coerced is the *condictio indebiti*, or, better still, the *condictio ob turpem causam*. As far as I can see, there is no such text.

Another argument can be taken from the effect duress had as regards third parties. D. 4,2,14,5 is quite clear.[18]

> Hence, some think that a buyer in good faith from a person who has brought force to bear is not liable, nor is one who accepted the property as a gift or was left it as a legacy. But Vivianus very rightly held that even such persons are liable, in order that the duress which I suffered should not cause me loss. Pedius also in his eighth book writes that the discretion of the judge in the matter of *restitutio* is such that he may indeed order the person who brought force to bear to make *restitutio* even if the property is in the hands of another and further that he may order the person in whose hands it is to make *restitutio*, even though it was another who exercised duress. For duress exercised by one person ought not to be the means of another's advantage.[19]

---

16 See in this respect the discussion under the Common law about the effect of duress on the validity of contracts, especially with regard to the theory that duress 'overbears the will' of the party coerced, so there is no consent. This theory has been invoked in the cases accepting economic duress. See e.g. *Pao On v Lau Yiu* [1980] AC 614, and especially 635–636. A criminal case on the defence of duress to a charge of murder, however, rejects this theory. *Lynch v Director of Public Prosecutions for Northern Ireland* [1975] AC 653. Lord Wilberforce e.g. states that duress does not negative intention, but that it is a matter of *coactus volui*, at 680. Lord Simon gives the fullest analysis, at 685 *seq*., and discusses the text of Paul (D. 4,2,21,5), 694 *seq*. See P.S. Atiyah, "Economic Duress and the 'Overborne Will' ", *LQR* 98 (1982), 197 *seq*., who calls the analysis of *Lynch* 'the sounder theoretical footing', at 202. The discussion was taken up by D. Tiplady in the next issue (*LQR* 99 (1983), 188 *seq*.), to which Atiyah responded at 353 *seq*. See now also *Borelli v Ting* [2010] UKPC 21, at fnt. 34 *per* Lord Saville: 'Duress is the obtaining of agreement or consent by illegitimate means', with a reference to *Lynch*.

17 Hartkamp, *Der Zwang*, 106 *seq*.

18 See Hartkamp, *Der Zwang*, 211.

19 Ulpianus, *libro undecimo ad edictum. Unde quidam putant bona fide emptorem ab eo qui vim intulit comparantem non teneri nec eum qui dono accepit vel cui res legata est. Sed rectissime Viviano videtur etiam hos teneri, ne metus, quem passus sum, mihi captiosus sit. Pedius quoque libro octavo scribit arbitrium iudicis in restituenda re tale esse, ut eum quidem*

Romanist literature once again used to be more engaged with the question whether this opinion is classical, or whether the horrible Byzantines have laid their hands upon it.[20] As far as Justinianic law is concerned the text speaks for itself. Third parties, even *bona fide* ones, cannot profit from duress. Any dogmatic explanations are omitted from the reasoning.

A modern day civil lawyer would say the contract is avoided *ab initio*, which works retroactively. So the cause or title for the delivery to the coercer was not valid. The coercer did not acquire ownership and could not have transferred it to the third party. This kind of reasoning is absent from the Roman texts. As regards the question whether these contracts are considered to be void or voidable, and in the last case whether this works retroactively, they are silent, or at least inconclusive, but perhaps these kinds of questions are too modern to pose for Roman law proper. To understand this last remark, a comparison with the Common law will be useful.

English Law

The Common law in its wide sense, including Law and Equity, has the remedy of rescission at its disposal for contracts made as a consequence of fraud or duress.[21] This is already a bold statement, because the terminology is not quite settled. Rescission is used more in connection with fraud than with duress. Avoidance seems to be the term used in case of duress. Modern day literature uses the term indiscriminately in a variety of cases where a contract is robbed of its legal effects. The law of rescission has been called 'a jurisprudential jungle', by Lord Walker of Gestingthorpe, one of the Justices of the UK Supreme Court.[22] I will use the term both in cases of fraud and in cases of duress.

Rescission cannot be considered an exclusively equitable remedy. Rescission was possible both at Law and in Equity before the Common

qui vim admisit iubeat restituere, etiamsi ad alium res pervenit, eum autem ad quem pervenit, etiamsi alius metum fecit: nam in alterius praemium verti alienum metum non oportet. Translation by A. Watson *et al.*, *The Digest of Justinian* (Philadelphia: University of Pennsylvania Press, 1985).

20 See the references given by Kupisch, *In integrum restitutio*, 208.

21 See in general D. O'Sullivan, S. Elliott and R. Zakrzewski, *The Law of Rescission* (Oxford: Oxford University Press, 2008) and e.g. H.C. Black, *A Treatise on the Rescission of Contracts and Cancellation of Written Instruments* (Kansas City, Mo.: Vernon Law Book Company, 1916), who deals with the matter in no less than 1780 pages.

22 Foreword to O'Sullivan *et al.*, *The Law of Rescission*, v.

Law Procedure Act 1854.[23] The way in which it was done, however, and the grounds for doing so differed. In the Common law courts rescission was something which the innocent party chose to do and the court merely gave effect to this choice. Let us take the case of fraud. On the discovery of the fraud perpetrated by the other party, the defrauded party could rescind the contract and treat it as void. If, for instance, in a sale of goods procured by fraud the innocent vendor had delivered the goods to the fraudulent buyer, the vendor could choose which form of action he preferred. If he wanted to claim damages he could use the writ of deceit. Deceit was, and is, a tort which was actionable against the defrauder, based on the fraud committed.[24] The innocent vendor could also choose to rescind the contract and then reclaim the goods delivered.[25] Rescission meant title revested in the vendor. The buyer lost title and no longer held the goods on the basis of the contract of sale, which had been rescinded. His refusal to hand the goods back voluntarily to the owner meant he committed what originally was the tort of detinue, but which later came to be absorbed by the tort of trover.[26] 'Trover' was an Anglo-Norman word meaning 'to find', just like the French 'trouver'. It came to be used for claims regarding things lost and found. The finding of lost things was, of course, not tortious. But if a finder refused to hand back found goods to the owner who reclaimed them he committed the tort. The loss and finding later became fictionalized.[27] Any refusal to hand back goods to the owner by anyone not having a right to possession constituted trover. Trover then became conversion as the tort is known nowadays.[28]

As regards the effect of fraud on the contract induced by it, the case of *Load v Green* seems to be of importance.[29] The case was decided by the Court of the Exchequer and the judgment was delivered by Baron Parke. It was a case concerning, among other things, handkerchiefs bought by Bannister from the plaintiffs, Load and another. At the trial, before Chief Baron Pollock, the jury found that Bannister had bought the goods with

---

[23] See e.g. O'Sullivan *et al.*, *The Law of Rescission*, 47 *seq.*

[24] See on the history of deceit e.g. T.A. Street, *The Foundations of Legal Liability I: Theory and principles of Tort*, (Northport: Edward, 1906), 374 *seq.*

[25] See *Towers v Barrett* (1786) 99 Eng. Rep. 1014.

[26] See on the history of trover e.g. J.W. Salmond, "Observations on trover and conversion", *LQR* 21 (1905), 43 *seq.*; J.B. Ames, "The history of trover", *HLR* 11 (1897), 277 *seq.*; and more recently S. Green and J. Randall, *The Tort of Conversion* (Oxford: Hart, 2009), 5 *seq.*

[27] See also O'Sullivan *et al.*, *The Law of Rescission*, 51, fnt. 15.

[28] See the Common Law Procedure Act 1852, S. 49. See also e.g. *OBG Ltd v Allan* (HL) [2008] 1 AC 87 *seq. per* Baroness Hale.

[29] (1846) 153 Eng. Rep. 828.

the fraudulent intention of not paying for them. The goods were delivered to him and a few days later he was declared bankrupt.[30] The defendants, Green and others, were the assignees in bankruptcy who took the goods into their possession. The plaintiffs 'elected to treat the contract as void' and brought an action in trover against the assignees.[31] Baron Parke stated as his opinion that 'as the goods were obtained by a fraudulent purchase, the plaintiffs had a right to disaffirm it, to revest the property in them, and recover their value in an action of trover against the bankrupt'.[32] So the plaintiffs had a right to recover their value in the hands of the assignees as well.[33] In another passage he gave as his opinion the plaintiffs 'had a right to annul the contract, and be again the real owners'.[34] By way of *obiter dictum* he stated that 'the transaction is not absolutely void, except at the option of the seller: he may elect to treat it as a contract, and he must do the contrary before the buyer has acted as if it were such, and resold the goods to a third party.'[35]

Prior to this decision it was not clear whether a sale of goods obtained by fraud changed the property in the goods, and, in other words, whether the contract was void or voidable. There were decisions pointing in the direction of nullity.[36] Holdsworth points to the interchangeability with

---

30 At least it was assumed to be so for the sake of the decision, although in fact the bankruptcy had been declared before the date of the sale and subsequent delivery. The outcome of the case was declared to have been the same in both sets of circumstances: 153 Eng. Rep. 828, at 830. See *infra*, fnt. 33.

31 The assignees claimed to have the right to possess the goods under the Bankruptcy Act (S. 72, 6 Geo. 4 (1825), c. 16; formerly 21 Jac. 1 (1624)). This Act was designed to bring within the power of the assignees in bankruptcy everything which was in the possession of the bankrupt with the consent and permission of the true owner. This permission of the true owner enabled the future bankrupt to appear worthy of credit. This should not be to the detriment of the creditors who relied on the apparent ownership of the debtor, so that 'everything whereby the trader obtained fictitious credit' was 'within the power of disposition of the assignees', as was said on behalf of the assignees, 153 Eng. Rep. 828, at 829.

32 153 Eng. Rep. 828, at 830.

33 Unless the assignees had been entitled to the goods under the Act, which they were not, because the debtor who bought the goods had become the true owner, not just the apparent owner, until the moment of rescission. For the Act to be applicable the goods had to be in the possession of the bankrupt as apparent owner before bankruptcy was declared. If he had already been declared bankrupt at the moment he came into possession of the goods, as was in fact the case, the Act was not applicable anyhow.

34 153 Eng. Rep. 828, at 831.

35 153 Eng. Rep. 828, at 829, with reference to the cases of *Parker v Patrick* (1793) 101 Eng. Rep. 99; and *Wright v Lawes* (1801) 170 Eng. Rep. 649.

36 See e.g. *Ferguson v Carrington* (1829) 109 Eng. Rep. 22, at 23. See O'Sullivan *et al.*, *The Law of Rescission*, 48 *seq.*

which the terms void and voidable were used.[37] In most cases it did not matter whether the contract was considered void or voidable. The consequences would be the same between the defrauded party and the defrauder. The difference would only be felt in a case where the rights of a third party were concerned. The *obiter dictum* of Parke B was therefore the clearest indication of his opinion that the contract was voidable, not void.[38] He said, if I read him correctly, that sale by the fraudulent buyer to an innocent third party would defeat the possibility of restitution. The title of the fraudulent buyer was defeasible as long as he had not passed it on to a third party. Trover against the third party would not lie. Of course, deceit against the defrauder would be possible.

This decision has been followed since then, and rights of innocent third parties acquired before rescission are unassailable. This means there is no retroactivity involved in rescission, although one speaks of avoidance *ab initio*. I have not found this stated explicitly anywhere, but how can it be otherwise. Perhaps this betrays the way of thinking of a civil lawyer as opposed to a common lawyer. In this respect the common lawyer seems to have more in common with the Roman lawyer. The conclusion of Parke B that the contract is voidable instead of void seems to have followed his conclusion, based on the cited cases, that the buyer had title, and could pass it on until the moment of rescission. That appears to be a somewhat odd conclusion, 'but it reflected both the primacy of the regime of the forms of action at the time, and also a dynamic in which principles of substantive law emerged as by-products of the availability of particular forms of action.'[39]

Modern day civil law would base its conclusions on the requirement of *iusta causa*. After rescission there never would have been a valid cause for transfer of property, so title never passed and could never have been passed on, cases of bona fide purchasers of goods excepted. Retroactively, the transfer is feigned never to have happened. When *bona fide* purchasers

37 W.S. Holdsworth, *A History of English Law* VIII (London: Methuen, 1925), 66 *seq*.

38 See on 'The Rise of the Will Theory' and the influence of Pothier in this respect e.g. D. Ibbetson, *A Historical Introduction to the Law of Obligations* (Oxford: Oxford University Press, 1999), 220 *seq*., 232 *seq*.; P.S. Atiyah, *The Rise and Fall of Freedom of Contract* (Oxford: Clarendon, 1979), 406.

39 O'Sullivan *et al.*, *The Law of Rescission*, 53. W.J. Swadling has argued *Load v Green* was wrongly decided and that rescission should not carry with it revesting of title: "Rescission, Property, and the Common Law", *LQR* 121 (2005), 123 *seq*. According to him the cases used by Parke B applied the principle of abstraction, so the third party acquired and kept title independent of the fate of the rescindable contract. See on this D. Sheehan, *The Principles of Personal Property Law* (Oxford: Hart, 2011), 170 *seq*.

are excepted, this means they are exempted from the *nemo plus*-rule, or the *nemo dat*-rule as the common lawyer would say. Under the Common law there is no such general exception to the *nemo dat*-rule. The innocent second buyer becomes owner because he bought from the first buyer who was still owner before rescission took place.[40]

Rescission at law also meant that the defendant availing himself of that opportunity was provided with a defence at Law to a claim to enforce the contract, whether it was a deed or a parole agreement.[41] With regard to deeds the defence of duress had long been established.[42] However, this came to be seen as an anomaly. In one of his lectures on 'Points in Legal History' given at Harvard Law School in the year 1886–87, entitled 'Specialty Contracts and Equitable Defences', James Barr Ames stated this opinion as follows.

> The general rule, that the misconduct of the obligee in procuring or enforcing a specialty obligation was no bar at common law to an action upon the instrument, was subject to one exception.

Ames goes on to say that 'as far back as Bracton's time' an action on a deed could be defeated by pleading 'duress practised upon the defendant by the plaintiff'. He calls it 'the anomalous allowance of the defense of duress at Common law', which 'may be due to some forgotten statute'. He disapproves of it and stresses that 'the defense of duress does not differ in its nature from the defense of fraud', which, according to him, was

40 See e.g. *White v Garden* (1851) 135 Eng. Rep. 364. See now Sale of Goods Act 1979, S. 23: 'When the seller of goods has a voidable title to them, but his title has not been avoided at the time of the sale, the buyer acquires a good title to the goods, provided he buys them in good faith and without notice of the seller's defect of title'; and e.g. Sheehan, *Principles*, 68 *seq*., 197 *seq*. The continental reader should remember that sale of goods itself transfers title under the Common law, not delivery. The notion of abstract or causal transfer of title is hardly discussed in this respect, but see now Swadling and Sheehan, mentioned *supra*, 170, fnt. 39.

41 See O'Sullivan *et al.*, *The Law of Rescission*, 272 *seq*. (contracts) and 669 *seq*. (deeds). Ibbetson, *Historical Introduction*, 71, points to the fact that in early cases the question of the voluntariness of the contract was 'raised to the surface' only in actions based on a deed, 'for in actions based on oral transactions any dispute about voluntariness would commonly be concealed behind the general denial of liability away from the gaze of the legal historian.' See the question as regards the formal contracts under Roman law, *supra*, 162 *seq*.

42 See Holdsworth, *HEL* VIII, 51 for Year Book authority. See Ibbetson, *Historical Introduction*, 71 *seq*.; J.B. Ames, *Lectures on Legal History and Miscellaneous Legal Essays* (Cambridge, Mass.: Harvard University Press, 1913), 113; O'Sullivan *et al.*, *The Law of Rescission*, 671 *seq*. The leading case was *Whelpdale's case* (1604), 77 Eng. Rep. 239, at 240.

no defence at Law, but only in Equity. Ames makes a comparison with Roman law which is telling.

> The Roman law was more consistent than the English law in this respect. For, by the *jus civile*, duress, like fraud, was no answer to a claim upon a formal contract. All defenses based upon the conduct of the obligee were later innovations of the praetor, and were known as *exceptiones praetoriae*, or as we should say, equitable defenses.[43]

According to O'Sullivan *et al.*, Ames was successful in promoting the notion that, unlike duress, fraud was not a defence to a deed at Law, as opposed to Equity.[44] Ames' view was based on two authorities, *Mason v Ditchbourne and Sarson* and *Wright v Campbell*.[45] As O'Sullivan *et al.* show, these decisions do not provide convincing support for Ames' view.[46] *Mason* was effectively reversed on appeal, a fact which Ames does not mention.[47] Nevertheless *Mason* was followed in *Wright*. So *Wright* appears to be a decision given *per incuriam* and therefore not binding. Apart from that, a group of other decisions taken in the 1830s and 1840s did in fact recognize fraud as a defence at Law to an action based on a deed.[48] O'Sullivan *et al.* conclude that both fraud and duress provided grounds for a defence to an action upon a deed at Law, but that, whereas the duress defence was long established, the fraud defence was first accepted during the first half of the 19th century.[49] Here we have a fine example of a comparison to Roman Law and Equity which did not make things easier for English Law and Equity, at least for a while.[50]

---

43 Ames, *Lectures*. The lecture was later published in *HLR* 9 (1895–1896), 49 seq. (at 57) and collected in the work cited in the previous note.

44 O'Sullivan *et al.*, *The Law of Rescission*, 672, with reference to Ames, *Lectures*, 106 (= *HLR* 9 (1895–1896), 51). See e.g. W.T. Barbour, "The History of Contract in Early English Equity", in *Oxford Studies in Social and Legal History* IV, ed. P. Vinogradoff (Oxford: Clarendon, 1914), 1 *seq.*, at 23; D. Ibbetson, *Historical Introduction*, 72.

45 *Mason* (1835) 174 Eng. Rep. 158; *Wright* (1861) 175 Eng. Rep. 1111.

46 *The Law of Rescission*, 673 *seq.*

47 See 174 Eng. Rep. 158, at 159 (end note). See *Connop v Holmes* (1835) 150 Eng. Rep. 304, at 305 (note a).

48 O'Sullivan *et al.*, *The Law of Rescission*, 674 mention *Edwards v Brown, Harries and Stephens* (1831) 148 Eng. Rep. 1436; *D'Aranda v Houston* (1834), 172 Eng. Rep. 1342; *Connop v Holmes* (1835) 150 Eng. Rep. 304 and *Spencer v Handley and Burges* (1842) 134 Eng. Rep. 169. These decisions were confirmed in *Evans v Edmonds* (1853) 138 Eng. Rep. 1407, and *Canham v Barry* (1855) 139 Eng. Rep. 558.

49 *The Law of Rescission*, 675.

50 It appears duress was not the basis of an action in tort. Statements to the effect that duress is actionable as a tort have been recent and *obiter*. See e.g. Lord Scarman in *The Universe Sentinel* [1983] AC 366, at 400.

So if rescission in case of fraud or duress was possible at law, where is the role of Equity in all this? Chancery provided remedies where the Common law courts could not achieve justice. Even the judges themselves admitted it, according to Chancery. 'We find that the judges themselves in their own courts, when there appeared unto them matter of equity, because they by their oath and office could not stay the judgments, except it be for some small time, have directed the parties to seek relief in Chancery.'[51] Equity acted differently. It was not the party defrauded who rescinded the contract, as at Law. A defrauded party wishing to rescind in Equity asked the court to do so instead.[52] Consequential relief could also be asked. All this was asked by bringing a bill. If the Court of Chancery found grounds to do so, it would itself effect rescission. This could be done in either of two ways. In case of an executory contract, a contract which still had to be performed, the court could grant orders for injunction and cancellation. The injunction served to prevent an action at Law.[53] The order for cancellation served to invalidate instruments such as a deed. In case of an executed contract, a contract already performed, the orders were for restitution to the plaintiff, for counter-restitution, if necessary, and for any other relief which was necessary. Most of these forms of order were not available at Law.

The grounds for granting equitable relief for fraud were also wider than at Law. Lord Hardwicke, Lord Chancellor in 1750, described the grounds for rescission in the case of *The Earl of Chesterfield and others against Sir Abraham Janssen, Baronet*.[54] He did so by defining 'fraud'. 'This court can certainly relieve against all kinds and species of fraud,' he stated. Fraud could be clear and express fraud, *dolus malus*, but it also could arise from circumstances and the necessity of the person at the time. Hard and unconscionable bargains could also be construed as fraudulent. Even the Common law had done so. In this case a bond had been taken by the defendant, Janssen, for a debt of £ 5.000 of John Spencer, Esq. The bond was for payment of £ 10.000, with a penalty of £ 20.000. The debt was not paid in full by Spencer before he died and his executors brought a bill to be relieved against Janssen's demand of payment of the penalty, as an unconscionable bargain, and a usurious contract. Lord Hardwicke went on to define fraud and stated:

---

51 Cited from Holdsworth, *HEL* V, 326, fnt. 1.

52 See for the following in particular O'Sullivan *et al.*, *The Law of Rescission*, 62 *seq.*

53 *Pennell v Millar* (1857) 53 Eng. Rep. 68, at 71.

54 26 Eng. Rep. 191, at 224–25.

> this court will relieve against presumptive fraud, so that Equity goes further than the rule of law, for there fraud must be proved, and not presumed only. To take an advantage of another man's necessity, is equally bad, as taking advantage of his weakness, and in such situation, as incapable of making the right use of his reason. [...] Fraud has been constantly presumed, or inferred from circumstances, and conditions of parties; weakness and necessity on one side, and extortion and avarice on the other, and merely from the intrinsic unconscionableness of the bargain.

Fraud defined in this way covered fraud in the traditional sense, but also duress and undue influence, and unconscionable bargains in general. Innocent misrepresentations as well as fraudulent misrepresentations could lead to rescission.[55] Fraudulent misrepresentations could lead to rescission at Law as well, but innocent misrepresentations could not. Relief for duress was limited in its scope at Law. Only force or threats of force directed against persons could found a plea of duress.[56] Duress with regard to goods and economic duress, threats to economic interests, did not lead to remedies until comparatively recently.[57] Undue influence was developed by Equity, as we saw just now, as a ground for rescission.[58]

The effect of rescission was made clear in Equity after the decision at law in *Load v Green*. Until then it had not been clear in Equity whether a contract induced by fraud was void or voidable, but after that decision the Court of Chancery began deciding as well that those kinds of contracts were voidable, and valid until rescinded or 'set aside', as the new expression came to be.[59] The discussion about the voidability or voidness of contracts made under duress appears to have been given a new lease

55 *Redgrave v Hurd* (1881) 20 Ch. D. 1.

56 The leading case was *Skeate v Beale* (1840) 113 Eng. Rep. 688. See for the following O'Sullivan *et al.*, *The Law of Rescission*, 137 *seq.*, especially 144 *seq.*

57 These possibilities were first recognized by Kerr J in *Occidental Worldwide Investment Corp. v Skibs A/S Avanti (The Siboen and the Sibotre)* [1976] 1 Lloyd's Law Reports 293, at 335–336. See also the discussion of 18th- and early 19th-century cases by Mocatta J in *North Ocean Shipping Co Ltd v Hyundai Construction Co Ltd and Another* [1979] QB 705, at 715 *seq.* See now for economic duress *Universe Tankships Inc of Monrovia v International Transport Workers Federation (The Universe Sentinel)* [1983] AC 366, at 383 *seq.*

58 See e.g. Lord Nicholls in *Royal Bank of Scotland v Etridge (No 2)* [2002] 2 AC 773, at 795 *seq.* Compare S. Wagner, "Undue influence—mögliche Einflüsse des Civil law vom Ende des 16. bis Anfang des 19. Jahrhunderts", *ZSS* 123 (2006), 248 *seq.*, who in general denies any influence of the civil law on the institution of undue influence.

59 *Clark v Malpas* (1862) 45 Eng. Rep. 1238, at 1240. See O'Sullivan *et al.*, *The Law of Rescission*, 65.

of life, but perhaps only temporarily, in 1966 by Lanham.[60] He pleaded for voidness.

With regard to the effect of rescission against third parties the equitable doctrines were, of course, that a *bona fide* purchaser for value could not be sued by the defrauded party, but a purchaser with notice or a volunteer could.[61] These principles were the same at Law. The question remained whether Equity imposed a trust when property was obtained by means which permitted rescission. This question appears to have been resolved in 1861 in *Phillips v Phillips* by Lord Westbury LC.[62] That decision came to be understood as having decided that title passes under a voidable contract, at Law as well as in Equity, and that pending rescission no equitable title existed, but that the right to rescind was merely an 'equity'.[63] So equitable rescission had the same effect as rescission at Law. In the end it was accepted in Equity as well that rescission was effected by the choice of the party concerned.[64]

60 D.J. Lanham, "Duress and Void Contracts", *Modern Law Review* 29 (1966), 615 *seq.*

61 See O'Sullivan *et al.*, *The Law of Rescission*, 66. Whether the acquisition of an indefeasible title by a *bona fide* purchaser for value before rescission has taken place also excludes the possibility to rescind the contract of sale of goods with the party who gave cause for rescission has been the subject of debate. One tends to speak of the third party rights bar to rescission, which may or may not exist. This problem concerns the legal consequences of a contract of sale of goods under the Common law. The contract itself in this case transfers title and so it is reasoned that if the contract can be avoided retroactively, after a third party in good faith has bought the asset, this will automatically result in the retroactive loss of the title of the third party, yet this last result is in conflict with authority (see *White v Garden*, *supra*, 171, fnt. 40). So in order to make the defeasibility of the title of the third party impossible, it is said that, after a third party acquires title, the seller is barred from rescinding his contract with the buyer who gave cause for rescission. This, however, creates a problem for the seller, who cannot sue the third party, to hold his buyer accountable for damages, because as long as the contract is valid there is no ground for claims based on unjust enrichment, and tort actions are not always available, as we have seen. That is why it has been suggested to decouple the contractual aspect of the contract of sale from the proprietary effect to abolish the third party rights bar to rescission. See B. Häcker, "Rescission and Third Party Rights", *Restitution Law Review* (2006), 21 *seq.*, especially 36 *seq.* More fundamental are the objections of O'Sullivan *et al.*, *The Law of Rescission*, 475 *seq.*, who find no authority for this bar, apart from its being 'difficult to justify in point of principle'. They argue it has not been explained why rescission of the contract between the seller and the buyer necessarily has the effect of divesting the innocent third party of his title, and distinguish between 'the contractual effect of destroying the bargain and the proprietary effect of revesting title'. Furthermore, they do not understand why a wrongdoer should profit from the protection which is afforded to the third party.

62 45 Eng. Rep. 1164.

63 O'Sullivan *et al.*, *The Law of Rescission*, 70.

64 *Reese River Silver Mining Co Ltd v Smith* (1869), LR 4 HL 64. This created difficulties which remain today. See O'Sullivan *et al.*, *The Law of Rescission*, 72 and ch. 10, 11, 12 and 15,

Conclusion

Law and Equity offer a view of the effects of contracts made under duress or the influence of fraud which would have been more familiar to a Roman lawyer than to a modern day civil lawyer. The forms of action were all-important, just like the remedies granted by the praetor, regardless whether they were designed to enforce the *ius civile* or to correct its effects. In both Roman and English law tort actions led the way to restitution, supplemented by restitution ordered and shaped by the Court of Chancery or the praetor. English law, in this respect, was not less consistent than Roman law. Dogmatic niceties like retroactivity of rescission were for a later day when Roman law served as the basis of the civil law systems. Systematic thinking and rigid logic was not the Roman cup of tea. For Roman law proper, just as for the common law in its extended sense, the phrase of Oliver Wendell Holmes holds true. 'The life of the law has not been logic, it has been experience.'[65]

par. 15.67–15.74. The decision was criticized by J.B. Ames, "Purchase for Value Without Notice", *HLR* 1 (1887), 1–2.

[65] O.W. Holmes Jr, *The Common Law* (Boston: Little, Brown and Company, 1881, repr. New York: Dover Publications, 1991), 1.

CHAPTER EIGHT

LAW AND EQUITY AT ODDS: LIABILITY OF A PRINCIPAL FOR ACCIDENTAL LOSSES SUFFERED BY HIS AGENT

W.J. Zwalve

Introduction

In the long history of the relation between equity and law, there is hardly a text in Justinian's Corpus Iuris that has drawn so much attention as the opinion of the Roman lawyer Paul on the liability of a principal for accidental losses sustained by his agent in the execution of his commission.[1] In my translation, the text reads as follows:

> D. 17,1,26,6: He [the agent] shall not charge to his principal everything he would otherwise not have expended, for example that he has been robbed by highwaymen or has lost property in a shipwreck or has made expenditures due to illness of himself or his relatives, since these things must be attributed to an Act of God rather than the commission.[2]

I intend to show how opinions on the equity of this provision have varied over time, from the Middle Ages until recent Dutch legislation on this issue. I will start with a discussion of the text according to classical Roman law.

---

[1] See *supra*, 17.

[2] Paulus, *libro trigesimo secundo ad edictum. Non omnia, quae impensurus non fuit mandator<i> imputabit, veluti quod spoliatus sit a latronibus aut naufragio res amiserit vel languore suo suorumque adpraehensus quaedam erogaverit: nam haec magis casibus quam mandato imputari oportet.* I have emended the word 'mandator' in the first phrase to 'mandatori', not only because it makes sense of an otherwise incomprehensible text, but also because it is consistent with the medieval Vulgate-tradition. It is, furthermore, generally accepted that *mandator* should be read as *mandatori*. See A. Watson, *Contract of Mandate in Roman Law* (Oxford: Clarendon, 1961), 157.

Classical Roman Law

The equity of the provision just cited has been criticized ever since the Accursian gloss. Yet it does not seem to be all that objectionable at first, the less so since the contract of mandate belonged to the *contractus bonae fidei* of Roman law,[3] meaning that Paul at least considered his opinion as conforming to what 'good faith' implied under the circumstances. The first question to be dealt with here is, therefore, what Roman lawyers meant by the concept of 'good faith' (*bona fides*).

It is usual among civilians[4] to distinguish between *bona fides* in an 'objective' sense and *bona fides* in a 'subjective' sense. The latter refers to the conscience of a subject only, meaning that he is considered to be *bona fide* if he is without notice of any circumstances inconsistent with the law (such as a *bona fide* possessor), the '*bona fides* of not knowing'. The former refers to legal standards directing the actions of a subject, 'the *bona fides* of acting'. This conceptual distinction between two kinds of *bona fides* may easily lead to the mistaken assumption that they are two totally unrelated concepts. They are not,[5] since even when taken in an 'objective' sense *bona fides* always refers to the conscience of a subject in the sense that he is acting unconscionable towards his counterpart by disregarding certain standards on which his counterpart is relying. It is on this reliance (*fides*) that the liability of a person acting *mala fide* is based. This is fundamental to the understanding of Roman *contractus bonae fidei*, since they were, initially, not based on the *ius civile*, but on *bona fides* directly.[6] They were, so to speak, originally reliance-based contracts by definition. Consequently, in asking what *bona fides* (in an 'objective' sense) implied, the crucial point was the answer to the question what the parties to a contract had (and could have) relied on as implied in their contract.[7] This amounts to a construction of that contract on the basis of the intentions of the contracting parties, rather than on the basis of what they have said

[3] See the list in Inst. 4,6,28.

[4] See for example the influential study by M. Voigt, *Die Lehre vom jus naturale, aequum et bonum und jus gentium der Römer* I (Leipzig: Julius Günther, 1856), 584.

[5] There is an important article on this issue (in Dutch, since it is about modern Dutch law) by P. van Schilfgaarde, "Over de verhouding tussen de goede trouw van het handelen en de goede trouw van het niet weten", in *Goed en Trouw, Opstellen aangeboden aan prof. mr. W.C.L. van der Grinten*, ed. E.A.A. Luijten *et al.* (Zwolle: Tjeenk Willink, 1984), 57–70.

[6] On this issue see W. Kunkel, "Fides als schöpferisches Element im römischen Schuldrecht", in *Festschrift Paul Koschaker* II (Weimar: Zentralantiquariat, 1939), 1–15; M. Kaser, *Das römische Privatrecht* I (Munich: Beck, 1971), 200.

[7] D. 19,2,21: *bona fides exigit, ut quod convenit fiat.* See also D. 45,1,35,2.

or written.[8] In the process of discovering the true intentions of the parties, a judge may have recourse to custom[9] *and* to certain standards of conduct that should have been taken for granted by the parties within the special circumstances of the case at hand. This is the point, indeed, where *aequitas* comes into consideration, but it is always related to the subjective expectations of the contracting parties. That is why, even in this 'objective' approach to *bona fides*, reliance (*fides*) is a decisive factor. The same reasoning applies, *mutatis mutandis*, to the '*bona fides* of not knowing', since the standard of 'not knowing' includes *constructive* notice. I ought to add that Roman lawyers never make a clear distinction between the *bona fides* 'of not knowing' (subjective) and the *bona fides* 'of acting' (objective), since to them the basic correlation between both aspects of *bona fides* was still obvious. We can now return to the case in D. 17,1,26,6.

In deciding a particular case of mandate, a Roman judge had to ask himself what the parties to a contract such as this might have expected of each other, or, in other words, what they had mutually relied on. In doing so, Roman lawyers concentrated on the intentions of the parties, rather than what had been written in the document testifying to that contract, or what had been literally said in reaching an oral agreement. What counted was their true intention (*id quod actum est*).[10] In the specific case of D. 17,1,26,6 the judge had to ask himself whether the agent could have reasonably relied on compensation by his principal for accidental losses sustained on account of robbery or illness. A question like this cannot be answered in the abstract, and that is one of the reasons why the provision of D. 17,1,26,6 has caused so much controversy, certainly so among modern scholars, since the question raised by that text is being treated *in abstracto* and on the basis of abstract principles such as the utility principle ('Utilitätsprinzip')[11] and the principle that 'no one has to sustain losses in executing a commission' (*nemini officium suum damnosum*). The latter

---

[8] D. 50,16,219: *In conventionibus contrahentium voluntatem potius quam verba spectari placuit.* See also D. 18,1,6,1.

[9] D. 21,1,31,20: *ea enim, quae sunt moris et consuetudinis, in bonae fidei iudiciis debent venire.*

[10] D. 50,16,219 (*supra*, fnt. 8). See also D. 18,1,6,1: *in emptis enim et venditis potius id quod actum, quam id quod dictum sit sequendum est.*

[11] For this see H. Honsell, "Die Risikohaftung des Geschäftsherrn", in *De iustitia et iure: Festgabe für Ulrich von Lübtow zum 80. Geburtstag*, ed. M. Harder, G. Thielmann and U. von Lübtow (Berlin: Duncker & Humblot, 1980), 485–500; D. Nörr, "Die Entwicklung des Utilitätsgedanken im römischen Haftungsrecht", *ZSS* 73 (1956), 91 *seq.*

'principle' (if principle it is) is derived from a discussion by the Roman lawyer Africanus in D. 47,2,62(61),5 describing the opinions of his teacher Julian. It concerns a case where someone had commissioned someone else to buy a specific slave. The commissioner executed the commission, but before the slave was handed over to the principal, the slave had stolen from the agent. Can the commissioner sue the principal for his losses on account of the theft by the slave? The question is answered in the affirmative and the reason is usually[12] found in a rather casual remark by Africanus, stating that it is only fair that 'no one suffers losses on account of a commission he has not executed on behalf of himself, but on behalf of the person with whom he has contracted'.[13] Africanus further states that in a case like this a commissioner can rightly (*iustissime*) refer to the fact 'that he would not have suffered the loss, if he had not accepted the commission'.[14] The Accursian Gloss adds that in this particular provision (and especially the comment of Africanus) equity prevails over the rigor of the law,[15] thus suggesting an antinomy between the opinions of Paul in D. 17,1,26,6 and Africanus/Julian in D. 47,2,62(61),5, a suggestion taken for granted by most modern scholars.[16] The latter Roman jurists are supposed to have allowed a claim for compensation on account of the principles just mentioned, a claim Paul is supposed to have declined. However, in attributing the use of principles like these to Roman lawyers great caution is called for, since, as Paul states elsewhere, a 'principle' (*regula*) is always a derivative of the law as it is and never the other way round: *non ex regula ius sumatur, sed ex iure quod est regula fiat.*[17] A principle is but the summary expression of a case (*causae coniectio*),[18] whereas the law as it is, is to be found in the facts of the case, *not* in the rule derived from it. Alfenus summarized this idea in his famous dictum *ius est in causa positum.*[19]

---

[12] R. Zimmermann, *The Law of Obligations* (Cape Town/Johannesburg: Juta, 1990), 430.

[13] D. 47,2,62(61),5: (*post alia*) *nemini officium suum, quod eius, cum quo contraxerit, non etiam sui commodi causa susceperit, damnosum esse.*

[14] D. 47,2,62(61),5: (*post alia*) *iustissime enim procuratorem allegare non fuisse se id damnum passurum, si id mandatum non suscepisset.*

[15] Gl. 'Damnosum' on D. 47,2,62(61),5: *hic nota aequitatem rigori praeferri.*

[16] Zimmermann, *The Law of Obligations*, 430–431; P. Stein, "Julian and Liability for Loss Suffered in the Execution of a Contract in Roman Law", *Butterworths South African Law Review* 1956, 64–69. P. Gröschler, "Schadens- und Aufwendungsersatz bei Julian, Afrikan und Paulus", in *Africani quaestiones, Studien zur Geschichte und Dogmatik des Privatrechts*, ed. J.D. Harke (Berlin/Heidelberg: Springer, 2011), 17–36, is less certain about this (at 30), but fails to outright deny the antinomy.

[17] D. 50,17,1.

[18] Sabinus in D. 50,17,1, and, for a definition of 'causae coniectio', Gaius 4,15.

[19] D. 9,2,52,2.

This *cautela* applies here as well. If the facts of the case in D. 47,2,62(61),5 are carefully scrutinized, it is clear that the true *ratio decidendi* is not a principle, but a simple fact distinguishing this case from the one dealt with by Paul. Africanus says this:

> As far as mandate is concerned, he [Julian] says it is doubtful whether one should say equally that losses are always to be compensated and yet it should be held, even more so than in the previous cases, that he [the principal] is liable for damages anyway, even if he did not know that *the specific slave* he commissioned to buy was a thief. That the commissioner can rightly allege that he would not have suffered the loss, if he had not accepted the commission; and this is evidently so with deposit, since, although it is reasonable in other cases that a man should not sustain more damage on account of a slave than the slave is worth, yet it is even more reasonable that no one suffers losses on account of a commission he has not executed on his own behalf, but on behalf of the person with whom he has contracted. As with the contracts dealt with earlier, sale, lease and pawn, *viz.* that the gross negligence of someone who has knowingly kept silent is to be punished, so it is with these contracts [deposit and mandate], where those on behalf of whom has been contracted should suffer the consequences of their own negligence themselves. For a principal who has commissioned to buy such a slave on his behalf, and similarly someone who has deposited, is obviously at fault for not having been more diligent in cautioning what kind of a slave he deposited.[20]

The text relates to a typically Roman topic, i.e. thievery by slaves. The owner was vicariously liable for all damages caused by the tortious behaviour of his slaves, but he could escape his obligation to pay damages by surrendering the tortfeasing slaves to the injured person (noxal liability), because, says Gaius, 'it is unreasonable that their torts cause more damage

---

20 Africanus, *libro octavo Quaestionum. Quod vero ad mandati actionem attinet, dubitare se ait, num aeque dicendum sit omni modo damnum praestari debere, et quidem hoc amplius quam in superioribus causis servandum, ut, etiamsi ignoraverit is, qui* certum hominem *emi mandaverit, furem esse, nihilo minus tamen damnum decidere cogatur. Iustissime enim procuratorem allegare non fuisse se id damnum passurum, si id mandatum non suscepisset: idque evidentius in causa depositi apparere. Nam licet alioquin aequum videatur non oportere cuiquam plus damni per servum evenire, quam quanti ipse servus sit, multo tamen aequius esse nemini officium suum, quod eius, cum quo contraxerit, non etiam sui commodi causa susceperit, damnosum esse, et sicut in superioribus contractibus, venditione locatione pignore, dolum eius, qui sciens reticuerit, puniendum esse dictum sit, ita in his culpam eorum, quorum causa contrahatur, ipsis potius damnosam esse debere. Nam certe mandantis culpam esse, qui talem servum emi sibi mandaverit, et similiter eius qui deponat, quod non fuerit diligentior circa monendum, qualem servum deponeret* (emphasis added).

to their owners than the value of their bodies'.[21] Consequently, whenever a slave was worth less than the damage he had caused, the injured party was left with residual damages. The question raised in D. 47,2,62(61),1 is whether an injured party may hold the owner of the slave liable for the residual damages in contract, rather than tort, in case the injured party had been in possession of that slave as a bailee of the owner on account of a deposit, *or a mandate*, by the owner, or when that slave had been leased to him by the owner.

In case of a mandate to buy a certain slave, the question at issue here presupposes that the principal was already owner of the slave which the commissioner had bought on his behalf, even before the latter had handed over that slave, since the principal can only surrender a slave to the commissioner on account of his (noxal) liability if he is the owner of that slave. In other words, the principal must have acquired title to the slave by way of an intermediary, the commissioner. Now this seems to be rather problematic in view of Gaius's famous *dictum* 'that we cannot in any way acquire rights through the intervention of a free person'.[22] Nevertheless, under Justinianic law acquisition of ownership through the intervention of a third party was not problematic since Justinianic law recognized but one mode of transfer of title, i.e. by way of *traditio*. In as far as *traditio* was concerned, it was already trite learning in classical law that possession and consequently title could be acquired by an agent on behalf of his principal.[23] However, our text concerns a slave who, according to classical law, had to be transferred by *mancipatio* rather than *traditio*. This raises the (rather neglected) question whether in classical law acquisition of ownership by the principal by way of *mancipatio* was also possible through the intervention of an intermediary. There is a curious passage in Gaius where he states that a slave could *in mancipando* acquire title on behalf of his master if he inserted his master's name in the formula of the *mancipatio*.[24] This is curious since the master would have acquired title even without that insertion on account of the fact that a master always acquired title to anything a slave acquired, whether or not the latter did so in the name of his master.[25] I believe a free person, for example a *libertus*, could *in mancipando* acquire title on behalf of a third party as well by inserting the name of that third party in the formula of the *mancipatio* in a similar way, provided of course that he had a *iussum*

[21] Gaius 4,75 (*post alia*) *erat enim iniquum nequitiam eorum ultra ipsorum corpora parentibus dominisve damnosam esse.*

[22] Gaius 2,95: *Per liberos homines [...] nulla ex causa nobis adquiri posse.*

[23] Gaius 2,95 *i.f.* and see explicitly D. 41,1,13 pr. (Neratius): *Si procurator rem mihi emerit ex mandato meo eique sit tradita meo nomine, dominium mihi, id est proprietas adquiritur etiam ignoranti.* See also C. 7,32,1 and Inst. 2,9,5.

[24] Gaius 3,167.

[25] Gaius 2,86.

> to that effect.[26] Our text (D. 47,2,62(61),1) contains strong (though indirect) evidence of this, since it presupposes that the principal could dispose of the slave by way of *noxae deditio*.[27]

The provision of D. 47,2,62(61),1 decides that the commissioner could sue the principal for the residual damages in contract because the principal had commissioned to buy a *specific* slave (*certum hominem*). In doing so, the principal accepted the risk for all deficiencies of that slave, such as thievishness, potentially causing damage to the commissioner, even when the principal was not aware of them. This risk allocation is emphasized in the last phrase of the text, where the deficiencies of the slave are attributed to the negligence (*culpa*) of the principal because he had explicitly commissioned to buy such a slave (*talem servum*).[28] This is a clear indication that the principal's liability in this case is not based on some general principle, such as the utility principle ('Utilitätsprinzip'), but on the specific facts of the case. The risk would have fallen elsewhere if the principal had commissioned to buy *a* (unspecified) slave, since then it would have been the commissioner, not the principal, who decided which slave was to be bought and he should therefore bear the consequences of his choice, provided, of course, that the principal did not have notice of the deficiencies of the slave his commissioner was about to buy, since if he had, he was bound to warn the commissioner:

> D. 17,1,26,7: But when a slave, whom you have bought on my commission, steals from you, Neratius holds that you can bring an action on account of the commission in order to have the slave surrendered to you, provided

---

26 So does A. Corbino, "Forma librale ed intermediazione negoziale", in *Sodalitas: scritti in onore di Antonio Guarino* V, ed. V. Giuffrè (Naples: Jovene, 1984), 2258–2271. It seems to me that even in classical times Gaius's famous dictum applied to choses in action only. For this see: D. 45,1,126,2 (Paulus): *per liberam personam quae neque iuri nostro subiecta est neque bona fide nobis servit*, obligationem *nullam adquirere possumus*. (emphasis added)

27 Honsell, "Risikohaftung", 489 and Gröschler, "Schadens- und Aufwendungsersatz", 20 do not take up this point, although they both acknowledge that the slave must already have been at the disposition of the principal some way or another: 'bei wirtschaftlicher Betrachtung' (Honsell); 'bereits der Sphäre des Auftraggebers [zuzurechnen]' (Gröschler).

28 Honsell, "Risikohaftung", 491 and Zimmermann, *Law of Obligations*, 430, fnt. 134, believe the last phrase of D. 47,2,62(61),5 to be interpolated. As they see it, the interpolation purported to remove the evident contradiction they feel exists between the provision of D. 47,2,62(61),5 and D. 17,1,26,7. As will be shown in the text, there is no such contradiction, even without the last phrase of D. 47,2,62(61),5. Gröschler, "Schadens- und Aufwendungsersatz", 28–29, also believes the phrase is interpolated. His reasons for doing so deserve some attention. He thinks that the reasoning in that phrase has 'mit dem Utilitätsgedanken, auf den sich Julian wirklich stützt, nicht mehr zu tun. Es muss sich *daher* um einen nachklassischen Zusatz handeln.' (emphasis added)

> this has happened without any negligence on your part. However, if I knew that he was such a slave and have not forewarned you, so that you might have taken precautions, then all damages you have sustained must be compensated.[29]

This is the sequel to Paul's immediately preceding *dictum* that a commissioner may not expect to be compensated for all damages sustained in the execution of his assignment, especially not damages due to illness or robbery. If, however, the agent had bought an unspecified slave[30] on the commission of his principal and that slave had stolen from the agent, the principal could meet his liability to pay damages by surrendering that slave, since he was liable in his capacity as owner of that slave. Residual damages were only due to the commissioner if the principal was at fault, for example by not notifying the commissioner that the slave the latter was about to buy suffered from kleptomania (D. 17,1,26,7), or by commissioning to buy a specified slave (D. 47,2,62(61),5). Consequently, there is no contradiction at all between the opinions of Africanus/Julian in D. 47,2,62(61),5 and Paul in D. 17,1,26,6 and 7.[31] To the contrary: both texts express the same underlying idea, that a principal is only liable for damages sustained by a commissioner in the execution of his assignment if these damages are one way (D. 17,1,26,7 *i.f.*) or another (D. 47,2,62(61),5) the responsibility of the principal.[32] If the facts of the case did not indicate

---

[29] Paulus, *libro trigesimo secundo ad edictum. Sed cum servus, quem mandatu meo emeras, furtum tibi fecisset, Neratius ait mandati actione te consecuturum, ut servus tibi noxae dedatur, si tamen sine culpa tua id acciderit: quod si ego scissem talem esse servum nec praedixissem, ut possis praecavere, tunc quanti tua intersit, tantum tibi praestari oportet.* See on the introduction of the possibility of *noxae deditio* in contractual, rather than tort-based, actions: Kaser, *Das römische Privatrecht* I, 633.

[30] Stein, "Julian and Liability", 67 seems to take for granted that there is a commission to buy a specific slave in the case of D. 17,1,26,7 as well ('a certain slave'). I have to admit that under this presumption there is indeed a clear contradiction between D. 47,2,62(61),5 and D. 17,1,26,7, but I do not believe the presumption is correct. Paul was perfectly capable of expressing himself unequivocally if he wanted to do so. See (in the very same context) D. 40,12,17 (Paulus): *si* certum *hominem mandavero emi* ('if I had commissioned to buy a *specific* slave'; emphasis added).

[31] The consonance of D. 17,1,26,6 and D. 17,1,26,7 on the one hand and D. 47,2,62(61),5 on the other was already explained in this manner by the Byzantine jurists of Justinian's time: see scholion no. 34 on Basilica 14,1,26 (= D. 17,1,26), BS II, 752, r. 17–19 (ed. Scheltema). See in the same way the Gl. 'Certum' on D. 47,2,62(61),5 and Azo, *Summa Codicis* (ed. Venice, 1596), on C. 4,35 (*Mandati*), no. 33, col. 392. See also (for a later legal humanist) Julius Pacius de Beriga (Giulio Pace, 1550–1635), *Enantiophanoon, sive Legum conciliatarum Centuriae VII* (ed. Lyon, 1618), 344.

[32] This is also the way in which the 19th-century German Pandektists explained these provisions. See B.J.H. Windscheid, *Lehrbuch des Pandektenrechts* II, 6th ed. (Frankfurt: Rütten & Loening, 1887), par. 410, fnt. 18 (at 573); H. Dernburg, *Pandekten* II, 4th ed. (Berlin:

fault or implied risk allocation, the rule in D. 17,1,26,6 applied, meaning that the principal was not liable for accidental personal losses sustained by a commissioner in the execution of his assignment (*occasione mandati*): *casus non praestantur.*[33]

Interlude

We can now turn our attention to the Accursian Gloss on D. 17,1,26,6. The last phrase of the Gl. 'Mandato' on D. 17,1,26,6 has caused a genuine division in the continental civilian tradition. Since it is very short and has caused so much confusion, I will leave it untranslated for the moment. It reads: *Item nec hic § de curialitate debet servari.* According to many medieval commentators, who were commenting the gloss, rather than Justinian's text, the phrase 'de curialitate' was synonymous to 'de aequitate',[34] suggesting that the gloss implied that the rule laid down by the law (D. 17,1,26,6) should be ignored by the judiciary. However, many medieval Italian jurists were not inclined to follow this suggestion.[35] One of them was the famous canonist Joannes Andreae (*c.* 1270–1348). He gives an example: 'if I commission a Genuese contractor to build a house for me on an island, for example Sardinia or Sicily, and the contractor loads his workers, ready money and building material on a ship that is shipwrecked en route, can the contractor charge me for his loss?'[36] The answer was no, at least in principle[37] and D. 17,1,26,6 was cited as deciding the question. Joannes Andreae is mentioned in this context for two reasons. Firstly, because his opinion is representative of the view of many contemporary

---

Müller, 1894), par. 116 2.b. (at 319) and the other jurists cited by Gröschler, *Schadens- und Aufwendungsersatz*, 23, fnt. 22.

[33] D. 50,17,23 (Ulpianus).

[34] See for example Albericus de Rosate (*c.* 1290–1354), *Commentarii in secundam Digesti Veteris partem* (ed. Venice, 1585 = repr. D. Maffei, E. Cortese and G. Rossi ed., *Opera iuridica rariora* XXII (Bologna: Forni, 1977)), on D. 17,1,26,6: *glossa quae dicit, quod* de aequitate *non debet servari* (emphasis added) and Baldus de Ubaldis (1327–1400), *In secundam Digesti Veteris partem* (ed. Venice, 1587) on D. 17,1,26,6: *non debet servari* de aequitate (emphasis added).

[35] See for example the comment of the influential civilian Cinus de Pistoia (1270–1336) in his *Lectura Codicis* on C. 9,12,6, where he condemns this suggestion as 'nonsense' (*truffa*).

[36] *Novella in secundum librum Decretalium* (ed. Venice, 1581), on X. 2,24,29, no. 12 (*f.* 198*r.*). Andreae refers to the famous commentary on the 'Liber Extra' by Sinibaldus Fliscus, the later pope Innocent IV. See on the latter's doctrine *infra*, 188–189.

[37] But see the important distinction *infra*, 187–189.

canonists, illustrating that the famous *aequitas canonica* did not find fault with Paul's opinion in D. 17,1,26,6, thus rejecting the suggestion that the provision should be ignored.[38] Secondly, because his opinion became quite an embarrassment to himself when, in 1328, he ran into trouble as an ambassador. In that year the city of Bologna, where Andreae was teaching canon law at the time, sent him to Avignon as an emissary of that city to pope John XXII. On his way back he was captured by highwaymen, robbed of all his belongings, and only released after a ransom of 4000 florins had been paid to his captors.[39] Back in Bologna he wanted to be compensated for all his losses. The problem was put to all the professors of the Bologna faculty and they decided, on the basis of D. 17,1,26,6, that there was no strict legal obligation on the part of the city to reimburse its emissary, an opinion that must not have come as a surprise to Andreae. One of the professors who surely must have participated in this was Bartolus's teacher Jacobus Butrigarius (*c.* 1273–1348), who was professor of civil law in Bologna from 1307 until his death in the same year as Andreae. We know Butrigarius rejected the suggestion implied by the Gl. 'Mandato'.[40] Nevertheless, we also know that the city decided to ignore the advice of the law faculty and to reimburse the unlucky canonist.

> This is a first indication of the true meaning of the phrase 'de curialitate' in the Gl. 'Mandato'. As stated by Azo (*c.* 1150–1223), Accursius's teacher, the Italian cities at the time used to compensate their ambassadors for losses such as Andreae had suffered in the execution of his mission, in spite of the fact that there was no strict legal obligation to do so (D. 17,1,26,6).[41] It was just not done, not courteous (*de curialitate*), to rely on that provision and deny compensation to someone who had suffered accidental losses while executing a commission.[42]

---

[38] For this see Guillaume Durant (*c.* 1237–1296), *Speculum iuris* (ed. Basle, 1574), lib. IV, part. ii (*De iudiciis*), par. 3 (*Specialia*) no. 5 (= repr. Frankfurt: Vico Verlag, 2009, II, 127). Durant's book is, if not the most influential, certainly one of the four most authoritative legal treatises of the Middle Ages, the other three being Azo's *Summa Codicis*, the Accursian gloss and Bartolus's commentaries.

[39] See on this incident F.C. von Savigny, *Geschichte des römischen Rechts im Mittelalter* V, 2nd ed. (Heidelberg: Mohr & Zimmer, 1850; repr. Bad Homburg: Hermann Gentner, 1961), 106–107.

[40] See his comment on D. 17,1,26,6: *In primam et secundam Veteris Digesti partem* (ed. Rome, 1606; ed. D. Maffei, E. Cortese and G. Rossi, *Opera iuridica rariora* XIV (Bologna: Forni, 1978)), 193: *Nonne hic est rigor, cui repugnat aequitas, quae debet praevalere? Sol.: haec aequitas non est scripta, rigor sic.*

[41] Azo, *Summa Codicis* (ed. Venice, 1596), on C. 4,35 (*Mandati*), no. 33, col. 392: *de consuetudine urbanorum est ut procuratori restituant damna.*

[42] See further on this *infra*, 192.

The case of Joannes Andreae and the advice of the Bologna law faculty were to become standard elements in later medieval commentaries on D. 17,1,26,6, for example in the very authoritative commentary of Bartolus de Saxoferrato (1313–1357), one of the most influential jurists in legal history. He must have heard the story from his teacher Butrigarius and leaves no doubt about his opinion on the suggestion to ignore the provision of D. 17,1,26,6:

> Take care at the end of this gloss, where it is said that this provision should be ignored *de curialitate*. Does the gloss suggest that this provision should not be applied on equitable considerations, since equity is to be preferred over the rigor of the law? [...] This is not true here, since the rigor of this provision is written law and therefore to be applied (although it contains a hardship), notwithstanding an equity which is not enacted.[43]

In the rest of his commentary on D. 17,1,26,6 Bartolus makes a fine distinction which apparently had first been suggested by the early glossator Aldericus († *c.* 1177)[44] and elaborated by the canonists, most notably among them by the great lawyer-pope Innocent IV (Sinibaldo Fieschi, 1243–1254). Before going into the opinion of the latter, some attention should be paid to the opinion of Aldericus himself, more especially to the specific context of his distinction, which has come down to us in a gloss on D. 17,2,52,4, a text which seems to flatly contradict the opinion of Paul in D. 17,1,26,6. It reads as follows:

> Some persons had gone into a partnership in the textile industry. One of them went on a journey to purchase commodities and ran into robbers. He lost his money; his slaves were wounded and he lost his own belongings. Julian says that the loss is to be shared and consequently he must bear half the damage on account of the partnership action [*actio pro socio*] both

---

43 Bartolus in his commentary on D. 17,1,26,6, *In secundam Digesti veteris Partem* (ed. Venice, 1570), *f.* 113*r*., in the middle, s.v. 'Cave de fine istius glossae': *Cave de fine istius glossae quando dicit, quod hic § de curialitate non debet servari. Vult glossa dicere quod iste § de aequitate non debet servari: quia aequitas rigori praefertur [...] quod non est verum hic: cum rigor iuris huius § sit scriptus et immo tenendus, licet duritiam contineat, non obstante aequitate quae non est scripta.* I should add that older editions of Bartolus's commentary on the second part of the *Digestum vetus*, like the Milanese 1570 edition and the 1527 Venetian edition (De Tortis) do not have this passage. There is, however, no reason to suppose this passage is a later addition and not by Bartolus. Later editors may have used better manuscripts and, more convincingly, Bartolus's opinion agrees with the concurring opinion of his teacher Butrigarius (see *supra*, 186). See on the text-constitution of Bartolus's commentary to the *Digestum vetus* Savigny, *Geschichte* VI, 162–165 and more recently H. Lange and M. Kriechbaum, *Römisches Recht im Mittelalter II, Die Kommentatoren* (Munich: Beck, 2007), 723.

44 See the reference to Aldericus in Bartolus's commentary.

> for the money and for the other things, which the partner would not have brought with him but to buy merchandise for the common venture. But Julian also rightly approves that, if he has made expenses for medical treatment, the partner must bear his part. Moreover, if he has lost something in a shipwreck, since commodities are usually not transported other than by ship, both must bear the loss, since as the profit is to be shared, so is the loss, provided there is no negligence on the part of the partner.[45]

Here we have the same contingencies as in D. 17,1,26,6, robbery, illness and shipwreck, but whereas the damages sustained because of them were to be borne by the commissioner alone, an associate was, at least partly, to be compensated by his partner.[46] Why? The Gl. 'Mandato' on D. 17,1,26,6 provides the beginning of an answer by pointing to the *ius fraternitatis* among partners, attested in D. 17,2,63 pr. But it is in the Gl. 'Commune' on D. 17,2,52,4 that Aldericus is referred to as contending that, in case of a commission, the principal is liable to the commissioner for the accidental loss of property which the commissioner would not have taken with him but for the execution of his assignment.[47] Here is the root of a distinction to the doctrine as expressed by Paul in D. 17,1,26,6 that was to make (legal) history. Pope Innocent IV picked it up in his commentary on X. 2,24,29.

Innocent emphasizes that it would be a *magna absurditas* to contend that a principal is liable for *all* losses sustained by a commissioner in the execution of his assignment. He clearly rejects the suggestion implied by the Gl. 'Mandato' that the provision of D. 17,1,26,6 should not be applied by the judiciary and makes a distinction instead, elaborating on the distinction already suggested by Aldericus. He introduces the example, later repeated by Joannes Andreae, of the contractor with a commission to build a house on an island who loses his money, slaves and building materials in a shipwreck while en route to the island. Innocent makes a

---

[45] Ulpianus, *libro trigensimo primo ad edictum. Quidam sagariam negotiationem coierunt: alter ex his ad merces comparandas profectus in latrones incidit suamque pecuniam perdidit, servi eius vulnerati sunt resque proprias perdidit. Dicit Iulianus damnum esse commune ideoque actione pro socio damni partem dimidiam adgnoscere debere tam pecuniae quam rerum ceterarum, quas secum non tulisset socius nisi ad merces communi nomine comparandas proficisceretur. Sed et si quid in medicos impensum est, pro parte socium agnoscere debere rectissime Iulianus probat. Proinde et si naufragio quid periit, cum non alias merces quam navi solerent advehi, damnum ambo sentient: nam sicuti lucrum, ita damnum quoque commune esse oportet, quod non culpa socii contingit.*

[46] Needless to say, the provision of D. 17,2,52,4 played its part in the controversy over the supposed contradiction between D. 17,1,26,6 and D. 47,2,62(61),5 just discussed in the text above. I will come to this *infra*, 191

[47] Gl. 'Commune' on D. 17,2,52,4: *Aldericus dicit ut mandator teneatur de his rebus, quas non detulisset mandatarius, nisi mandatum suscepisset, de aliis autem non agit.*

distinction between materials already belonging to the contractor before he accepted his commission and materials he had purchased in order to perform his commission. The former were already at the risk of the contractor before he accepted his assignment and the loss of them should therefore not be charged to the principal, whereas the latter would not have been bought but for the commission and could therefore be charged to the principal.[48] Here is the origin of a doctrine, which, not in the least because it was adopted by Bartolus, was to find its place in the civilian tradition throughout the ages to come. In applying D. 17,1,26,6 a distinction should be made between the accidental loss of property in the execution of the commission (*ex occasione mandati*) and the accidental loss of property because of the commission (*ex causa mandati*).[49] I should stress that this distinction presupposes the acceptation of the rule in D. 17,1,26,6 and the implicit rejection of the suggestion instigated of the Gl. 'Mandato' that it should be ignored by the judiciary. The overwhelming majority of medieval Italian commentators did indeed reject that suggestion.[50] It was incompatible with the position of a judge to overrule a provision of positive law on purely (i.e. unenacted) equitable considerations. It was the privilege of the sovereign to rule on the equity of D. 17,1,26,6.[51]

The French experience with the rule in D. 17,1,26,6 was quite different from the Italian, primarily because of the extraordinary constitutional position of the French 'parlements', especially the Parlement de Paris. In France, the idea that the judiciary ought to ignore the rule in D. 17,1,26,6 and charge a principal with *all* losses, including accidental losses, incurred by a commissioner in the execution of his commission, was attributed to the Gl. 'Mandato' and wholeheartedly embraced by the courts: 'nous suivons la glosse, non le texte'.[52] The doctrine attributed to the Accursian

---

48 *Apparatus Innocentii* (ed. Venice, 1491), on X. 2,24,29. Innocent refers for this to a number of texts from the Digests (D. 12,4,5; D. 17,1,8,10; D. 17,1,10,5; D. 17,1,10,9; D. 17,1,27,4 and D. 17,1,56,4), all of them are concerned with compensation for expenses, rather than for damages. I will return to this rather arbitrary distinction between expenses and damages *infra*, 198.

49 An influential proponent of this doctrine was Hugo Donellus (1527–1591), *De iure civili*, in *Opera Omnia* III (repr. Florence, 1861), lib. XIII, cap. XII, no. 15, at col. 905–906. Pothier was another: see *infra*, 195, fnt. 73.

50 I refer to Albericus de Rosate and Baldus de Ubaldis in their commentaries on D. 17,1,26,6.

51 C. 1,14,1. See my contribution earlier in this volume, *supra*, 17–18.

52 Bernard Automne (1574–1666), *Conférence du droict françois avec le droict romain, civil et canon* I (ed. Paris, 1644), on D. 17,1,26,6, at 182, referring to two decisions of the

Gloss was followed in France throughout, i.e. including the districts traditionally under Roman law ('pays de droit écrit') in the south, where the influence of the Italian tradition had always been stronger than in the north ('pays de droit coutumier').[53] Its authority was considerably enhanced by the support of the high priest of legal humanism, Jacques Cujas (1522–1590).[54] This doctrine found its way from France to the southern Netherlands ('Belgium')[55] and from there to the northern Netherlands. It was not only due to the influence of French authorities, however, that the purported doctrine of the Gloss was widely accepted in the Netherlands, but also because of the extraordinary impact of the *Codex fabrianus*, an enormous collection of law reports first published in 1606 by the chief justice of the High Court (*Senatus Supremus*) of the autonomous principality of Savoy, Antoine Favre (Antonius Faber, 1557–1624). Favre's *Codex fabrianus* was the single most influential collection of judicial decisions of the European legal 'ancien régime'. It was widely utilized, not only in Italy and France, but also in the Netherlands and the German territories, and served as a model for many later collections of its kind published elsewhere on the continent. One of the cases reported by Favre[56] concerns the rule in D. 17,1,26,6. It was about a person sent on a mission by a public corporation (*universitas*), who accidentally lost his horse in the course of

---

Parlement de Paris from 1565 and 1590. See also his addition at 309: *glossema Accursii [...] quae sententia usu comprobata est.* See also Antoine Mornac (1554–1619), *Observationes in XXIV libros Digestorum et in IV libros Codicis ad usum fori Gallici* (ed. Paris, 1631), on D. 17,1,26,6, at 421: *Subtilitas huius legis* [D. 17,1,26,6] *emendata est non modo a glossa, sed ab ipso Senatu Parisiensi,* referring to a decision of the Parlement de Paris from 1589. I found a different opinion (following the text of D. 17,1,26,6, rather than the gloss) expressed in a decision of the Parlement de Paris from April 1, 1597, reported in his lifetime by Claude le Prestre, a 'conseiller' of the Parlement: *Questions notables de droict, décidées par plusieurs arrests de la cour de Parlement* (1st ed. Paris, 1645), cent. 1, ch. xvi (ed. Paris, 1652, at 42–43). French law reports from this period are notoriously unreliable and Le Prestre's reports are no exception, as is noted by a later editor of Le Prestre's reports, Gabriel Guéret (1641–1680), who had his doubts on the correctness of this particular decision: 'fort problématique' (*Questions etc.*, (ed. Paris, 1679), at 41 ('Nouvelles Remarques')).

53 For the 'pays de droit écrit' see Géraud de Maynard (1537–1607), *Notables et singulières questions de droict escrit* I (ed. Paris, 1608), livr. IV, ch. 16 (at 249), where the Gl. 'Mandato' is referred to as well.

54 Jac. Cuiacius, *Julius Paullus* (ed. Frankfurt, 1596), on Paul, *ad edictum* Book 32 (*l.* 26, par. 'omni'), 119. Cujas stated the opinion, shared by many modern scholars, that there was a clear contradiction between the doctrine of Paul in D. 17,1,26,6 and 7 on the one hand and the conviction of Africanus/Julian in D. 47,2,62(61),5 on the other. Cujas preferred the latter, because he felt it was more equitable.

55 Franciscus Zypaeus (Frans van den Zype, 1578–1650), *Notitia Iuris Belgici* (ed. Antwerp, 1635), lib. IV, tit. 'mandati' (at 151).

56 *Codex fabrianus* (ed. Geneva, 1659), lib. IV, tit. 26, *def.* 29 (at 410).

his commission and wanted to be reimbursed by his principal. The High Court of Savoy applied D. 17,1,26,6 and rejected the claim (*sic*). However, what counted was a comment on this decision by Favre, stating that it was exceptional since it concerned a commission originating from a public authority rather than a private person. If the commission had come from a private person, things would have been quite different since in that case, as Favre stresses, the principal would have been obliged to compensate the commissioner for all his losses. For this opinion he explicitly appeals to the Gl. 'Mandato', suggesting that he accepted the French tradition on this account.

> Favre was not only one of the most influential judges of his time, but a great scholar as well, the author of a number of excellent studies on Roman law in the style of Cujas. In one of them, his highly acclaimed *Rationalia* (an enormous commentary in five volumes on the first three *partes* of the Digests), he deals with D. 17,1,26,6 explicitly.[57] He stresses a point there, which is traditionally[58] insisted on by the opponents of Paul's doctrine in D. 17,1,26,6, i.e. that D. 17,2,52,4 seems to contradict Paul's doctrine for the contract of partnership (*societas*).[59] The traditional counter-argument[60] is, of course, that with a partnership all partners share in the profits and consequently also in the losses, whereas a commissioner has no claim against his principal on account of the profits the latter makes from his services. Favre conceded the logic of this, but decided to disregard D. 17,1,26,6 nevertheless.[61] He regarded the rule in that provision as 'rather hard' (*duriuncula*) and preferred (in view of the provision of D. 47,2,62(61),5) the doctrine attributed to the Gloss as more equitable.[62]

Favre's opinions impressed his contemporaries far beyond the Savoyard borders. The famous Dutch civilian Joannes Voet (1647–1713), for example, based his opinion that the provision of D. 17,1,26,6 had ceased to obtain in contemporary Dutch law (*hodie*) mainly on Favre.[63] Similar views were

---

57 A. Favre, *Rationalium in tertiam partem Pandectarum* V (ed. Orléans, 1626), *De mandato* (17,1), on D. 17,1,26,6 (66).

58 It is already in the Gl. 'Mandato' itself.

59 For this see *supra*, 187–188.

60 Already to be found in Innocent's *Apparatus* on X. 2,24,29.

61 'Logisch volkommen richtig, und dennoch verkehrt', as Jhering would have argued.

62 Favre's opinion corresponds with the view of Cujas (*supra*, 190, fnt. 54), whom he does not mention.

63 Johannes Voet, *Commentarius ad Pandectas* (ed. Geneva, 1757), 17,1, no. 13 *i.f.* Voet also refers to *Hollandsche Consultatien* IV (a massive collection of legal expert views, some of them by Grotius) (Amsterdam/Utrecht, 1728), cons. 385, at 708: 'zo werd [...] gehouden en verstaan dat de genoemde text niet behoord te werden gepractiseert als strijdende tegen alle redenen en aequiteit' ('it is held that the said text [D. 17,1,26,6] is disregarded, since it is contrary to reason and equity'), with a reference to the Gl. 'Mandato'. Johannes

expressed in Simon van Groenewegen's treatise on abolished and disused provisions in Justinian's Corpus Iuris, also with reference to Favre and French authorities.[64] However, in spite of the stain of iniquity that attached to the provision of D. 17,1,26,6, there was one voice strongly in favour of Paul's doctrine. It belonged to the influential Frisian civilian Ulrik Huber (1636–1694), who defended the equity of that provision in an important essay.[65]

What makes Huber's essay interesting, is his disclosure of the true meaning of the last phrase of the Gl. 'Mandato': *Item nec hic §* de curialitate *debet servari*. According to Huber it should not be read as it was in France, i.e. as an instruction directed at the judiciary to disregard the provision of D. 17,1,26,6, but as an advice to a principal not to insist on it out of courtesy (*de curialitate*) to a commissioner who had suffered accidental losses in executing his commission, and thus to compensate the commissioner for these losses too, although the law (D. 17,1,26,6) did not entitle him to it. Huber, moreover, explicitly denied the iniquity of D. 17,1,26,6 by stressing the absurd consequences of the opposite rule, implying as it does that the principal was liable to a commissioner for *all* accidental personal losses which the latter had suffered in the execution of the commission. Was it not far more equitable to make the commissioner bear these losses himself, rather than credit them to a principal who was in no way responsible for them? In support of his opinion, Huber refers to Ulpian's famous dictum that good faith (*bona fides*) implies in a contractual context that 'no one can be held responsible for losses suffered from robbery, riots, arson, floods and hold-ups by highwaymen'.[66] He further stresses that a commission is an economically and socially important legal instrument, making it counter-productive to burden a principal with the financial consequences of excessive risks.

Since 1964 we know for certain that in the former Dutch province of Holland the doctrine of Huber prevailed over the French tradition, the

Voet's father, Paulus Voet (1619–1667, professor of civil law in Utrecht), had expressed a similar opinion in his *In IV libris Institutionum* (ed. Gorcum, 1668), on Inst. 3,26,8 under no. 6, also emphasizing the 'iniquity' of D. 17,1,26,6 and referring to the Gl. 'Mandato'.

64 Simon à Groenewegen Van der Made, *Tractatus de legibus abrogatis et inusitatis* (ed. Leiden, 1649), on D. 17,1,26,6.

65 U. Huber, *Eunomia romana sive Censura censurae iuris Justinianaei* (ed. Amsterdam, 1724), 608–610.

66 D. 50,17,23 *i.f.*: *rapinae, tumultus, incendia, aquarum magnitudines, impetus praedonum a nullo praestantur.*

opinion of Favre and similar convictions held by Dutch jurists like Voet.[67] In that year the first volume was published of the *Observationes tumultuariae novae*, the private reports collected (in Latin, of course) by Willem Pauw (1712–1787), Justice and later Chief Justice of the Supreme Court ('Hoge Raad') of that province. Like the *Observationes tumultuariae* of Pauw's father-in-law Cornelis van Bynkershoek (1673–1743), also a Justice and Chief Justice of the 'Hoge Raad', Pauw's private reports were not intended to be published. But after the Dutch legal historian E.M. Meijers (1880–1954) was able to lay his hands on the manuscripts of both collections, they have been published at intervals since 1926. In a decision of 19 July 1754, the 'Hoge Raad' decided on the equity of D. 17,1,26,6.[68]

> It was a case concerning a commission given by a certain 'Titius' to 'Maevius', both living in the Dutch province of Zeeland, to collect a debt owed to Titius by someone living in Amsterdam and to buy an annuity in England for the price of £1000 with the proceeds. Maevius bought the annuity, though not with the proceeds of the outstanding debt. He ordered his correspondent in England to buy the annuity, for which that correspondent drew two bills of exchange on Maevius, which were accepted by him, indicating 'Seius' (obviously his banker) as the person who was to pay on his behalf. Somewhat later, Seius was declared bankrupt and Maevius suffered considerable losses. He lost the money already advanced to Seius in order to pay off the takers of the bills that were drawn on him, and since they were not paid by Seius, he was liable to the takers as well. He tried to charge Titius with these losses. Titius relied on D. 17,1,26,6; Maevius relied on Voet and the French tradition rejecting the rule in D. 17,1,26,6.

The Supreme Court of Holland, by unanimous decision, rejected the view that the rule in D. 17,1,26,6 had ceased to obtain in Holland. All the authorities to the contrary (Favre, Voet and Groenewegen) were taken into consideration but according to Pauw, the arguments of Huber had cleansed the provision of D. 17,1,26,6 'of all the stains of iniquity' (*ab omni labe iniquitatis*) attached to it ever since the Middle Ages. Consequently, the court rejected the claim of the plaintiff (Maevius). In doing so, the

---

[67] I should add that Huber was not the only one in the Netherlands holding this position. It was shared by S. van Leeuwen (1626–1682), *Censura forensis* (ed. Leiden, 1678), I, 4,24 under no. 12, but Van Leeuwen was a minor authority. The same cannot be said of the Leuven professor of civil law Antonio Perez (Perezius, 1583–1672), who shared Huber's opinion as well: *Praelectiones in XII Libros Codicis* (ed. Amsterdam, 1671), on C. 4,35 (*Mandati*) under no. 16 (at 299, r. col.), Perezius's book was very influential in the northern Netherlands at the time.

[68] W. Pauw, *Observationes tumultuariae novae* I, ed. H.F.W.D. Fischer *et al.* (Haarlem: Tjeenk Willink, 1964), no. 511 (at 386).

Supreme Court distanced itself from the French tradition and adhered to the Italian tradition. It was right to do so, since there is no manifest iniquity to Paul's rule in D. 17,1,26,6.

In closing this section, I should pay some attention to the doctrine of Robert-Joseph Pothier (1699–1772) on this issue, since, in a kind of historical Pavlovian response, his *Traité des Obligations* is regarded by many modern legal historians as the decisive influence on the drafters of the French civil code. Most of the time it is indeed, but not always and certainly not in this case. The writings of Pothier stand alone in French legal literature of his time. The discipline of Roman law was at a low tide in France when he began to study it in his native Orléans.[69] The candle of Roman law had been handed over to the Dutch universities, Leiden in particular. Pothier, for example, learned the first principles of Roman law from Arnold Vinnius's textbook on Justinian's Institutes.[70] Consequently, Pothier had to find his own way without sufficient guidance by contemporary French legal literature. This assessment is confirmed by his treatment of the matter at hand. In his *Traité du Contrat de Mandat* (*not* a source for the Code civil on this matter) he deals with the problem at issue here without a single reference to one of the French jurists just mentioned (Automne, Mornac, Cujas or Doneau). He found his inspiration in medieval treatises instead, especially in the writings of Bartolus.[71] He did so here as well. As we have seen,[72] Bartolus rejected the idea, suggested by the Gl. 'Mandato', to disregard D. 17,1,26,6. Instead, he followed the doctrine successively developed by Aldericus, Innocent IV and Joannes Andreae, distinguishing between accidental loss of property merely during the execution of the assignment (*ex occasione mandati*), which ought not to be compensated, and the accidental loss of property in the possession of the commissioner because of the assignment (*ex causa mandati*), which ought to be compensated. This medieval doctrine was adopted

---

69 A.F.M. Frémont, *Recherches historiques et biographiques sur Pothier* (Orléans/Tours: Gatineau/Mame, 1859), 29; J.A. Rogron and Firbach, "Dissertation sur la vie et les ouvrages de Pothier", in *Œuvres de Pothier* I, ed. J.A. Rogron and M. Firbach (Paris: Tilliard, 1835), II; A.J. Arnaud, *Les origines doctrinales du Code civil français* (Paris: Pichon et Durand-Auzias, 1969), 47 ('relâchement des études').

70 Frémont, *Recherches historiques*, 29; Arnaud, *Les origines doctrinales*, 112 and also G.F. le Trosne, *Éloge historique de Pothier* (Orléans, 1773), 60.

71 Frémont, *Recherches historiques*, 233 states that after his death two books stood out in Pothier's library because they had come apart by constant use: Justinian's Corpus Iuris and the commentaries of Bartolus.

72 *Supra*, 187.

by Pothier.[73] It was, at that time and considering the state of contemporary French law on this issue, a stark anachronism. It rests on the basic acceptation of D. 17,1,26,6, which was generally rejected in France at the time. This is the reason why Pothier was not followed on this issue by the drafters of the French Code civil. They knew that French law did not follow 'the law' (D. 17,1,26,6), but what was (wrongly, as it turned out) believed to be the doctrine of the Gloss: 'nous suivons la glosse, non le texte'.[74] This doctrine found its way into the French Code civil (1804), now as *aequitas scripta* rather than *non scripta*: (Art. 2000 Cc) 'Le mandant doit aussi indemniser le mandataire des pertes que celui-ci a essuyées *à l'occasion de sa gestion*, sans imprudence qui lui soit imputable.'[75]

The Equity of D. 17,1,26,6 Reconsidered

The Netherlands may not have the world record in the sheer number of successive civil codes, but it certainly holds the European record. No other European country can boast of a succession of no less than four civil codes over a period of less than two hundred years (1809–1992). In all of these successive codes, except the last one (1992), the French tradition of the Code civil is obvious, certainly where our topic is concerned. Art. 1846 of the old Dutch civil code (OBW, in force in the Netherlands from 1838 until 1992) was a literal translation of Art. 2000 Cc. It is rather remarkable that,

---

73 *Traité du Contrat de Mandat*, par. 76 (in *Œuvres de Pothier* VI, Paris 1819, 380). Pothier's doctrine on this issue was not, as Honsell, "Risikohaftung", 492 believes, inspired by natural lawyers (Grotius and Pufendorf). It is much older and Pothier knew that. Pothier generally ignores natural law and natural lawyers, since he detested them, with the only exception of Grotius.

74 Bernard Automne. See *supra*, 189, fnt. 52.

75 There is no connection between this article and the doctrines of Pothier, as is taken for granted by Honsell, "Risikohaftung", 493 and Zimmermann, *Law of Obligations*, 432, let alone of a 'Redaktionsversehen' (Honsell) by the drafters of this article. Art. 2000 Cc can easily be traced to the French tradition on the Gl. 'Mandato'. Although this article was passed without comment by the French legislator of the time (Locré, *La législation civile, commerciale et criminelle de la France* XV (Paris: Treuttel & Würtz, 1828), 215), it was commented on by one of the drafters of the Code civil, Jacques Maleville (1741–1824), in his *Analyse raisonnée de la discussion du Code civil au Conseil d'État* IV, 2nd ed. (Paris: Garnery & Laporte, 1807), 102. Maleville refers to D. 47,2,61,2 (must be 5) and the opinion of Claude Serres (1695–1768) as expressed in his *Institutions du droit français, suivant l'ordre de celles de Justinien* (ed. Paris, 1778), on Inst. 3,26(27),11 (must be 13): 'on juge que le mandataire doit être indemnifié *de toutes les pertes et même des cas fortuits* auxquels il s'expose dans l'exécution du mandat (p. 370).' For this, Serres refers to Géraud de Maynard, who, as we know (*supra*, 190, fnt. 53), based his opinion on the contemporary French reading of the Gl. 'Mandato'.

after following this French tradition for almost two centuries, the new Dutch civil code (BW, 1992) has finally returned to the rule in D. 17,1,26,6, all the more so since the recent return to the old rule from the Digests rests on the appraisal that the contrary French rule is obviously *inequitable*: 'it is nowadays unacceptable that a lawyer, breaking his leg while hurrying to court to plead a case on behalf of his client may charge all costs for medical treatment and nursing, let alone loss of income, to his client.'[76] Hence the abolition of the *aequitas scripta* of Art. 1846 OBW (Art. 2000 Cc) in modern Dutch law. The return to the old rule is even more remarkable in view of the fact that the person responsible for the new Dutch civil code, E.M. Meijers, had still praised the equity of Art. 1846 OBW (Art. 2000 Cc), preferring it to the doctrine of Pothier.[77] He would have been surprised (if not rather annoyed) to find precisely this doctrine, even more refined than it already was with Pothier, in the final redaction of his new Code.[78]

As discussed, the rule in D. 17,1,26,6 has traditionally been refined by a distinction originating for the most part in the writings of pope Innocent IV and canonized by Bartolus. So there is a certain historical logic to the fact that this distinction was introduced in the new Dutch civil code as well, for at a relatively late stage of the legislative process, the Dutch legislator was struck by the boldness of his decision to abolish the provision of Art. 1846 OBW (Art. 2000 Cc). Influenced by some observations of an early commentator on the original draft of the section dealing with mandate that considerable hardship might follow from it,[79] it was decided to add a new subsection to the article in the Code dealing with the principle of D. 17,1,26,6 (Art. 7:406 BW), designed to avoid such hardship. The full article reads as follows:

> (subs. 1) The client must reimburse the provider of services for the expenses related to the performance of the services to the extent that these are not included in the remuneration.

[76] Comments of the drafting committee on the repeal of Art. 1846 of the old Dutch civil code in: W. Reehuis, ed., *Parlementaire Geschiedenis van het nieuwe Burgerlijk Wetboek, Boek 7 (Invoering Boeken 3, 5 en 6)* (Deventer: Kluwer, 1991), 338.

[77] In his discussion of HR 27 May 1927, *NJ* 1927, 1341. Pothier's distinction is condemned there as being 'unfair and rather unsharp'.

[78] Meijers, the original sole drafter of the new Dutch civil code, died in 1954, before his draft was completed. His work was continued by a committee of experts who worked on it for the next forty years until it was finally completed in 1992.

[79] H.C.F. Schoordijk, "De ontwerpregeling van de opdracht in het zevende boek", *Nederlands Juristenblad* 24A, 1973, 42 *seq.*, at 48.

> (subs. 2) The client must repair the damage suffered by the provider of services as a result of the occurrence of a particular hazard related to the services, which is not attributable to the latter. Where the provider of services has acted in the conduct of his profession or business, the preceding sentence only applies if that hazard exceeds the risks which follow from the nature of the conduct of that business or profession. Where the services are performed otherwise for remuneration, the first sentence only applies if, in the determination of the remuneration, no account has been taken of the hazard.[80]

Subsection 1 (the original article) contains the repeal of the old rule of Art. 1846 OBW (Art. 2000 Cc) and the *de facto* return to the rule of D. 17,1,26,6: a provider of services, such as a commissioner, may claim expenses, but there is no liability on the part of the principal for accidental losses suffered by the commissioner in the execution of his commission. It is a (relatively) clear provision. The added subsection (2) however bears, by the sheer complexity of it, all the obvious marks of a quick fix. During the preparation of the German civil code (BGB, 1900), which also abides by the rule in D. 17,1,26,6,[81] similar suggestions were made to introduce distinctions to the general principle that a commissioner can only claim expenses, but not reimbursement for accidental losses.[82]

> Such suggestions as have been made in the Netherlands and Germany to somehow correct the rule in D. 17,1,26,6 illustrate the dilemma that rule creates.[83] Though it is evidently unreasonable to burden a principal with the cost of all the accidental losses a commissioner has sustained in the execution of his assignment, it is also true that under special circumstances the rule may work out in an unsatisfactory way. German courts have tried to solve the dilemma of what is called in German 'risikospezifische Zufallschäden' in various ways, sometimes by a very extended construction of the concept 'Aufwendungen' (expenses), mentioned in par. 670 BGB, sometimes by working with the stratagem of an implied condition to the contract, meaning that the principal has guaranteed to reimburse the commissioner for all

80 Translation taken from H.C.S. Warendorf *et al.*, *The Civil Code of the Netherlands* (Deventer: Kluwer, 2009).

81 See par. 670 BGB: 'Macht der Beauftragte zum Zwecke der Ausführung des Auftrags Aufwendungen, die er den Umständen nach für erforderlich halten darf, so ist der Auftraggeber zum Ersatz verpflichtet.'

82 For these suggestions see B. Mugdan, *Die gesammten Materialien zum Bürgerlichen Gesetzbuch für das Deutsche Reich II, Recht der Schuldverhältnisse* (Berlin: Von Decker, 1899), 951–952.

83 For this see J. von Staudinger and M. Martinek, *Staudingers Kommentar zum Bürgerlichen Gesetzbuch: par. 657–704, Geschäftsbesorgung* (Berlin: Sellier-De Gruyter, 2006), par. 670, Rn. 17–30.

accidental losses suffered in carrying out his assignment.[84] As far as the first method is concerned, I should draw attention to the fact that German law makes a sharp distinction between expenses ('Aufwendungen') and damages ('Schaden'), as does the Dutch legislator in Art. 7:406, cited above. This distinction is, I believe, rather imprecise, if not arbitrary. It is sometimes very hard to make a clear distinction between expenses and damages.[85] Be that as it may, a third method of approaching this problem has been suggested in modern German law. It has long standing, for it was already contended in the 19th century, when Germany was still under Roman law, that the generally accepted rule in D. 17,1,26,6 should be somewhat mitigated by making a distinction between accidental losses sustained as a consequence of the execution of the assignment ('als Folge der Ausführung des Mandats') and accidental losses due to incidents merely occurring during the execution of the assignment ('nur bei Gelegenheit dieser Ausführung').[86] This is, as the reader will no doubt have recognized, the old distinction between losses *ex causa mandati* and losses *ex occasione mandati*. It is now seriously advanced again by modern German jurists as an alternative way of solving the problem of 'risikospezifische Zufallschäden'.[87]

The suggestions to somehow mitigate the rule in D. 17,1,26,6 (par. 670 BGB) have not resulted in legislation in Germany, since it was felt that too much depended on the peculiarities of the individual case, making it impossible to force all contingencies into a provision in the code,[88] as has been so awkwardly attempted by the Dutch legislator in Art. 7:406, subs. 2. That was a wise decision of the German legislator, if only because the assessment which damages are to be regarded as accidental losses

---

[84] Staudinger and Martinek, *Staudingers Kommentar*, par. 670, Rn. 18–19.

[85] I refer the reader to Revigny's example purported to illustrate the iniquity of D. 17,1,26,6, discussed earlier in this book (*supra*, 17 and 36). Revigny was so appalled by the conduct of the clerks in the Rota that he qualified their conduct as sheer robbery. This qualification implies that the moneys paid to the clerks were accidental damages, in principle not to be compensated on account of the rule in D. 17,1,26,6. By another way of looking at it, they may well be qualified as necessary expenses that had to be compensated as a matter of course (D. 17,1,12,9). I know of at least one decision of the Dutch Supreme Court on mandate (HR 27 May 1927, *NJ* 1927, 1341), where *damages* were awarded to a commissioner on the basis of the old rule of art 1846 OBW (Art. 2000 Cc) for *expenses* he had made in executing his commission and which were due to him as a matter of course on account of Art. 1845 OBW (Art. 1999 Cc).

[86] For this distinction see J. Unger "Handeln auf fremde Gefahr", *Jherings Jahrbücher für die Dogmatik des bürgerlichen Rechts* 33 (1894), 329–330. Unger's suggestion met with the approval of the renowned Pandektist Heinrich Dernburg (*Pandekten* II, 319, fnt. 14).

[87] Staudinger and Martinek, *Staudingers Kommentar*, par. 670, Rn. 23, where the old idea that 'no one should suffer losses on account of a commission he has not executed on behalf of himself, but on behalf of the person he has contracted with' (*nemini officium suum damnosum*) is resuscitated. See on this *supra*, 179–180.

[88] See Mugdan, *Die gesammten Materialien* II, 302.

suffered *ex causa mandati* ('a particular hazard related to the services', 7:406, subs. 2 BW) and which damages are to be regarded as losses sustained *ex occasione mandati* rests primarily on the construction of the contract at hand. A distinction like the one just mentioned suggests a problem of causation, whereas the true problem involved is not a problem of causation,[89] but of construction. When seen from this perspective, the question about the 'equity' or 'iniquity' of the rule in D. 17,1,26,6 becomes futile, since everything depends on the intentions and assumptions of the parties to the contract. For example, even when it is *in confesso* that accidental damages have been directly sustained by the agent in the course of the execution of his assignment and are caused by contingencies directly related to the character of that assignment too, it is still be possible that principal and agent have agreed that the risk is to be borne by the agent in spite of these factors, or that the principal may reasonably rely on his assumption that the agent would bear the risk.

> I give an example from a recent Dutch court decision.[90] A horse-breeder had contracted with a veterinary to inoculate his horses. The vet began to perform his task, but after inoculating some of the horses in the stable of the breeder, he was struck by a panicking horse and was severely wounded. Due to his injuries, he became largely incapable of continuing his practice. The vet was not insured and sued the horse-breeder, though not on the basis of the contract but in tort, since according to modern Dutch law the possessor of an animal is strictly liable for all damages caused by that animal (Art. 6:179 BW). The horse-breeder countered by alleging that he had relied on the assumption that the vet bore the risk of a contingency like this as a matter of course, since he was a professional veterinary and as such subjected to risks like these continuously.

In situations like these everything depends on the construction of the agreement between principal and commissioner.[91] The construction of a particular contract is treated in the civil law as a matter of *fact*, rather than of law, which led to a rather unsatisfactory result in the case just mentioned. The lower court had (singularly, but most probably on account of poor pleading by counsel for the defendant) decided that, considering all the facts and circumstances of the case, the horse-breeder could not have relied on his assumption that the vet bore the risk of a contingency like

---

89 As Unger (*supra*, 198, fnt. 86) believed.

90 HR 27 April 2001, *NJ* 2002, 54.

91 See the remarks to this end by C.J.H. Brunner, professor of private law in Groningen and an authority on the Dutch law of obligations, in his discussion of HR 27 April 2001, *NJ* 2002, 54.

this as a matter of course. Due to the peculiarities of the law of procedure before the Dutch Supreme Court, a factual assessment like this cannot be challenged in the Supreme Court.

It should be clear by now why causation-inspired distinctions such as the old distinction between accidental damages *ex causa mandati* and accidental damages merely *ex occasione mandati,* and the new one concocted by the Dutch legislator in Art. 7:406, subs. 2, are really unhelpful, since the question of causation is completely absorbed by questions relating to the content, the purpose and the construction of the contract under consideration. Reassuring as it may be to a legal historian to find a distinction, already advanced by the jurist Aldericus in the 12th century, enacted in a code destined for the 21st century and beyond, I do believe it is an unnecessary (and even unhelpful) addition to the rule in D. 17,1,26,6 (Art. 7:406, subs. 1). Everything depends on the facts of the case: *ius est in causa positum*. One thing is certain though: 'Dutch equity' does not help here.[92] One does not need such external standards to let 'good faith' (*bona fides*) do its job. The Roman lawyer Celsus strongly felt that an appeal to 'reasonableness and fairness' (*bonum et aequum*) often leads to serious error. Paul agreed with that. The history of the equity of D. 17,1,26,6 confirms it.[93]

---

92 Unless one is inclined to contend that a Dutch judge has the discretion, on the basis of art. 6:2 and 6:248 BW (cited *supra*, 35–36), to decide a case on purely equitable grounds, irrespective, that is, of what the law lays down as a rule or what has been agreed and relied on. This would be making a 'sticky mess' of private law indeed. See J.H. Nieuwenhuis, *Ex libris Hans Nieuwenhuis, 43 Conclusies van antwoord* (unpublished, 2012), 60, a reaction to the interesting article by W.L. Valk, "Uitleg en het onderscheid tussen autonome en heteronome normen", in *Ex libris Hans Nieuwenhuis*, ed. A.G. Castermans *et al.*, (Deventer: Kluwer, 2009), 391–402.

93 D. 45,1,91,3 (Paulus, *libro decimo septimo ad Plautium*): *esse enim hanc quaestionem de bono et aequo: in quo genere plerumque sub auctoritate iuris scientiae perniciose erratur.*

INDEX OF PERSONS

INDEX OF SOURCES

I Classical Period

I.1 Leges

I.2 Literary sources

I.3 Epigraphic sources

I.4 Jurists

II Postclassical Period

Codex Iustiniani

III Medieval Period (600–1600)

III.1 *Civil law*

III.2 *Canon law*

III.3 *English law*

IV Early Modern Period (1600–1800)

IV.1 *English law*

IV.2 *French law*

V Modern Period (from 1800)

V.1 *Dutch law*

V.2 *English law*

V.3 *French law*

V.4 *German law*

VI Cited Cases

VI.1 *Dutch law*

VI.2 *French law*

VI.3 *German law*

VI.4 *English law*

VI.4.1 Alphabetical Table of Named Cases

VI.4.2 Table of Cases cited by Year

www.ingramcontent.com/pod-product-compliance
Lightning Source LLC
LaVergne TN
LVHW010657300926
849161LV00005B/1151